ISLAMOPHOBIA /
ISLAMOPHILIA

Indiana Series in Middle East Studies

Mark Tessler, general editor

ISLAMOPHOBIA /
ISLAMOPHILIA

Beyond the Politics of Enemy and Friend

EDITED BY ANDREW SHRYOCK

Indiana University Press

Bloomington and Indianapolis

This book is a publication of

Indiana University Press
601 North Morton Street
Bloomington, IN 47404-3797 USA

www.iupress.indiana.edu

Telephone orders   800-842-6796
Fax orders   812-855-7931
Orders by e-mail   iuporder@indiana.edu

∞The paper used in this publication meets the minimum require-
ments of the American National Standard for
Information Sciences—Permanence of Paper for Printed Library
Materials, ANSI Z39.48-1992.

Manufactured in the United States of America

Library of Congress Cataloging-in-Publication Data

Islamophobia/Islamophilia : beyond the politics of enemy and
friend / edited by Andrew Shryock.
   p. cm. — (Indiana series in Middle East studies)
  Includes index.
  ISBN 978-0-253-35479-2 (cl : alk. paper) — ISBN 978-0-253-22199-5
(pb : alk. paper) 1. Islam—Public opinion. 2. Muslims—Public
opinion. 3. Islam and culture. 4. Islam and politics. I. Shryock,
Andrew.
  BP52.I855 2010
  297.09—dc22

                  2009054116

1 2 3 4 5 15 14 13 12 11 10

Contents

Part Three Violence and Conversion in Europe

Part Four Attraction and Repulsion in Shared Space

Acknowledgments

This book grows out of intellectual exchanges that began in October 2007 at "Islamophobia/Islamophilia: Beyond the Politics of Enemy and Friend," the inaugural conference of the Islamic Studies Initiative (ISI) at the University of Michigan. I would like to thank Mark Tessler, director of the International Institute at the University of Michigan, for the generous support he has given this project from start to finish. Alexander Knysh, director of the ISI, helped conceptualize the original conference; Bryce Adams handled logistics; and Juan Cole and Sherman Jackson provided early inspiration. Some of the conference participants could not contribute essays to this volume, but I would like to thank Engseng Ho, Marcia Hermansen, and Mayanthi Fernando for helping us map out topics and approaches that would ultimately be explored by others. Paul Silverstein, Sally Howell, Mucahit Bilici, and Naamah Paley came to the project late, while other duties weighed heavily on them. I thank them for their keen interest and ability to adapt ongoing work to the needs of this volume, which has been greatly improved by their efforts. To the other contributors, Tomaž Mastnak, Moustafa Bayoumi, Lara Deeb, Muhammad Qasim Zaman, and Esra Özyürek, I owe special gratitude for their persistence, good ideas, and gracious dealings with their editor. Finally, I would like to thank Rebecca Tolen, for shepherding the volume through to print, and the anonymous reviewer at Indiana University Press, who encouraged us to add additional layers of critical nuance to our essays.

ISLAMOPHOBIA /
ISLAMOPHILIA

Introduction

Islam as an Object of Fear and Affection

Andrew Shryock

The twenty-first century is still young, but it is already proving to be an especially bad time for relations between the Muslim world and the West. Or so it would seem, if we accept the grand collapse of geography, culture, and history conveyed in terms like "the Muslim world" and "the West." To speak more precisely, the U.S. military now occupies two Muslim-majority countries, where it faces multiple armed resistance movements, some explicitly Muslim in orientation, others less so. The violence exchanged by these forces is not confined to the roadsides of Iraq or remote villages in Afghanistan. It has produced bus and train bombings in Europe, attacks on globally dispersed targets linked to support for U.S. war efforts, and massive new government structures—again, global in scope—dedicated to the detention, questioning, and elimination of suspects and "combatants" who are, with few exceptions, Arab, Muslim, or both.

In the short-term memory of our media age, all of this began with the 9/11 attacks, and it will end when "terror" has been defeated. The link between terrorism and Islam was firm long before September 11, 2001,[1] but it has grown stronger in recent years as high-profile enemies in the war on terror have been defined, and have defined themselves, as Muslim. The result, now recognized by journalists, politicians, intellectuals, and other interested parties, is pervasive "Islamophobia," a generalized fear of Islam and Muslims. As a social and political problem, Islamophobia is almost always associated with the U.S. and Europe, although related strains of it are well developed in India and China, in several African states with sizable Muslim minorities, and even in Muslim-majority countries (Turkey, Egypt, Algeria, Lebanon), where prominent political parties and opposition groups are Islamist in orientation. The term "Islamophobia" could reasonably be applied to any setting in which people hate Muslims, or fear Islam, but the word is most frequently invoked, and has its richest connotations, when it is used to describe a sentiment that flourishes in contemporary Europe and North America.

In its American forms, Islamophobia is often posed as the motivation behind acts of mosque vandalism, hate crimes against individuals thought to be Muslim, sensational press coverage of "the Muslim threat," the selective policing and surveillance of Muslim communities, and electoral campaign smears in which a candidate is linked to Muslim extremists or (in the case of Barack Obama) is said to be a Muslim.[2] The latter claim is widely perceived to be a slur, not simply a mistake—and never a compliment—because of the suspicion, prevalent among even the most tolerant of bourgeois multiculturalists, that Islam is somehow antithetical to democratic values. In Europe, where many immigrants from non-European nations are Muslim, and where European-born Muslim populations are growing steadily, anti-Muslim sentiment is a prominent trend in right-wing political movements, and in more mainstream political culture as well. Laws preventing Muslim girls from covering their hair in school, for instance, seem entirely acceptable, even necessary, to most French citizens (Bowen 2007; Scott 2007).

Across all these contexts, acts of violence against Muslims, and legislation averse to certain traditions of Islamic practice, can be variously interpreted as racist, secularist, nationalist, or anti-immigrant. Islamophobia, as a unifying concept, brings all of these possibilities into a single framework, and the sensibilities nurtured within that framework produce a predictable range of stereotypes. Indeed, the content of this worldview has become so predictable that we can use it to generate a reliable profile, a stereotype, of the contemporary Islamophobe, who is apt to believe that Muslims are (openly or in the secrecy of their own mosques and languages) violent extremists, anti-Semitic and anti-Christian, averse to democracy, oppressive of women, culturally backward, and dedicated to establishing Islamic law around the world.[3] To the extent that such beliefs shape government policy in the U.S. and Europe, they pose a significant threat to the civil liberties of the tens of millions of Muslims who now live in Western countries. They also threaten the national security of Muslim-majority states, who must share global space with a suspicious and frequently hostile superpower.

This sketch of our current political climate is beset by the sins of wartime analysis, foremost among them the tendency to reduce very complex historical patterns to ideologically useful concepts. If terror is one of these, so is Islamophobia. Both terms are polemical in nature, and the people the terms are applied to seldom accept their validity. The FBI agent investigating a Muslim charity does not consider herself an Islamophobe, just as a Hizbullah militant does not identify as a terrorist. Applying these labels is an exercise in negative characterization, a fact that makes the labels invaluable for political purposes, but potentially misleading for analytical and interpretive ones. When seen as a condition akin to homophobia, Islamophobia is something one should denounce, or treat, or cure. Without denying the merit and urgency of such responses, one could also approach Islamophobia—much as critical scholarship has approached terrorism[4]—with different ends in mind: namely, to understand how the concept solves and creates problems for those who use it, why it is necessary, what alternative sensibilities it brings into relief, and what histories come embedded in the term and its usage.

These additional agendas are valuable because we know far too little about what Islamophobia signifies. Without a careful assessment of contemporary geopolitics and deep historical relations between Muslim and non-Muslim societies, it is hard to understand what people are afraid of when they fear Islam. Given the scant knowledge of Islam most Americans and Europeans bring to the creation of their anti-Muslim stereotypes, can we be sure that Islamophobia is ultimately about Islam at all? Perhaps it is better explained in relation to ideas adapted from Cold War polemics, in which formerly Red scares are now Green. Perhaps it depends for its imagery and appeal on ideological residue from much older contests between European and Ottoman powers. It is also obvious that Islamophobia draws its symbolism more from European and American models of race, empire, and human progress than it does from political symbolism dominant among Muslims, past or present. One could argue that American and European varieties of Islamophobia are especially powerful, and are most effective as tools of political mobilization, when the audiences receptive to them have little or no practical knowledge of Islam, and no sustained relations with Muslims except relations of real or imagined conflict. Finally, the tendency to fix Islamophobia, geographically, in North America and Europe is itself questionable in an age of pervasive globalization. Popular ideas about Islam have transnational consequences and are part of transnational political hierarchies; as a result, anxiety about Islamist movements and outright fear of particular Muslims can flourish in Muslim societies, just as (and largely because) modern forms of secularism and nationalism do.

A Troubling Term

As a label describing a distinctive form of intolerance, Islamophobia is demonstrably new. Widespread usage in the U.S. is a post-9/11 phenomenon—it is difficult, for instance, to find a book with Islamophobia in its title published before 2001—and the term first rose to prominence in Britain in the late 1990s. It was the centerpiece of *Islamophobia: A Challenge for Us All*, a report issued in 1997 by the Runnymede Trust, a think tank specializing in ethnic and racial diversity issues. The report was written in response to anti-Muslim sentiment in Britain, which had grown steadily following the Rushdie affair (1989) and the first Gulf War (1990–91). These events had mobilized and alienated British Muslims, turning them into a viable political constituency, but one widely viewed as alien in its values and desperately in need of national incorporation. The Runnymede document was intended to speed the latter process along. Islamophobia, according to the report, is "an unfounded hostility towards Islam" as well as "the practical consequences of such hostility in unfair discrimination against Muslim individuals and communities, and . . . the exclusion of Muslims from mainstream political and social affairs" (Commission on British Muslims and Islamophobia 1997: 4).

The insertion of an escape clause—*unfounded* hostility toward Islam—in the Runnymede definition has not insulated the concept of Islamophobia from criticism. It has been roundly denounced as an exercise in political correctness by politicians and pundits who would like to reserve their right to criticize Islamists (or Muslims, or Islam). Daniel Pipes, a neoconservative political commentator whose views on Islam and Muslims are consistently negative (see chapter 2), dismisses Islamophobia as a smokescreen that protects Muslim extremists. He also questions the idea that fear of Islam can be treated as irrational:

> What exactly constitutes an "undue fear of Islam" when Muslims acting in the name of Islam today make up the premier source of worldwide aggression, both verbal and physical, versus non-Muslims and Muslims alike? What, one wonders, is the proper amount of fear? . . . Muslims should dispense with this discredited term [Islamophobia] and instead engage in some earnest introspection. Rather than blame the potential victim for fearing his would-be executioner, they would do better to ponder how Islamists have transformed their faith into an ideology celebrating murder (Al-Qaeda: "You love life, we love death") and develop strategies to redeem their religion by combating this morbid totalitarianism. (http://www.danielpipes.org/3075/islamophobia)

Note how Muslims are depicted as a collective body that is (or ought to be) responsible for the misdeeds of its criminal element, who have "transformed" the faith into an ideology. References to murderous and totalitarian forces are ubiquitous among those who express such views, which often appear in coordinated political and media campaigns. In 2006, for instance, a collective of prominent literary types produced a public statement, "Together Facing the New Totalitarianism," in which a force called "Islamism" is likened to "fascism, Nazism, and Stalinism."[5] Islamism is never clearly defined in the document; it is simply portrayed as a dark ideology born out of fear, frustration, and hatred. According to the authors:

> Islamism is a reactionary ideology that kills equality, freedom and secularism wherever it is present.
>
> Its victory can only lead to a world of injustice and domination: men over women, fundamentalists over others.
>
> On the contrary, we must ensure access to universal rights for the oppressed or those discriminated against.
>
> We reject the "cultural relativism" which implies an acceptance that men and women of Muslim culture are deprived of the right to equality, freedom and secularism in the name of a respect for certain cultures and traditions.
>
> We refuse to renounce our critical spirit out of fear of being accused of "Islamophobia," a wretched concept that confuses criticism of Islam as a religion and stigmatization of those who believe in it.
>
> We defend the universality of the freedom of expression, so that a critical spirit can exist in every continent, towards each and every maltreatment and dogma.
>
> We appeal to democrats and free spirits in every country that our century may be one of light and not dark.

The signers included Salman Rushdie (who writes and thinks much better than this) and several other writers known for publishing work offensive to Muslims; Irshad Manji and Ayaan Hirsi Ali, two popular, highly inflammatory commentators on Islam (see chapter 3), were among them. The statement is simplistic and alarmist; hardly a phrase can withstand critical inspection (need we wait for the triumph of Islamism to experience a world of "domination and injustice"?), yet the most perplexing of these claims is the idea that Islamophobia is a "wretched" concept because it confuses critique of religion with the stigmatization of religious people. Distinguishing between those two activities is difficult in the abstract, and the joint statement, with its urgent appeal to a political morality of light and dark, makes such distinctions even harder to draw in practice.

The controversy surrounding Islamophobia is not confined to op-ed pages, however, nor is it inevitably expressed in crusading language. Academics and policy-minded intellectuals have different concerns. Islamophobia was originally intended to describe a new form of discrimination; as such, it entailed new forms of expertise (to diagnose it) and new institutional remedies (to offset it). Among scholars who study older platforms for discrimination, like race, ethnicity, or class, and especially among activists committed to anti-racist politics, the popularization of the Islamophobia concept has not been warmly received. Because they privilege religious identity and call for solidarity with causes organized in relation to religious affinities, campaigns against Islamophobia are often hard for members of the secular intelligentsia to embrace, whether their tendencies are liberal, progressive, centrist, or conservative (Werbner 2005). The experts who must respond to claims of a growing Islamophobia and prescribe solutions for it are, with few exceptions, members of the secular intelligentsia.

In France, where Muslims have long been studied not as Muslims per se, but as immigrant populations, or North Africans, or Arabs (Cesari 2002; Wieviorka 2002), Islamophobia is still not a popular analytical term among scholars, many of whom think it is "imprecisely applied to very diverse phenomena, ranging from xenophobia to anti-terrorism" (Cesari 2006: 6), reducing complex forms of discrimination and government policy to a single concept that cannot adequately explain them. In Britain, anti-racists and Muslim activists often have very different perspectives. According to Tariq Modood, anti-racists give great moral and explanatory weight to the relationship between skin color and relative disadvantage, whereas British Muslims are more likely to assess their status in relation to that of Islam: "their sense of being and their surest conviction about their devaluation by others comes from their historical community of faith and their critique of the 'West'" (2005: 104). In the U.S., scholars and activists have tended to close this gap by focusing on "the racialization of Islam" (Naber and Jamal 2008), or they have considered the role of racial thought and racism in the development of Muslim communities in North America (Dannin 2002; Jackson 2005), or they have argued that Muslim identity is no longer exclusively religious, but has ethnic and racial dimensions as well (Leonard 2003). These approaches allow individual analysts to blend religious themes with color politics, just as American Muslims tend to do in practice, in effect bringing Islamophobia and racism into the same analytical frame.

Meanwhile, beyond the academy, advocacy groups and governing bodies in North America and Europe have, in the years following the 9/11 attacks, made Islamophobia a target of policy and public education. Both the European Union and the United Nations have embraced the concept, organizing high-profile international conferences that address Islamophobia and adding it to the several varieties of racism and intolerance they monitor and combat (see chapter 1). Activist organizations, ranging from the international (Organization of the Islamic Conference), to the national (Council on American-Islamic Relations), to the thousands of regional and municipality-based Muslim associations now active throughout the Western countries, are mobilizing to oppose Islamophobia in public institutions and political life (Sinno 2009). These efforts, whether undertaken on a local or global scale, have a similar goal: namely, the favorable incorporation of Muslims, as citizens and communities, in nation-states that are assumed, or encouraged, to be secular, pluralistic, and democratic.

The definition and defeat of Islamophobia is, at heart, a governmental agenda. Its principal concern, since the Runnymede report debuted in 1997, has been to facilitate the participation of Muslim minorities in non-Muslim societies, especially those of Europe and North America. Moreover, the efflorescence of this agenda after the Rushdie affair, the first Gulf War, the 9/11 attacks, the Madrid and London train bombings, the Danish cartoon affair, and other episodes of violent conflict between antagonists defined as Muslim and non-Muslim, suggests that anxieties about Islamophobia—both the social problem and the analytical term—are part of a larger disciplinary regime. The primary subjects of this regime are Muslims living in the West (who must be made into good citizens), and the societies that must accommodate them (and must do so efficiently and effectively). These imperatives are played out simultaneously on a global stage. The exemplary Muslim citizen, member of the tolerant and inclusive (Western) society, has his equivalent in the modern Muslim-majority state, member of a tolerant and inclusive (Western-dominated) family of nations. Lurking behind this formula, thwarting and distorting it, is the "deal breaker": the Muslim radical, the extremist, the terrorist, or, just as problematic, the Muslim person or Muslim-majority state that does not want to be incorporated on these terms.

It is important to understand the terminological disputes triggered by the concept of Islamophobia because they are ultimately linked, across the political spectrum, to this larger governmental paradigm. Those who reject the term "Islamophobia" sometimes do so out of an unwillingness to accommodate certain kinds of Muslim difference, which are considered genuinely incompatible with Western values, and therefore deserving of vigorous critique. Sometimes rejection of the term signals a refusal to admit that Islam, or religious belief, could really be the difference that matters most in modern nation-states, in which racism and immigrant status should explain more. Rather than choose sides in these debates, the contributors to this volume look instead at a wide range of contexts in which Muslims and particular forms of Islam are understood, with varying degrees of anxiety and affection, as problems that must be solved, or as solutions to problems. At stake in all these contexts are values and political investments that make collective life possible, *but only on certain terms.* The fact that these terms—security, citizenship, democracy, and religious freedom—are being renegotiated at a rapid pace, globally and locally, even as people insist on defending them, is a contradiction central to this volume. It generates Islamophobia and, for now, is securing Islam's relationship to violence, especially forms of violence widely believed to threaten the physical and cultural integrity (and thus the continued existence) of a group, whether this group is Muslims in Britain, the French nation, Europe as a whole, or the global *ummah* of Islam.

The Politics of Inversion: From Phobia to Philia

As stock characters, the Muslim and the Islamophobe stand in an ideologically perfect relationship when they can see each other, first and last, as "enemies" in exactly the sense described by Carl Schmitt, who argued that politics itself is an activity based on the drawing of fundamental distinctions between enemies and friends. Muslims are enemies (just as Greeks and Persians were, or communists and capitalists are) when they are judged to be adversaries who, in Schmitt's words, intend to negate their "opponent's way of life and therefore must be repulsed or fought in order to preserve one's own form of existence" (1996: 27). The starkness and analytical utility of this formulation for a discussion of Islamophobia lies in the capacity of "enemy status" to render moral nuance irrelevant, even if the diverse qualities of the enemy can still be discerned. As Schmitt puts it:

> The political enemy need not be morally evil or aesthetically ugly; he need not appear as an economic competitor, and it may even be advantageous to engage with him in business transactions. But he is, nevertheless, the other, the stranger; and it is sufficient for his nature that he is, in a specially intense way, existentially something different and alien, so that in the extreme case conflicts with him are possible. (1996: 27)

The decision to cast Muslims in this role is a political act; moreover, it is one that can be contested. Not everyone agrees that Muslims are existentially alien, and Muslims who live as citizens in the U.S. or France or Canada are not, by strict legal reckoning, Others or strangers, even when their fellow nationals see them as outsiders. This overlap of inside and outside, an artifact of global immigration and modern regimes of citizenship, is what drives Islamophobia and imbues it with missionary zeal. People must be convinced and reminded that Muslims, even the ones who live here with us, as us, are really Them.

If we grant that Islamophobia fits this simple profile and poses a real danger not only to Muslims, but also to models of citizenship and human rights that aspire to include Muslims and non-Muslims as equals in the same political community, should we not also be concerned about political distortions that might arise from attempts to offset Islamophobic agendas? This question is difficult to consider, and easily misconstrued. To put it differently, the insidious nature of Islamophobia is not located in fear alone, or in hate; nor is it found in the designation of enemies as such, since a society or group can define its enemies, or be defined as enemies, for entirely legitimate reasons. One can, for instance, consider al-Qaeda an enemy, fear their policies, and hate the violence they espouse without being an Islamophobe. What is most problematic about Islamophobia is its essentializing and universalizing quality, which casts both Islam itself and all Muslims as real or potential enemies in a way that, if similarly applied to Jews or Christians, would seem delusional at best, vile at worst. The extent to which this universal application is deeply rooted in European history, and is still actively deployed in anti-Muslim polemics, will be explored throughout this volume. What is harder to assess is the challenge of countering Islamophobic impulses in ways that do not simply invert or reinforce them by cultivating their opposite: the image of the Muslim as "friend," as a figure identified with the Self, characterized as familiar, and with whom legitimate conflict is not possible. This image, too, is impervious to nuance, and it can be coercive when applied to Muslims, who might have differences—with non-Muslims and fellow Muslims alike—they think are worth asserting and maintaining. When "friendship" is subordinated to the demands of sameness—whether conceived in national or human terms—it can be just as coercive, just as prone to misrecognition, as the sentiments of hostility it is meant to correct.

Islamophilia, understood as a generalized affection for Islam and Muslims, comes with its own political costs. If, as some analysts would argue, Islamophobia has little to do with real Islam as practiced by actually existing Muslims, then constructing selectively positive images of Islam in response to Islamophobic propaganda will have less than helpful, and sometimes bizarre, results. One of these, now widely recognized, is the spread of "good-Muslim/bad-Muslim" binaries (Mamdani 2004), in which the good Muslim (the friend) is the real Muslim, and the bad Muslim (the enemy) is a creature who violates the good Muslim code; he can and should be vigorously opposed. The "good Muslim," as a stereotype, has common features: he tends to be a Sufi (ideally, one who reads Rumi); he is peaceful (and assures us that jihad is an inner, spiritual contest, not a struggle to "enjoin the good and forbid the wrong" through force of arms); he treats women as equals, and is committed to choice in matters of hijab wearing (and never advocates the covering of a woman's face); if he is a she, then she is highly educated, works outside the home, is her husband's only wife, chose her husband freely, and wears hijab (if at all) only because she wants to. The good Muslim is also a pluralist (recalls fondly the ecumenical virtues of medieval Andalusia and is a champion of interfaith activism); he is politically moderate (an advocate of democracy, human rights, and religious freedom, an opponent of armed conflict against the U.S. and Israel); finally, he is likely to be an African, a South Asian, or, more likely still, an Indonesian or Malaysian; he is less likely to be an Arab, but, as friends of the "good Muslim" will point out, only a small proportion of Muslims are Arab anyway.

Islamophilic discourse returns consistently to this array of features, which are found, in varying degrees of completeness, in millions of real Muslims. Of course, these traits are lacking in millions of real Muslims as well, but it is not their empirical presence or absence that matters as much as the moral connotations these traits carry when they are used to define the modern, safe, and acceptable Muslim. The same is true of Islamophobic discourses. There are Muslims who advocate and practice violence, oppress women, hate Jews, would like to see the universal establishment of shari'ah law, and so on. Counting them and calling them out is not as important, or as dangerous, as the categorical stigmatization that occurs when phobic portrayals of Muslims come to dominate a political field, thus setting the terms on which Islam is deemed pre/modern, un/safe, and un/acceptable.

In this light, the resemblance between the good Muslim and the Muslim who could serve most effectively as a counter to the anti-Muslim propaganda now being disseminated by Islamophobes is all too apparent,[6] as is the affinity between the values of the good Muslim and those of the good citizen of the liberal democratic state. When drawn to these specifications, the good Muslim certainly appears less malign than his evil twin, but the traits that define the good Muslim are just as likely to be based on wishful thinking and a politics of fear. If we persist in portraying Islamophobia as an irrational force of mis-perception, or the result of malicious stereotypes, we might render ourselves oblivious to its ultimate causes and consequences, and the corrective imagery we develop in response to it might, in the manner of a bad diagnosis, end up reinforcing the very syndrome it was meant to counteract. In our rush to identify Muslim friends who think and act like "us," we turn those who think and act differently into potential enemies.

Analytical Interventions

To explore these issues in greater depth, this volume brings together a diverse group of scholars whose research has equipped them to think critically and creatively about Islamophobia and Islamophilia as political projects. Ranging from the Middle Ages to the present day, from North America to South Asia, the work presented here will challenge popular discourses about Islam as an object of dread and desire. Our contributors do not advocate a uniform perspective, but they are motivated by shared analytical commitments. First, they do not accept at face value the key terms under discussion. While recognizing the dangers of a generically anti-Muslim politics, our contributors are wary of the reductive moral discourses that result when Islam is portrayed as an objectified form, as a thing, to be fondly embraced. The idea that Islamophobia and Islamophilia function as opposites is singled out for special critique, as is the assumption that only non-Muslims can view Islam, or aspects of Islam, through a phobic lens. Generally, the contributors are keen to avoid the analytical dead ends that await scholarship (and political action) that accepts a "good-Islam/bad-Islam" dichotomy as its starting point. A secular outlook, a language of analysis that does not privilege belief or disbelief, prevails in these essays, and this tendency raises special challenges of its own, which I will discuss below.

Apart from these shared sensibilities, our authors bring together several distinctive approaches that generate reciprocal arguments and themes. I have arranged the essays in hopes of creating conversations among the authors, sometimes relying on clear contrasts in subject matter or approach, sometimes playing on unexpected similarities. In the remainder of this introduction, I will provide a road map to the book that emphasizes conceptual advances these authors achieve in their discussions of (1) historical continuities and discontinuities in relations between Muslims and non-Muslims in what are now called Western societies, (2) the centrality of ideologies of modernity to Islamophobic and Islamophilic thought, (3) the odd realignments and misrecognitions that pervade these ideologies, making them highly resistant to critique, and (4) the extent to which Muslims and non-Muslims inhabit spaces, both global and local, in which their differences are increasingly defined by the moral qualities and political identities they share.

Continuities and Transformations

Since Islamophobia is a term of recent vintage, it is important to situate it in larger historical contexts and to specify what about it is genuinely new. In chapter 1, Tomaž Mastnak provides much of this framing, arguing that the elaboration of a fundamentally hostile Latin Christian attitude toward Muslims was an outcome of the deep internal crisis of the Western Christian world in the eleventh century. This crisis in Europe led to the Crusades and to an assemblage of anti-Muslim sensibilities that has survived for centuries. Mastnak's account is sobering. It shows not only how entrenched, and how particular, the history of anti-Muslim politics is in Europe (and, by extension, in Europe's colonial domains), it also shows how the very notion of Europe is based in a legacy of violent interactions with Muslim Others. Much of this legacy has been successfully reproduced in the present. Contemporary forms of Islamophobia are shaped (or haunted) by a worldview in which Europe and the Christian world are clearly set apart from an Oriental and Muslim world. These civilizations, in the formula made famous by Samuel Huntington, persist in a state of clash. Indeed, as Mastnak suggests in his revealing account of the U.N.'s Alliance of Civilizations initiative, contemporary forms of Islamophilia are shaped (and haunted) by the same moral geography.

The great irony of this historical complex is its simultaneous relevance and rather obvious outdatedness. In chapter 2, Naamah Paley offers a telling contrast to Mastnak's material by showing how radically the terrain on which Muslims and non-Muslims interact today has shifted. Paley describes the recent controversy in New York City over the opening of the Khalil Gibran International Academy, a public school that features Arabic-language instruction and a practical focus on Arab world societies and cultures. Opposition to this school was intensely Islamophobic and anti-Arab. It invoked age-old models of the Muslim enemy, but several of Mastnak's key variables have changed: the Muslims in question are now members of the larger society, the line between Self and Other must be enforced (often in tones of outrage and panic) because this line has already been crossed, and the role of the anti-Muslim, European Christian has been replaced, in Paley's case, by anti-Muslim American Jews, who figured prominently in the campaign against the school. As Paley argues, the Islamophobia displayed by opponents of the Gibran Academy is best understood as a function of collapsed boundaries, contests over shared public space, and the inability to recognize the Arab/Muslim as American.

The Islamophilia on display is similarly vexed by boundary issues; according to Paley, organized support for the Gibran Academy is oriented toward intra-communal Jewish concerns and the search for "good Muslims" with whom to form secure partnerships.

Modern (Self) Criticism

The juxtaposition of Mastnak and Paley shows nicely the conditions that distinguish contemporary forms of Islamophobia from patterns of hostility that prevailed before the age of European imperialism and the institutionalization of today's global political and economic systems. Millions of Muslims are now resident in Western nation-states, where they provoke old and new anxieties, and this pervasive change is part of the massive restructuring of the Muslim world accomplished during the colonial period, when infrastructures of modernity were imposed on and variously resisted, taken up by, and adapted to the needs of Muslim populations. However collaborative this world-transforming process was in practice, Europeans long held the upper hand, and the ideological equivalence between modernity, civilization, historical progress, and Western values became, and remains, a hegemonic reality Muslims can hardly ignore.[7] As three of our authors argue, this ideological climate has produced phobic and philic accounts of Islam among Muslims themselves, who are compelled to criticize and defend Islam, and its institutions, against backdrops of modernity that are now global in scope.

In chapter 3, Moustafa Bayoumi subjects the writings of popular Muslim American public intellectuals after 9/11 to a withering critique. Focusing on best-selling books by Ayaan Hirsi Ali, Irshad Manji, and Reza Aslan, Bayoumi shows how a supposed failure to achieve a convincingly modern state of being is the inspiration for defiant apostasy (in the case of Hirsi Ali), anti-Muslim polemic (in the case of Manji), and a conciliatory apologetics that holds out (in the case of Aslan) for the possibility of a future Islam that is progressive and reformed. Not only does Bayoumi think these authors cater to the prejudices of Jewish and Christian readers—obviously, with great success in the marketplace—but he also insists that both the Islamophobia of Hirsi Ali and Manji and the Islamophilia of Aslan share a common Orientalist heritage. All three authors focus attention on the origins and essences of Islam, removing them from history and producing comfortable alibis for readers who, in Bayoumi's opinion, find it difficult (or counterproductive) to situate Islam within a secular world of politics and responsibility.

In chapter 4, Lara Deeb follows themes of modernity and self-criticism into Muslim-majority society, where they generate very different discourses. Building on her research among Lebanese gender activists affiliated with Hizbullah, Deeb examines how U.S.-based transnational discourses about Muslim women provoke alternative gender ideologies explicitly designed to offset depictions of Islam as sexist and oppressive towards women. For her interlocutors in the Shi'a suburbs of Beirut, concerns over the proper teaching and public representation of Islam, and of women's role in Muslim society, are acutely developed, and criticisms of tradition, backwardness, and uncivilized behavior are as vehement among Muslims as they are among non-Muslims, although the intent of these critiques differs radically, producing Islamophilia, not Islamophobia. What is more, the critical concerns of Muslims and non-Muslims often resemble each other, responding directly to each other—or to similar political forces—across what are believed to be vast religious divides. Deeb shows, for instance, how fear of Shi'a in Lebanon, as expressed by their Sunni and Christian opponents, makes heavy use of the images and claims that predominate in American propaganda against Iran.

In chapter 5, Muhammad Qasim Zaman develops an equally counterintuitive analysis, pushing the boundaries of phobia and philia even further into Muslim cultural space by exploring how, over the last century, Muslim scholars across the Middle East and South Asia have criticized madrasas (religious schools). With the introduction of European-style secular curricula, which were associated with modernity and progress, the effectiveness of what came, by contrast, to be described as "traditional" Islamic education was open to debate. And the debate, as recounted by Zaman, has been vigorous, with 'ulama (Muslim scholars) taking up diverse positions on how best to reform the madrasa, either by blending religious education with the modern, secular sciences, or by marking off their jurisdictions more carefully. This tradition of contestation, Zaman argues, was in place long before Western policy analysts discovered (and demonized) the madrasa. While some Muslim scholars have claimed that the madrasa is politically and pedagogically retrograde, others have insisted that madrasa training can produce an elite stratum ideally prepared to lead fully modern, fully Muslim societies. Zaman's careful exploration of these debates is an illuminating corrective to biased Western accounts of madrasas. It also reveals competing models of religious authority in contemporary Islam, each of which fosters patterns of anxiety (about other Muslims) and affection (for Islamic tradition) that are internal to the Muslim community, yet which resonate far beyond it.

Violence and Conversion in Europe

Contemporary Europe is filled with Muslims, a state of affairs the inhabitants of Christendom or early modern Europe could only have equated with military defeat. Indeed, many Europeans today liken the growing Muslim presence in their countries to an invasion of cultural spaces that are historically Christian and politically secular.[8] It would be hard to envision a discussion of Islamophobia that did not give attention to French campaigns against the expression of Muslim religious identity in national/public space or the elaborate policies of incorporation and exclusion directed at Turkish immigrants by German authorities. Two of our authors explore the systematic racism and violence experienced by Muslims in Europe, but from points of view rarely taken up in treatments of Islamophobia in its French and German forms. Themes of mistaken identity and cross-dressing emerge in both essays, with some French Muslims identifying politically with Jews and Israel, and some German Muslims harboring intensely anti-Turkish prejudices in the name of Islam. This ambiguity of identity labels, felt among Muslims as well as non-Muslims across Europe, can sometimes make phobic and philic attitudes hard to distinguish.

In chapter 6, Paul Silverstein interprets violence against French Muslims within larger contexts of French post/colonial history. Noting the remarkable degree to which accusations of Muslim intolerance—especially instances of anti-Semitism—are used as ideological cover for discrimination against Muslims, Silverstein traces current patterns of Islamophobia in France back to foundational moments in French colonial policy in North Africa, when sharp distinctions were drawn between French settlers, Arabs, Berbers, and Jews in personal status law. These distinctions privileged Jews and Berbers, and handicapped Arabs (who were associated with a fanatical and essentially backward Islam). Much of contemporary Islamophobia in France is a national re-enactment of this original assessment of the Arab Muslim as inassimilable, and much of fashionable Islamophilia, expressed in conversion to Islam and the embrace of Muslim popular culture among oppositional French youth, is closely identified with support for Arab political causes. Many Berber activists, themselves Muslims, have sought to distance themselves from French disdain for Arabs by promoting a cultural heritage, and a political posture, that downplays Islam and is openly philo-Semitic, calling for recognition of Israel and stressing Jewish elements in Berber folklore and communal ritual.

Meanwhile, prominent French Jewish intellectuals stir up Islamophobic sentiment, and North African youth battle riot police and special security forces
in their suburban enclaves. These phobic and philic trends, Silverstein argues,
are the legacy of French colonialism which institutionalized, and has now
internalized, a regime of citizenship in which Muslims cannot be authenti-
cally French.

Germany does not have the same colonial history, but similar ideas of
authenticity pervade German nationalism. As Esra Özyürek demonstrates in
chapter 7, the fact that a true German is not, or should not be, a Muslim is inconsistent with a reality in which Turks are acquiring German citizenship and
Germans are converting to Islam. The latter trend, one might suppose, is a classic instance of Islamophilia, but as Özyürek shows, this love of true Islam often
breeds disdain for Muslims, especially Muslims of immigrant backgrounds.
Although they usually come to Islam through personal relationships of love
and friendship with "foreign" Muslims, German converts are apt to conclude
that it is Muslims who give Islam a bad name. The solution to this problem is
a more German Islam, or an Islam that is less beholden to immigrant culture,
much of which is construed, in the mind of the convert, as a set of beliefs and
behaviors antithetical to proper Islam. Ironically, this position is also widespread among the children of Muslim immigrants in Western countries, who,
like Özyürek's German converts, must place a strategic distance between Islam
(which must be loved) and Muslim immigrants (who clearly are not).

Attraction and Repulsion in Shared Space

The essays in this volume suggest that conversion, transregional migration,
colonial histories, and imperial politics in the present are culminating not in a
starkly divided world of rival Western and Islamic civilizations, but are instead
producing diverse zones of interaction and contest, each filled with complex,
overlapping patterns of attraction and repulsion between actors defined as
Muslim and non-Muslim.[9] Two of our contributors carefully dissect these
patterns. What they find is a remarkable amount of common ground, and a
growing perception of common sense, on which transcommunal alliances can
be built. The building materials discussed here are Muslim "ethnic humor,"
which is now popular among young Muslims in the U.S. and Canada, and
dreams of upward mobility, which Muslim immigrants share with members of
the larger, non-Muslim society. The social projects that emerge in these common frameworks are integrative, but fragile; they put the reality of cultural
sharing to the test, and they sometimes fail.

In chapter 8, Mucahit Bilici takes us on a fast-paced tour of Muslim comedy, a genre that has flourished in the aftermath of 9/11, much to the surprise of community observers, who did not see humor as a form of social criticism available to Muslims in societies that consider them a security threat. Indeed, the idea that Muslims could be funny (and were not simply people to be made fun of) was not widespread before the 9/11 attacks. Bilici explores the peculiar confluence of tragedy, scapegoating, and a practical sense of citizenship—of belonging in the U.S. or Canada—that makes Muslim comedy good to think about and, in a deeply cathartic sense, funny. The Muslim stand-up comedian, Bilici contends, is entering a tradition of ethnic humor that accentuates the status of the Muslim (as it did the status of the Jew) as a marginal figure who is wise to the habits of the majority and his own minority group, and can tease both at once. Thus, it is second-generation American Muslims who are often the funniest, and second-generation Muslims who laugh loudest at the jokes. Muslim comedy is an inversion of Islamophobia, pulled off by artists who can love Islam and poke fun at their co-religionists, all the while participating in American popular culture *as Muslims*. The growth of this genre, Bilici suggests, is proof that anti-Muslim stigma can be harnessed and put to creative use, not only to engender affection for Muslims, but to reveal the backdrop of common sense against which Islamophobia appears ridiculous.

In chapter 9, Sally Howell explores grassroots Muslim community work in greater Detroit, an urban landscape that has been home to Muslims for over a century. The social and political gains made by Detroit-area Muslims can be seen in their relationships with public schools, which now cater to Muslim students, providing Arabic-language instruction, observing Muslim holidays, and hiring Muslim staff. As Howell shows, there is now intense competition to attract immigrant Muslims to low-income areas of Detroit, where their conservative social values and strong family structures can be used to stabilize poor neighborhoods. Recent attempts by the beleaguered Highland Park Public Schools to lure immigrant Muslims from neighboring districts of Hamtramck and Detroit have failed, ironically, because the Muslim-oriented magnet school Highland Park established was so successful. As Howell argues, the moral virtues of Muslim communal life that appealed most to the administrators of this poor, African American school district could not be effectively shared. The magnet school had an entirely Muslim enrollment, but few of its students were from Highland Park. The racial, class, and ethnic divisions that set Highland Park apart from its immigrant-rich neighbors were accentuated, not dampened, by this experiment in applied Islamophilia. The struggles for upward mobility and inclusion now being fought by Detroit's Muslims, Howell concludes, are making Muslims part of the city's pervasive structures of inequality, an outcome that creates new friends, and new enemies, for Muslims and the local institutions that compete for them.

Beyond the Politics of Enemy and Friend

At first glance, Islamophobia would appear to be the product of a rigid, polarized worldview. It demands that Muslims be seen negatively, as threatening figures who want to dominate the West, a geopolitical space in which they do not belong and to which they cannot adapt. Yet the essays featured in this volume suggest that appearances can be misleading. In practice, Islamophobia owes more to the convergence of cultural and political spaces than to their separation. Polarization is what Islamophobes desire, but cannot quite achieve. The Muslim presence in the West has been growing steadily for over a century, through immigration and conversion. Mosques can be found in every major city of Europe and North America, and the idea that Muslims can only be foreigners is now a position that must be vigorously argued, with obvious ideological bias.[10] At the same time, however, the inclusion of Muslims in Western societies as citizens is a conflicted process, and it too requires immense ideological effort. To reverse our formulation, a generalized affection for Muslims is what Islamophiles desire, but cannot quite achieve, as evidence of Muslim difference persists and wars against Muslim-majority nation-states and Islamist militant groups reanimate a time-tested imagery of crusade and jihad.

The conditions that make the language of enemy and friend so appealing, and so inadequate, are part of a politics of interaction between Muslims and non-Muslims that no longer describes our world accurately, but has yet to be replaced by politics of a new kind. This older political language is grounded in reductive patterns of malign and benign misrecognition, and its conceptual weaknesses are easy to diagnose once the extensive overlap of Self and Other is acknowledged, and once attempts to assert distance between Muslims and a stereotypically non-Muslim West are analyzed as political agendas that make, and do not simply reflect, the realities they purport to describe. In this volume, the move beyond opposed categories of enemy and friend is accomplished through secular criticism, whether historical, cultural, or political. Islam as a doctrinal system is seldom the focus of analysis, but Muslims as social actors always are, and Muslims are assumed to be participants in the politics of enemy and friend, not simply its passive victims. This tendency explains why our contributors so often detect signs of Islamophobia in Muslim countries (as well as in the U.S. and Europe) and why they attribute these phobic signs to modernity and its hierarchy of values, not to correct or incorrect understandings of Islamic tradition. For the person of faith, this analytical tendency will not necessarily be welcome. The German converts who criticize Turks as poor representatives of Islam in Germany invoke hadith and Quranic verses to justify their position, as do Muslim scholars who criticize madrasas in Egypt and India, or Hizbullah gender activists who criticize the sexism of their co-religionists in Beirut. One can add to these examples a growing literature that shows how young Muslims in the U.S. call on Islamic tradition, properly (re)interpreted, for support in developing their own arguments against what they perceive to be the racism, political docility, and cultural insularity of their parents.[11]

These attempts to shift stigma and relocate religious identity are themselves devoted to the recalibration of the enemy/friend binary. As such, they can be read as Americanizing, or Germanizing, or simply modernizing moves. Inevitably, they bring many of the prejudices and cherished values of a larger, non-Muslim world into Muslim communities that must adapt to life in a new society, or a new age. The Muslim American, or the Hizbullah activist, who tries to purify Islam of cultural accretions that corrupt it and expose it to ridicule is not likely to see her agenda as phobic in relation to the aspects of Islam she deems "backward," "unnecessary," or "mistaken"—the latter are not properly Islamic, in her view—but there is a clear sense in which the Islam that emerges from this process of adjustment has been tempered by an awareness of phobic and philic tendencies prevalent in larger, non-Muslim interpretive contexts. Everywhere, Muslims must take into account the prejudices and expectations of an imagined, non-Muslim observer. As a result, new distinctions between Self and Other are constantly woven into Muslim self-definitions, and this creative response to the disciplinary pressures applied to Muslims by non-Muslim observers (or by fellow Muslim critics) is often rewarded with higher levels of political influence and societal inclusion.[12] In the case of Muslim comedy in North America, these new distinctions, and the insights they provoke, are rewarded not only with laughs, but with an expanded media presence, a bigger market share, and, most important of all, with new perceptions of a common humanity in which Islam is present, and real, but can no longer be the dominant frame in which Self and Other are viewed. Muslim comedy, in this sense, bears a strong resemblance to more "serious" forms of immigrant incorporation.

The limits of this disciplinary process are visible on almost every page of this book: in police brutality, the failure of schools, political scapegoating, accusations of primitiveness, and the self-loathing manifest by prominent Muslim critics of Islam. The transformative success of the process is also evident: in the growing political incorporation of U.S. Muslims (not only in Detroit, but across urban America),[13] in the literal spread of Islam as a faith into terrain once forbidden to it, in the conspicuously modernizing variants of Hizbullah activism in Lebanon, in the careful blends of Western science and Islamic learning now being developed in educational establishments of the Muslim world, and in the ability of Muslims to model their identities on those of other ethnoracial and religious minorities who have used humor, civil rights activism, anti-defamation campaigns, and grassroots constituency politics to secure their place in national cultures that once excluded them from public life.

The irony of disciplinary inclusion, as applied to Islam and Muslims, is the extent to which it turns phobic and philic sentiments into the very architecture of identity formation. It constructs Muslim enemies even as (or precisely because) it stipulates the qualities of Muslim friends, and it encourages the latter to control and marginalize the former, a contest that unfolds in the self, the family, the community, the nation-state, and the transregional diaspora. As hegemonic as it now seems, the moral peculiarity of this political style is revealed immediately, and quite shockingly, if one tries to apply it to Christians or Jews as such. An application of this kind is forbidden in polite, metropolitan society; indeed, the ban defines polite metropolitan society, a space in which a person's enemy or friend status does not follow immediately from their status as a Christian or a Jew. The argument that Christianity (or Judaism) is, in key respects, antithetical to democracy, or national identity, or even to modernity, is not often made today, and those who care to pursue the argument in depth will be treated as intolerant cranks or denounced as anti-Semites.[14] The space given over in public discourse—in the U.S. or elsewhere in the world of Anglophone mass media—to the consideration of Christianity and Judaism as security threats, to the links between these belief systems and terror, and to the difficult task of turning Jews and Christians into viable, constructive members of modern society, is minuscule. Yet these themes are common in discussions of Islam, in the West and in the Muslim world, and they are as likely to surface in arguments made by Muslims, in religious terms, as they are by non-Muslim critics and allies. This predicament is explained, by our authors, not in reference to Islam as a set of universal beliefs and practices, but through reference to the stigmatizing and valorizing powers of modernity and the ideologies of personhood, citizenship, faith, and society it favors.

Because diverse possibilities for incorporation and exclusion are conveyed in these ideologies, understanding their histories, and their politics, is one of the most important social justice issues of our day.[15] Numerous commentators have argued that, if the twentieth century was defined by problems of race and the color line, the twenty-first will be defined by Islamophobia and the problem of integrating Muslims into modern, democratic societies, both in the West and in the Muslim world. These grand pronouncements bring with them a multitude of problematic assumptions, and they need to be given the same rigorous intellectual attention that has been devoted to the analysis of racism, class inequality, sexism, and other forms of political oppression. The contributors to this volume eagerly take up this task, exposing the tactical ignorance, malign and benign, that suffuses educated opinion on all things Muslim. Neither Islamophobia nor Islamophilia has cornered the market on mis/representation. The essays assembled here offer a deeper, more critical understanding of how these patterns of anxiety and attraction are continually reinvented, how they are expressed in multiple languages of identity, and how they relate to prevailing ideas—of race, gender, citizenship, secularism, human rights, tolerance, and pluralism—that are important to Muslims and non-Muslims alike.

Notes

1. A tandem reading of Edward Said's *Covering Islam* (1981) and Melani McAlister's *Epic Encounters* (2001), books written twenty years apart, shows the extent to which post-9/11 terror talk is a rhetorical continuation of the durable, anti-Muslim motifs that pervade Western media cultures.

2. Incidents of anti-Muslim violence and discrimination are catalogued by several watchdog groups, ranging from the American Civil Liberties Union to the American Arab Anti-Discrimination Committee. The annual reports provided by CAIR (the Council on American-Islamic Relations) are especially detailed and are available online at http://www .cair.com/Home.aspx. More specifically, CAIR's assessment of Islamophobia in the U.S. is available at http://www.cair.com/Issues/Islamophobia/Islamophobia.aspx.

3. Who thinks this way, exactly? Lists of prominent American Islamophobes are easy to generate, and I would rather not add another canon to the many now in circulation. For a concise and current naming of names, with a focus on the American punditocracy, one should consult the special report produced by FAIR (Fairness and Accuracy in Reporting), a media watchdog, at www.smearcasting.com. To sample the Islamophobic discourse in its most well-developed academic forms, one should tour the Campus Watch website, http:// www.campus-watch.org/, where the common fixations of the genre are on full, unapologetic display. Run by Daniel Pipes, this site is dedicated to exposing anti-American, anti-Israeli bias among Middle East studies scholars. Scholars who propagate such bias are, by the standards of Campus Watch, very likely to be Islamophiles.

4. A sampling of this scholarship would include McAlister (2001), Chomsky (2003), Gregory (2004), Beinin (2003), Mamdani (2004), Lincoln (2006), and Asad (2007). In

discussing terrorism, these authors are never far from a critique of Islamophobia. The two topics are virtually inseparable.

5. The full statement can be viewed at http://news.bbc.co.uk/2/hi/europe/4764730.stm.

6. Evelyn Alsultany (2007) catalogues recent public relations campaigns sponsored by the Council on American-Islamic Relations (CAIR), showing how they play on positive imagery available to American Muslims in an attempt to improve the image of Islam in the United States. Many of the themes I have identified as Islamophilic are front and center in CAIR publicity.

7. The manner in which these imperial encounters were based on fundamental inequalities, yet were also collaborative, transforming colonizers and the colonized, is demonstrated with great sensitivity in Ussama Makdisi's *Artillery of Heaven* (2008). This study of American Christian missionaries in nineteenth-century Lebanon/Syria contends with earlier forms of the Islamophobic and Islamophilic ideologies explored in this volume.

8. This sensibility is vividly on display in Bat Yeor's *Eurabia* (2005). For a fresh historical account of the last historical period in which Muslim political powers could effectively invade Christian Europe as such, garnering territory and converting Christians to Islam, see Marc Baer's *Honored by the Glory of Islam* (2008). The latter, with its sophisticated account of why and how Ottomans extended their domains into Christian realms, is especially useful in developing genealogies of Islamophobia in Europe; in many ways, it is the perfect complement to Mastnak's essay in this volume, and his earlier study on the origins of the crusading movement in Latin Christendom (2002).

9. Needless to say, this model of the contemporary world contradicts the popular "clash of civilizations" imagery developed by Samuel Huntington (1996). One might argue that investment in civilizational models, and the idea of necessary civilizational clashes, is an intellectual attempt to hem in processes of transregional cultural interaction that have become too promiscuous.

10. For a disturbing meditation on the place of Islam in Europe, see Talal Asad's "Muslims and European Identity" (2000). Written before the 9/11 attacks, this essay concludes that Muslims cannot be represented in Europe as Muslims under current regimes of citizenship, secular nationalism, and European identity. Asad's position, read in the aftermath of 9/11, seems only to replicate the problems of representation it analyzes. Throughout North America and Europe, Muslim activists and intellectuals are now making vigorous, successful bids for national inclusion, as Muslims, in terms Asad's analysis could not have foreseen. For one of the most challenging arguments in this new vein, see Tariq Ramadan (2005).

11. Examples of this generational revisionism are discussed in Naber (2005), Grewal (2009), and Ewing (2008).

12. For detailed accounts of how this process of discipline and inclusion can yield substantial political gains for Muslims, see Lara Deeb's (2006) study of Hizbullah activism in Lebanon and Jenny White's (2003) study of Islamist mobilizations in Turkey. How this process has unfolded among Arab Muslims in Detroit, in the years after 9/11, is described by Howell and Shryock (2003) and Howell and Jamal (2008).

13. The unexpected success of Muslim political mobilization in the U.S. after 9/11 is charted in recent work by Bakalian and Bozorgmehr (2005).

14. Despite the market appeal of anti-religious manifestoes like Christopher Hitchens's *God Is Not Great* (2007) or Richard Dawkins's *The God Delusion* (2008), such books have almost no policy-making potential, and as intellectual exercises, they are widely portrayed as the products of curmudgeonly minds.

15. This equation of historicism and political criticism with social justice is a common trope, and I see good reason to be skeptical. Secular academics, who believe religiously in history and its effects on the present, underestimate the advances that can be made by dispensing with the past. Movement beyond the politics of enemy and friend might require a prudent dose of tactical forgetting, or forgiveness.

Works Cited

Alsultany, Evelyn. 2007. "Selling American Diversity and Muslim American Identity through Non-Profit Advertising Post-9/11." *American Quarterly* 59(3): 593–622.

Asad, Talal. 2000. "Muslims and European Identity: Can Europe Represent Islam?" In *Cultural Encounters: Representing "Otherness,"* ed. Elizabeth Hallam and Brian Street, 11–27. London: Routledge.

———. 2007. *On Suicide Bombing.* New York: Columbia University Press.

Baer, Marc. 2008. *Honored by the Glory of Islam: Conversion and Conquest in Ottoman Europe.* New York: Oxford University Press.

Bakalian, Anny, and Mehdi Bozorgmehr. 2005. "Muslim American Mobilization." *Diaspora* 14(1): 7–43.

Bat Yeor. 2005. *Eurabia: The Euro-Arab Axis.* Madison, N.J.: Fairleigh Dickinson University Press.

Beinin, Joel. 2003. "Is Terrorism a Useful Term in Understanding the Middle East and the Palestinian-Israeli Conflict?" *Radical History Review* 85: 12–33.

Bowen, John. 2007. *Why the French Don't Like Headscarves: Islam, the State, and Public Space.* Princeton, N.J.: Princeton University Press.

Cesari, Jocelyne. 2002. "Islam in France: The Shaping of a Religious Minority." In *Muslims in the West: From Sojourners to Citizens,* ed. Yvonne Haddad, 36–51. New York: Oxford University Press.

———. 2006. *Securitization and Religious Divides in Europe: Muslims in Western Europe after 9/11—Why the Term Islamophobia Is More a Predicament than an Explanation.* A Challenge research project funded by the European Commission. http://www.liberty-security.org/article1167.html.

Chomsky, Noam. 2003. *Pirates and Emperors, Old and New: International Terrorism in the Real World.* Cambridge, Mass.: South End Press.

Commission on British Muslims and Islamophobia. 1997. *Islamophobia: A Challenge for Us All.* London: Runnymede Trust.

Dannin, Robert. 2002. *Black Pilgrimage to Islam.* New York: Oxford University Press.

Dawkins, Richard. 2008. *The God Delusion.* New York: Mariner Books.

Deeb, Lara. 2006. *An Enchanted Modern: Gender and Public Piety in Shiʻi Lebanon.* Princeton, N.J.: Princeton University Press.

Ewing, Katharine Pratt, ed. 2008. *Being and Belonging: Muslims in the United States Since 9/11.* New York: Russell Sage Foundation.

Gregory, Derek. 2004. *The Colonial Present.* Oxford: Blackwell.

Grewal, Zareena. 2009. "Marriage in Colour: Race, Religion, and Spouse Selection in Four American Mosques." *Ethnic and Racial Studies* 32(2): 323–45.

Hitchens, Christopher. 2007. *God Is Not Great: How Religion Poisons Everything.* New York: Twelve Books.

Howell, Sally, and Amaney Jamal. 2008. "Detroit Exceptionalism and the Limits of Political Incorporation." In *Being and Belonging: Muslims in the United States Since 9/11,* ed. Katherine Pratt Ewing, 47–79. New York: Russell Sage Foundation.

Howell, Sally, and Andrew Shryock. 2003. "Cracking Down on Diaspora: Arab Detroit and America's 'War on Terror'." *Anthropological Quarterly* 76(3): 443–62.

Huntington, Samuel. 1996. *The Clash of Civilizations and the Remaking of the World Order.* New York: Simon and Schuster.

Jackson, Sherman. 2005. *Islam and the Blackamerican: Looking Toward the Third Resurrection.* New York: Oxford University Press.

Leonard, Karen Isakson. 2003. *Muslims in the United States: The State of Research.* New York: Russell Sage Foundation.

Lincoln, Bruce. 2006. *Holy Terrors: Thinking about Religion after September 11.* Chicago: University of Chicago Press.

Makdisi, Ussma. 2008. *Artillery of Heaven: American Missionaries and the Failed Conversion of the Middle East.* Ithaca, N.Y.: Cornell University Press.

Mamdani, Mahmood. 2004. *Good Muslim, Bad Muslim: America, the Cold War, and the Roots of Terror.* New York: Pantheon Books.

Mastnak, Tomaž. 2002. *Crusading Peace: Christendom, the Muslim World, and Western Political Order.* Berkeley: University of California Press.

McAlister, Melani. 2001. *Epic Encounters: Culture, Media, and U.S. Interests in the Middle East, 1945–2000.* Berkeley: University of California Press.

Modood, Tariq. 2005. *Multicultural Politics: Racism, Ethnicity, and Muslims in Britain.* Minneapolis: University of Minnesota Press.

Naber, Nadine. 2005. "Muslim First, Arab Second: A Strategic Politics of Race and Gender." *The Muslim World* 95(4): 479–95.

Naber, Nadine, and Amaney Jamal, eds. 2008. *Race and Arab Americans Before and After 9/11: From Invisible Citizens to Visible Subjects.* Syracuse, N.Y.: Syracuse University Press.

Ramadan, Tariq. 2005. *Western Muslims and the Future of Islam.* New York: Oxford University Press.

Said, Edward. 1981. *Covering Islam.* New York: Pantheon Books.

Schmitt, Carl. 1996. *The Concept of the Political.* Chicago: University of Chicago Press.

Scott, Joan Wallach. 2007. *The Politics of the Veil*. Princeton, N.J.: Princeton University Press.

Sinno, Abdulkader, ed. 2009. *Muslims in Western Politics*. Bloomington: Indiana University Press.

Werbner, Pnina. 2005. "Islamophobia: Incitement to Religious Hatred—Legislating for a New Fear?" *Anthropology Today* 21(1): 5–9.

White, Jenny. 2003. *Islamist Political Mobilization in Turkey: A Study in Vernacular Politics*. Seattle: University of Washington Press.

Wieviorka, Michel. 2002. "Race, Culture, and Society: The French Experience with Muslims." In *Muslim Europe or Euro-Islam: Politics, Culture, and Citizenship in the Age of Globalization,* ed. Nezar AlSayyad and Manuel Castells, 131–46. Lanham, Md.: Lexington Books.

Part One Continuities and
Transformations

1

Western Hostility toward Muslims: A History of the Present

Tomaž Mastnak

"Islamophobia" is a new word but not a new phenomenon. The term is a close cousin of "xenophobia," and like other words in this family, it has proven useful in recent decades as transregional immigration and shifting national boundaries have produced political climates in which fearful, or overtly antagonistic, relationships to difference are resurgent. Whereas xenophobia signifies hostility toward a wide array of foreigners, or those perceived to be foreign, Islamophobia denotes hostility directed specifically at followers of Islam, at Muslims. As a target of hostility, Islam is hardly uniform. It is understood to be many things by non-Muslim observers, and Muslims themselves, who can be secular in their outlook, have equally divergent views of their faith. Those who could be described as "Islamophobes" do not correspond to a monolithic category, either. They are hostile to Muslims for a variety of reasons, and they cultivate this hostility in a diversity of cultural and political contexts.

Today Islamophobia is a global phenomenon. Because the contemporary world system is dominated by Western states, several of whom colonized Muslim territories in the recent past and still dominate them today, the forms of Islamophobia that pervade international media and global political discourse tend to reflect the interests and anxieties of Western, metropolitan societies. Despite the fact that multicultural pluralism and a general commitment to tolerance are central to the political self-image of the West, animosity toward Muslims is commonplace throughout Europe and North America, and Islam is often portrayed as a serious threat to secularism, or democracy, or, on a far grander scale, to Western civilization itself (see introduction). These sentiments did not emerge out of thin air, and the conflicts of the last decade, no matter how intense, are not sufficient to explain them.

The ideological complex we now refer to as Islamophobia is rooted in far older traditions of hostility toward Muslims. These traditions have, over a span of centuries, shaped Latin Christianity and European identity in fundamental ways. The temporal depth, enduring tropes, and political tenacity of these traditions are the bedrock on which contemporary Islamophobia is built; even cultural trends that are conspicuously Islamophilic (that endorse a supportive, congenial relationship to Islam and Muslims) are colored by this legacy. A greater awareness of the antiquity and persistence of Western hostility toward Muslims is a necessary element of any political or intellectual agenda that hopes to overcome it.

I.

Deep-seated animosity toward Muslims was created at a particular moment in history. That moment coincided neither with the advent of Islam nor with the Muslim threat to, and incursions into, regions now called "the West." Even a clear Muslim threat to Christian lands in the early Middle Ages did not trigger an all-embracing war. Islam and Christianity are not naturally, automatically, or necessarily inclined toward an all-consuming conflict.

Muslim conquests in the Iberian Peninsula in the early eighth century, which followed repeated raids into southern Italy and Sicily in the preceding half century, were recorded by Latin Christians in the dry language of chronicles. But the religion of the invaders did not itself stir much curiosity. Some seventh- and eighth-century Western pilgrims to the Holy Places did not even notice religious differences between Christians and Muslims, whom Latin Christians usually called Saracens.[1] In the East, Christian polemics against the new religion seem to have appeared soon after Muslim conquests in the region, but only with John of Damascus (almost a century after Muhammad's revelation) did this discourse cover the ground and take the form that would later become stock in trade in the West. When and how Eastern Christian polemics against Islam were transmitted to the West begs more research.

In the lands where Christianity and Islam originated, the two religions appear to have peacefully coexisted in the early years of Islam. Travelogues by Western pilgrims give a picture of an apparently undisturbed Christian religious life. One can read reports that, in some cases, Christians and Saracens "shared a church."[2] When, in the seventh and eighth centuries, Muslims reached the European peninsula, Latin Christians saw them as one among many pagan, infidel, or barbarian enemies. Among this host, Muslims were assigned no privileged place. Western Christians saw neither Muslims nor Islam as a special threat to the Christian religion.

The Latin Christians' early response to Muslims was not friendly, but it was quite moderate in tone. Seventh- and eighth-century Merovingian chroniclers represented Saracen conquests as secular wars no different from the many other wars they recorded. Their Carolingian successors wrote of the anti-Saracen campaigns as an element in the Carolingians' endeavors to strengthen their rule in what is today southern France. Neither the Muslim nor the Christian wars were seen as specifically religious wars. Christian scribes did not vilify Saracens and lacked interest in the invaders' religion.[3] Muslims played a relatively unimportant role in Carolingian portrayals of the cosmic struggle between Good and Evil, and while the Carolingians occasionally waged wars against Muslims, they also maintained diplomatic relations with them.

Christian views of Muslims began to shift in the mid–ninth century. One moment in that shift was the episode of the "martyrs of Córdoba." In the 850s, Muslim authorities decapitated close to fifty Christians found guilty of blasphemy. Those Christians had publicly insulted Islam and reviled Muhammad. The Christian community was split in its reaction to these "martyrs." On the one hand, Christian townsfolk of Córdoba pointed out that the Cordoban authorities had not persecuted the Christians. They refused to recognize their fanatical co-religionists as legitimate martyrs because they had "suffered at the hands of men who venerated both God and law."[4] On the other hand, the "martyrs" enjoyed support from the outlying monasteries.

This extremist confrontation with Islam seems to have been an expression of anxiety over the loss of Christian identity. The walls the Muslim conquerors initially built to separate themselves from the Christians soon began to crumble. Assimilation and acculturation advanced in both directions, but especially toward Islam. Numerous Christians were employed in the public administration, immersed themselves in Arabic literature, and accumulated wealth in a prosperous commercial empire.[5] In response to such appeasement, the "martyrs" and their apologists worked to affirm the exclusivity of Christianity. If one accepted that the "martyrs" were killed by men who "worship God" and have a valid "cult or law," the apologists Eulogius and Alvarus asserted, "the strength of the Christian religion must necessarily be impaired." In order to support their exclusivist claim and defend Christianity, the martyrs' apologists attacked Muhammad as a "demoniac full of lies," who could not speak the truth, as one "enveloped in fallacies," who could not establish law, and as a "perverse grove," unable to produce good fruit. As one who had formed "a sect of novel superstition at the instigation of the devil," Muhammad was called "heresiarch" and "antichrist."[6]

The other impetus for the change in Christian views of Islam came from Rome. Faced with the military presence of the Saracens in southern Italy and with local Christians making alliances with the invaders, Pope John VIII (872–82) promoted a new, uncompromisingly hostile view of the Muslims and banned Christians from making alliances with them. He pictured the *impia gens Saracenorum,* hateful to God, as a grave danger to the Christian way of life.[7] He pronounced that divine law prohibited any social links between the faithful and the unfaithful and, in particular, the crafting of treaties and alliances with the infidels. Those who made unclean alliances with Saracens acted against Christ himself.[8] Even keeping peace with the "most evil" was a crime. The faithful, Pope John pronounced, had to desist from making peace with the enemies of God.[9]

In practice, John VIII's efforts to break the "impious alliances" were unsuccessful. The two centuries that passed between John VIII's papacy and the launching of the First Crusade saw continuing contacts between Christians and Muslims and lacked any clear focus on the latter as enemies. The monastic reform at the turn of the millennium, which radiated from Cluny, appears to have inspired some French monks to cross the Pyrenees in order to take possession of mosques or simply "to kill a Moor."[10] The eleventh-century Church reformers, especially Pope Leo IX (1049–54) and Pope Gregory VII (1073–85) and their polemicists, however, considered bad Christians their worst enemies—more detestable than Jews and pagans, among whom Saracens were hardly ever named. Neither did the imperial writers of the period regard Muslims as *the* enemy.

In sum, before the end of the eleventh century, Christian animosity toward non-Christians was diffused. Muslims were not yet the chosen enemy people. In general, Latin Christians were indifferent to Muslim culture and religion, of which even the educated among them knew virtually nothing. They regarded Muslims as "only one of a large number of enemies threatening Christendom from every direction, and they had no interest in distinguishing the primitive idolatries of Northmen, Slavs, and Magyars from the monotheism of Islam, or the Manichean heresy from that of Mahomet," and there appears to be little evidence that, before the launching of the First Crusade, "anyone in northern Europe had even heard the name of Mahomet."[11]

A momentous change occurred with the Crusades. When Pope Urban II launched the First Crusade in 1095, he did not so much raise hostility toward Muslims, which had hitherto in the main been dormant in the Latin West, to new heights.[12] Rather, he eliminated the ambiguities in Christian views of Muslims (which had characterized such a great figure of that age as Pope Gregory VII)[13] and fixed the image of the Muslim as the focal point for Christian animosities. In his theology of history, Pope Urban saw his time as the age of confrontation with the Muslims: God fought the Muslims through the Christian soldiers. In a letter to Bishop Peter of Huesca, written during the First Crusade, Pope Urban said that God had "in our days with the help of Christian forces combated the Turks in Asia and Moors in Europe, and through special mercy restored to his worship once famous cities."[14] Christian military successes in Spain and the Orient were a turning point in redemptive history. Fighting Muslims, Christians found atonement with their God.[15]

At a point in history when Muslims presented no threat in any real terms to Christendom, Muslims became *the* enemy of Christianity and Christendom: their normative, fundamental, quintessential, universal enemy. They represented infidelity as such, the embodiment of evil and the personification of the very religion of the Antichrist. The Muslim world became no less than "the antithetical system, the social Antichrist."[16] Whereas, in fact, Christians had been on the offensive against Muslims in the Mediterranean for roughly a century, they still felt threatened and dislocated. Within the Latin West, anarchy was widespread, violence was endemic, the millenary of Christ's birth and passion dominated mental horizons, and time was rife with eschatological, apocalyptic, and chiliastic fears and expectations.[17] The clear-cut image of the Muslim enemy must have been a welcome response to the internal drama of Christendom, facing all the calamities of that age, accounting for its own sinfulness, searching for a public order, and hoping for salvation. Against the Muslim enemy, Christians could unite in peace. Their peace efforts, which had been under way for a century, could be enhanced and came to fruition in a God-willed war against Muslims, the sworn enemies of Christ's name.

With the Crusades, Christendom as a specific historical form of Latin Christian unity came of age.[18] The construction of the Muslim enemy was an essential moment in the articulation of the self-awareness of the *res publica christiana*. The antagonistic difference between themselves and Muslims became at this crucial point a constitutive element of the Latin Christians' collective identity. The work of that collective identity or, rather, that collective identity at work was the Crusade itself, the war against the fundamental enemy. The mobilization for and leadership of the Crusade was a powerful lever that helped to settle power struggles among the ruling orders of society and thus to define the contours of public order. The setting up of an internal order in Christian society and, among particular Christian entities, in Christendom was at the same time the shaping of a global order. A defining trait of that global order was the fundamental unacceptability to Western Christians of the existence of the Muslims as Muslims.

II.

With the waning of the Middle Ages, one historical form of Western unity, Christendom, was succeeded by another: Europe. Roughly coinciding with that change, one image of the Muslim enemy, the Saracen, gave way to another: the Turk. What did not change was animosity toward Muslims. In fact, the establishment of the Muslim as *the* enemy, which was integral to the Crusades, was of direct relevance for the articulation of Europe as the new historical form of the broadest community of Western Christians. In response to the fall of Constantinople to the Turks in 1453, Latin Christian ecclesiastical and secular leaders and leading intellectuals drew on that heritage. They took over the symbolic figure of the Muslim enemy as the "reconciler of brethren." They seized on fundamental animosity toward Muslims, forged during the First Crusade and cultivated over the next three centuries, and reformulated it in such a way that the sense of "us-ness" it invoked began to refer to the entity called Europe.

Facing the Muslim enemy, Aeneas Sylvius Piccolomini (1405–64) asserted a fundamental unity of European culture. His illustrious career as a humanist man of letters and political man of action was crowned by his election as Pope Pius II in 1458. When Constantinople fell, Piccolomini was inspired to write of Greek culture as the well of Europe's sciences and arts. The studies cultivated by the Latins were only rivulets flowing from the Greek spring. With the Ottoman capture of Constantinople, the stream of learning had been cut off; the spring of muses had dried up; Homer, other illustrious poets, and Plato had died a second death.[19] Against the Turks as the enemies of both Greek and Latin culture, Europe appeared as a cultural whole. Against the Turks, Piccolomini represented Europe as a religious unity as well. Because Christians had fled and left victory to *Maumeto*, Christianity had been reduced to Europe, and Europe became identical with Christianity.[20] As a geographically well-defined cultural and religious whole, Europe became the Christians' homeland. Piccolomini warned his contemporaries that "we are persecuted by the enemy's hand in Europe, on our own soil."[21] "In former times," he continued, "we namely suffered damage in Asia and Africa, that is to say, in foreign lands; but now we are most badly struck in Europe, that is, in our *patria*, in our own home, in our dwelling-place."[22]

When Europe became the reference point for the sense of "us-ness" directed against the Turk, the Muslim became the enemy of Europe. The rallying cry, which transformed Christendom into Europe and Latin Christians into Europeans, was to "liberate Europe," to "chase the Turk out of Europe." Muslims were now seen as threats to the geographical integrity of Europe, to its common culture, its freedom, religion, and way of life. The Muslim was the existential enemy and action against him—of which Europe was the agent, the arena, and the goal—was accordingly nihilistic.[23] Europe was born under the aegis of cleansing. Along with "chasing the Turk out of Europe," the mobilizing slogans were to "erase the Turkish name from Europe" and to "exterminate the Turk in Europe."

These formulae encapsulated intense intellectual developments. Piccolomini was but one among many lay intellectuals and ecclesiastical men of power who participated in the militant birth of Europe. The slogan of "chasing the Turk out of Europe" became, in the mid–fifteenth century, a humanist commonplace. Poggio Bracciolini, Orazio Romano, Andrea Contrario, Nicolao Sagundino, Flavio Biondo, Panormita, and Francesco Filelfo, among others, had much to say on that account. On the fringes of the intellectual elite, the programmatic catchphrase of "chasing the Turk out of Europe" was recorded by chroniclers from Burgundy to the Czech lands and was duly taken up by writers of historical treatises dealing with the "Turkish question."

The vision of "driving the Turks out of Europe" was also embraced by the people. They listened to the preaching of the crusade, joined in daily prayers against the Turks, and paid crusading taxes. The new printing press was mobilized to further the case of war against the Turks. The printers "kept the Turkish peril before the eyes of an ever-expanding reading public" not only by printing books and booklets (often containing vivid, suggestive pictures of the "cruel Turk") but also by publishing broadsides and newssheets (proto-newspapers).[24] It is significant that the first German book printed by Gutenberg addressed the "Turkish question." In the "Turkish Calendar" for the year 1455, the verses for each month of the year called on a particular Christian prince or people to wage war against the Turks. The booklet closed with a prayer to the Lord, beseeching him to help drive out the evil Turk and his people, so that none of them would be left alive "neither in Turkey, Greece, Asia, nor Europe."[25]

The calls on Christians—and on Christian princes in particular—to end their quarrels and wars and join forces against the Muslims were abundant in Western Christian literature of the period. This "crusading commonplace"[26] was the basis of numberless plans and projects for peace and unity in Europe. At the beginning of this literary genre stands the "Grand Design" of the Duke of Sully, written early in the seventeenth century, in which Winston Churchill found inspiration for the integration of Europe in his day.[27] In Sully's plan, as soon as Europe had been pacified, a European army was to chase "strangers" from Europe and conquer "such parts of Asia as were most commodiously situated, and particularly the whole coast of Africa, which is too near to our own territories for us not to be frequently incommoded by it." The grand idea of the "Grand Design" was to "convert the continual wars among its several princes, into a perpetual war against the Infidels."[28]

Such perpetual war—I would call it a perpetual crusade—was a standard ingredient in the politics and political imagination of early modern Europe. As a formative principle and imperative, it was not shattered by deals and compromises made in practical politics. To a degree we should not underestimate, this perpetual crusade has framed Western policies and politics. The ideas and attitudes that constitute the perpetual crusade, and are reproduced by it, have crosscut religious, ideological, cultural, and ethnic divides among Christians. They have been voiced in different political languages across different historical periods, creating shared ground even among opponents and foes. They are inseparable from cherished Western ideals of liberty, rights, justice, peace, and humanity. They belong to the same web of thought and imagery as those ideals. They are part of what makes Western thought complex and, as such, not an unqualified good.

A brief—and correspondingly simplified—overview of the ubiquity of anti-Muslim attitudes in European intellectual and political history will substantiate these claims. It is best to start with the Christian humanists. The most influential of them, Erasmus of Rotterdam (1466/69–1536), is famous for his apparently uncompromising rejection of war. Yet he approved of war against the Turks on more than defensive grounds alone. If human nature was "quite unable to carry on without wars," why, Erasmus asked rhetorically, "is this evil passion not let loose upon the Turks?" War against the Turks, he argued, "would be a lesser evil than the present unholy conflicts and clashes between Christians."[29] He urged concord among Christian princes and employment of their arms against the Turks, whom he regarded as barbarians and called monstrous beasts, enemies of the Church, and a people contaminated by all manner of crimes and ignominies.[30]

Thomas More saw the Turks as representing the forces of darkness and Belial, and he wrote about their "high malice and hatred" and "incomparable cruelty."[31] He joined the choir calling for peace and concord among Christians so they could successfully fight the common enemy and defend God's name. In his polemics against Luther, whom he saw as doing now what "Mahomete dyd before," More took issue with Luther's position (which Luther himself later abandoned), "that it is not lefull to any crysten man to fight against ye Turke / or to make agaynst hym any resystence / thoughe he come in to crystendome with a grete army and laboure to destroy all." For More, this was one among the Lutherans' many heresies.[32] In his own view, there was "no reason to loke that crysten pryncys sholde suffer the catholyke crysten people to be oppressed by Turkys / or by heretykes worse than Turkys."[33] More admitted that Christ and his holy apostles exhorted "euery manm to pacyence and sufferaunce / without requytynge of an euyll dede or making any defence / but vsyng further sufferaunce / and doynge also good for euyll." Yet that "counsayll" was not absolutely binding. In case of "necessyte agaynste the comen nature," man is allowed to defend himself as well as an innocent victim of invasion or oppression "by malyce." In such cases, a Christian was to follow Moses rather than the gospel: "bothe nature / reason / and goddys byheste byndeth / fyrste the prynce to the sauegarde of hys peple with the parell of hym selfe / as he taught Moyses to know hym selfe bounden to kyll Egypcyans in the defence of Hebrewe / and after he byndeth euery man to the helpe & defence of his good & harmles neyghbour / agaynst the malyce and cruelty of the wronge doer." Such "comen warre which euery peple taketh in ye defence of theyr countre" and which every man fights "of a crysten charyte," was not "only excusable but also commendable." War against the Turks was such a war par excellence: "Whych reason as it hath place in all batayle of defence / so hath it most especyally in the batayle by whyche we defende the crysten countrees agaynste the Turkys."[34]

Juan Luis Vives (1492–1540), the youngest of the group, gave much thought to Muslims. The only relation he could imagine with them was war. His writings were a reveille for Europe to unite against the Turk and to "rush with arms at the ready to destroy him."[35] He went beyond imagining a liberation of European nations from the Turkish yoke. He thought of conquest. Instead of fighting each other for the handful of soil they could wrest from one another, he argued, Europeans should march against the Turks as a united Christian army, crush their power, and take possession of the abundant land and wealth of Asia.

The "discovery" and colonization of America was, to a large degree, conceived in the framework of a crusading imagination. Columbus himself understood his "Indian enterprise" as a step towards the recovery of Jerusalem. The question of how the American natives were to be treated was decided on whether or not they were like the Turks. A case in point is the famous dispute between Las Casas and Sepúlveda. The disputants shared a hostile view of the

Muslims, but drew opposite conclusions from that common ground. Sepúlveda extended European attitudes toward the Turks to the Indians and used arguments for war against Turks to justify war against Indians. Las Casas, in line with theologians from Salamanca, endeavored to prove that Amerindians were not Turks and should, consequently, be treated differently—that is, peacefully. He agreed with the conquest against "Moors from Africa, Turks, and heretics who seize our lands, persecute Christians and work for the destruction of our faith." But as to America, "there should be no talk of conquest, as if the Indians were African Moors or Turks, but only the preaching of the gospel of Christ 'with gentle and divine words.'"[36]

The Reformation, likewise, did not shake European views of the Turk. To Protestants and Catholics alike, the Turk represented sin, or evil, itself. The divisive question was who represented the "Turks" in Europe—that is, who were "our Christian Turks" as opposed to the "Mohammedan Turks"—the Protestants or the Catholics?[37] To be called a "Turk" by a Christian adversary was to be denounced as the enemy of Christ. For Luther, Turks were servants of the devil and his instrument, a wild people under whom the Christian faith could not survive. Both Muhammad and the "Turkish emperor" were possessed by the devil, and their armies were the devil's own. The Turks' faith was scandalous, absurd, and filthy. The *Quran* was a foul, shameful, and abominable book that distorted Christianity even while it praised Jesus and Mary. It taught a disorderly doctrine of worldly government and commanded the Turks to plunder and murder, to devour and destroy everything around them. Unlike other powers that be, the Turkish *Regiment* was not a power ordained by God. *Mahmet,* the Prophet, was a son of the devil and the devil's apostle. The distinction between him and the pope was that *Mahmet* was the "rude devil" (*grobe Teuffel*), whereas the pope was the "subtle devil" (*subtile Teuffel*).[38] Because the "Turks or Saracens" took "that book of *Mehmet,* the *Alcoran,*" seriously, they did not "deserve to be called human," since their belief in the *Quran* was a proof that they were deprived of "common human reason." (But if they were human and did not lack reason, and believed in the *Quran* knowingly and willingly, they could not blame their perdition on anybody else.)[39]

On a more political level, Luther questioned papal power, condemned clerical participation in warfare, and rejected the efficacy of good works in the individual's search for salvation. As such, he consequently objected to the crusade—war under the pope's command, in which clerics took part and individuals looked for salvation. Luther saw Turkish military successes in Europe as divine punishment for Christians' sinful ways and, in his younger years, argued against resistance to Turkish attacks. He soon changed his stance, but he replaced crusades led by the pope and clerics with a war against the Turks (*Türkenkrieg*) conducted by lay princes. By the time the Turks held Vienna under siege, in 1529, Luther clearly declared his support for the *Türkenkrieg*—and accused the popes of never having seriously intended to fight the Turks.[40] Even when led by secular rulers, war against the Turks retained a godly character; it was *gotseligen Krieg*.[41] The Protestants helped to secularize, if not desacralize, war against the Turks.

The new humanists of the late sixteenth century differed from their Renaissance predecessors in that they were inspired by the political realist Tacitus rather than the moralist Cicero. But like the Renaissance humanists before them, they gave considerable time and energy to thinking about a common European military enterprise against the Turks. Justus Lipsius, a luminary of this new school, was surprisingly conventional when it came to the "Turkish question." Europe, broken by incessant wars and civil strife, needed "one head" which would be an "effective force for religious unity, for the well-being of all its subjects, and for the struggle against the common enemy, the Turks."[42] When, in his old age, the great humanist thought obsessively about making a crusade, he was not alone. In the late sixteenth and early seventeenth centuries, appeals for European unity against the Turks were frequent and crusading plans were many.

For men like Botero, Ammirato, Campanella, and Francis Bacon, leading figures of the second generation of new humanists, Christian and European unity against the Turks remained a central concern. Botero, for example, understood very well that armed forces were of vital importance for defense and maintenance of the state, and he regarded war as the best means for eliminating evil spirits and diverting people from dangerous thoughts. The question for him was, against whom could arms be legitimately used? Luckily, he stated, a Christian prince will always have a cause for war, for there will always be enough Turks, Moors, and Saracens against whom war will always be just, justified, and universally lawful. His advice was to attack the Turks in their own land instead of sitting at home and waiting for them to come.[43]

Later in the seventeenth century, the "Turkish question" was of grave concern to people all over Europe, and it was discussed with real passion. Men at the very center of European politics of the time, like Father Joseph (Richelieu's *éminence grise*) and the Duke of Nevers, worked on preparations for a crusade. And the best minds of Europe did not find it undignified to occupy themselves with the "Turkish threat" and war against the Turks. The great philosopher Leibniz is a case in point. Whereas he considered war within Europe both scandalous and futile, he regarded war against barbarian infidels as just. Wishing to divert French aggression from the Netherlands, obtain security for the German empire, and prevent war in Europe, Leibniz suggested to Louis XIV that he conquer Egypt. The conquest of Egypt was of great strategic importance, for it was in Egypt that the Ottoman Empire was most vulnerable. This conquest was urgent because it would preempt the reform of the Ottoman Empire that the sultan was about to undertake. The common good of Christendom and security of Europe, Leibniz argued, required that the Turks be kept in their deep slumber of ignorance.[44]

When, as a patriot, Leibniz worried about the decline of martial spirit among Germans, he proposed the formation of a new Teutonic Order to fight the *Türcken* and other enemies. Ideally, war against the Turks should be permanent, unceasing warfare.[45] As a European, the old and resigned philosopher wrote to Saint-Pierre that a remedy for the evil of wars disturbing Europe might be "to help the Emperor to chase the Turks out of Europe."[46] Abbé de Saint-Pierre (1658–1743) was a famous name during his lifetime. D'Alembert eulogized him as an "enemy of religious intolerance" and mentioned in the same breath that, as a "professed enemy of all the errors that debase and eat up the human race," the abbé "vowed a special aversion to the Muslim religion." Saint-Pierre regarded Islam as "one of the greatest scourges of the human race" and wanted to "extirpate Mohammedanism." The "speeding up of the annihilation of Mohammedanism" was "very much on his mind."[47]

Saint-Pierre indeed believed that *Mahometisme* had been declining in proportion to the growth of "universal reason" among the Mohammedans. All that was false, obscure, absurd, and incomprehensible in Islam—a religion founded by an impostor, deceiver, fanatic, and madman—was going to dissipate in the light of reason. The Muslims would be freed from the necessity of pilgrimages to Mecca, daily prayers, circumcision, fasting during Ramadan, and incessant washing. They would be liberated from the prohibition against eating pork and drinking wine, and from their own religious intolerance. As such, the Muslims would become "reasonable" and, as *Mahometans rézonables,* could be tolerated.[48] But until that time, said Saint-Pierre, Europeans had to get rid of the illusion that "the Arabs are men like us." "Utterly ignorant" as they were, they had to be put in their proper place.[49]

The imperative of keeping the Mohammedans in their place may be seen as Saint-Pierre's guideline for solving the "Muslim question." His plan for European unity and peace, for which he is mainly renowned, was a plan for a general crusade. He came to the conclusion that it was advantageous, convenient, and glorious for Christian sovereigns to go to war to "chase the Turk out of Europe and even out of Asia and Africa."[50] Saint-Pierre's European union was a device for "making the way to a universal crusade, incomparably more solid and better concerted than all the previous."[51] The great objective of this enlightened crusade was "the conquest of everything that the Turks possess in Europe and on the Mediterranean islands, in Asia and Africa."[52] Saint-Pierre thought of establishing "many new Christian sovereignties" on the ruins of the Turkish empire,[53] and he defined European union and peace as "the only means for making Europe and the European order [la police Europaine] reign in all parts of the world."[54]

Saint-Pierre was neither eccentric nor anachronistic. The crusading spirit was not alien to the Age of Reason. Voltaire, the very symbol of the Enlightenment, is a vivid example of this ethos. He wrote that the Turks were, along with the plague, the greatest curse on earth. He wanted to annihilate them. "It does not suffice to humiliate them," he said, "they should be destroyed."[55] He deplored the fact that "the Christian powers, instead of destroying the common enemies, were engaged in bringing each other to ruin," and he corresponded with the philosopher-king Frederick II about the hoped-for pleasure of seeing "the Muslims driven out of Europe."[56] In a letter to Catherine II of Russia, Voltaire confided in unequivocal terms: "Overcome the Turks, and I will die content." Toward the end of his days the great Enlightenment philosopher seems to have felt that his life was not complete, that there was more he could have done. "I wish," he wrote to the czarina, "I had at least been able to help you kill a few Turcs."[57]

In 1788, ten years after Voltaire's death and a year before the revolution, the French scholar and politician Volney tried to dissuade France from getting involved in the Russo-Turkish war. But Volney did not argue against anti-Turkish war as such. A man of a new age, he reflected on the universalization of civilization (radiating, of course, from Europe) and the gradual formation of a "great society" of humankind.[58] But Volney saw Asian despotism as an impediment to the improvement of the human race and considered the Ottoman "barbarians" a plague, and a vicious one at that, because "with their stupid fanaticism they perpetuate the contagion by renewing its germs." The Turks had, of course, to be "chased out of Europe." But Volney expected that other powers than France would do the job. Russia had a prominent role to play here. Volney was happy to imagine Catherine II becoming "the empress of Constantinople and restorer of the Greek Empire," and that "other peoples" might establish themselves where the Turks had lived.[59]

The French Revolution does not appear to have caused any drastic change in European attitudes toward the Muslim world. The conquest of Egypt, a very old idea, was an offspring of the revolution. It was a first step in the process that, in about a century, would bring three-quarters of the world's Muslim population under European domination.

After rivalries among the European powers had already brought about a world war, a great French historian of the crusades was inspired to describe, in a book written for a popular audience, French and English machinations in the Middle East as a replay of the old crusades. In 1914, he suggested, the "Franks" set foot in Syria again in order, four years later, to "deliver Tripoli, Beirut, and Tyre, the city of Raymond of Saint-Gilles, the city of John of Ibelin, the city of Philip de Montfort. As to Jerusalem, it was to be 'reoccupied' on December 9, 1917, by the descendants of King Richard under the command of Marshal Allenby."[60]

If this is not irreproachable historiography, it is a realistic political judgment. Its realism lies in understanding the presence and power of the crusading spirit in our lives. The French historian was mistaken only in his belief that the Crusades were finally accomplished. In fact, we are living with the consequences of that apparent final triumph. The Middle East had to be recovered again in our own day. A new crusade, still well under way, was declared on September 16, 2001.

III.

My narrative so far has dealt with Western animosity toward Muslims. The focus can easily be justified. When it comes to the Muslims and their world, Islamophobia is the dominant Western tradition, even though Christians lived securely in Muslim domains, as minorities, throughout the centuries I have described here.[61] When in our own day it comes to grappling with actual and looming political disasters, linked in one way or another to the relations between the West and the Muslim world, it is the Islamophobic tradition that is of greatest consequence for us. Next to Islamophobia, Islamophilia has always been marginal and full of contradictions. I want to conclude this paper with a note on Islamophilia.

In benevolent accounts of the Western tradition of Christian-Muslim relations, which apparently want to give us hope by playing down the uglier aspects of that tradition, there appear a set of figures who are said to have been peacefully and lovingly disposed to the Muslims. Some of them are represented as critics of the Crusades, opponents of the shedding of blood, proponents of dialogue, and advocates of coexistence between the followers of Christianity and Islam. I have shown elsewhere that there are clear limits to their criticism, irenism, and ecumenicalism.[62] Moreover, juxtaposed to their

Islamophilic utterances and gestures, or even as a (perhaps suppressed) part of them, one detects more conventional Islamophobic attitudes. Let me cite just a few examples.

Peter the Venerable, a great man of early-twelfth-century Christendom, wrote many a kind word about approaching "the sons of Ishmael, who observe the law of that one who is called *Mahumeth* . . . not in hatred, but in love."[63] He concluded, however, that the Muslim doctrine was the "foremost error of errors," the "dregs of all the heresies into which all the remnants of the diabolical doctrine have flown together, which came into existence since the very coming of the Saviour."[64] Ultimately, he set out to prove, as did so many Christian polemicists, that Islam was unreasonable, from which it followed that Muslims were not reasonable and were, as such, not human, since God endowed men with reason. In the end, he helped organize the Second Crusade.

St. Francis is often praised for choosing to address the Egyptian sultan with words rather than swords, bringing to the infidel prince the divine truth. But he approved of crusading. His Franciscan brethren did their own share of abusing Islam. Roger Bacon, one of the order, who lived in the thirteenth century, declared that he preferred preaching, in the hope of converting Muslims, to killing them. He abhorred the shedding of blood. Therefore, in case preaching to Muslims had no success, he devised a scientific scheme to use burning mirrors to destroy the enemy without blood being spilled.[65] Raimundus Lullus, a Franciscan tertiary who lived into the second decade of the fourteenth century, considered the Muslims a defect in the structure of the universe.[66] This much admired Majorcan "doctor of mission" thought out methods of convincing them of the truth of Christianity that remind me of the "sensory overload" employed by today's torturers. If such persuasion failed, he would rely on the sword. Père Joseph was later to sing of "Francia, Franciscus" as "fatalia nomina Turcis."[67]

Leaving aside Platonic Orientalism, a tradition rich in phobic and philic approaches to Islam, I want to place my focus on today's torturers, whom I see as practitioners of certain brands of Orientalism. These indispensable experts in what is marketed as "the war on terror" draw part of their expertise from Orientalist insights. A case in point is Raphael Patai's book *The Arab Mind,* which has acquired great notoriety since Abu Ghraib. It has been allotted a place of honor in the genealogy of torture methods to which Muslim suspects are subjected in our contemporary global gulag. Patai's case shows how thin the line between philia and phobia can be. This is how he described his book when he had just finished it: "Seriously though, I am convinced that if, in analyzing the Arab character, I occasionally deviate from strict objectivity, it is in the direction of a romantic sympathy with the Arabs which has been with me ever since my early youth. In the very personal preface I wrote to the book I tried to show the various roots of this incurable Arabophilism."[68]

Patai sent these words to Robert Graves, with whom he had written a book on Hebrew myths (which added hardly anything new to Louis Ginzberg's *The Legends of the Jews*). Graves, a prolific English writer, responded in kind: "I hope your *Arab Mind* is successful. My two closest friends, Sufis, are in direct senior descent from the Prophet (from whom I am also descended, like most of us English gentry, including the Queen, via Edward III and Spanish Alfonso line). So I have a love and sympathy with Arabs especially the medieval ones who civilized S. Europe and introduced the romantic love-motif. I am glad that you are similarly attached."[69]

Graves translated Patai's Islamophilia with an ethnic turn into Islamophilia proper. As the object of his philia he chose Sufism, which is easier to be loved by non-Muslims in the West because of its mysticism and the corresponding emphasis on the inner experience of the divine rather than on shari'ah—the "outer path," the Muslim law. Instead of common religious descent from Abraham, which is on offer, Graves established blood relations between the Prophet, English gentry, and himself. He picked up the idea of Muslim cultural and scientific—civilizational—influences on the backward Europe of the Middle Ages, popular at least since Hans Prutz's *Cultural History of the Crusades*[70] and standard fare for those who want to portray Islam in a positive light for Western audiences today. And he did not forget our debt to the Arabs for the "romantic love-motif." Had he lived a century earlier, he would certainly have added chivalry, as exemplified by Saladin. The motif common to the times between Walter Scott and Robert Graves was that of love, the longing for those "wilder shores of love" that lay beyond the sea. Ultimately, both Muslim and Christian civilizations are civilizations of love.

Why, then, should there be a clash of civilizations? The clash of civilizations, which is as a rule popularly understood to be a clash between the West and the Islamic world, is a result of politics and policies, as well as deeds and actions on the level of civil society, which generate it. Today, there are numerous efforts and initiatives to de-escalate the tensions. By an unexpected twist of fate, I happen to know one of these projects from the inside. After its inception and until our ways parted (December 2006–August 2007), I was the director of the Secretariat of the United Nations' Alliance of Civilizations initiative. The originator of the initiative was Spanish prime minister José Luis Rodriguez Zapatero, who had promised in his 2004 election campaign to pull Spanish troops out of Iraq. With the adoption of the initiative by the United Nations, the binary nature of the conflict the initiative was meant to address was built into the structure of the initiative itself. Started by a Christian country, Spain, the initiative had to be co-sponsored by a Muslim one, Turkey. It is hardly coincidence that these two countries were historically the site of intense Muslim-Christian conflict, as well as long periods of peaceful coexistence, and that both have a vexed relationship to Europe and to modernity, a place and a quality to which Spain and Turkey are widely believed to be marginal.

The new bloc division of the alliance was then reproduced in the High-Level Group, a body of dignitaries who, before the year was over, had to report to the U.N. secretary-general and present a package of "practical measures" to counter the rise of extremism (which, by tacit agreement, was predominantly understood to be Islamic extremism). The members of that group, which had to represent the global community, were chosen so as to give equal representation to the "West" and the "Islamic world." The West was a chimerical notion that resisted neat translation into a formal structure, so the de facto division of the High-Level Group became the Islamic world and the rest of the world. The Islamic world was represented exclusively by secular and moderate Muslims, the former outnumbering the latter.[71] Despite many good intentions, it seems fair to say that the initiative's main expressed concern turned out to be the threat of Islam, especially variants of Islam that were not subservient to current notions of moderation or subsumable in nostalgia for the declining Muslim secular elites. As with much older Christian polemics against Jews and Muslims, this threatening Other had no voice in the "alliance of civilizations."

Like any high-level political initiative, part of the raison d'être of the Alliance of Civilizations initiative was to provide a raison d'être for some very important persons temporarily out of very important positions. As such, the initiative at moments seemed to lack the passion needed to come to the root of the problem, which it had the mission to help solve. At the highest levels of the initiative it was generally assumed that the problem was known and its nature understood. Any shaking of that assumption was duly resisted. An extreme example of this tendency was the refusal to use statistical data on perceptions of the West in Muslim countries gathered by a prominent polling organization from the United States. On more than one occasion this intellectual resistance led to accepting current ideas and images of what had gone wrong in our world and to adopting terms of discussion favored in the metropolitan West and among Muslim secular elites. Unfortunately, these terms are a key part of the problem the initiative was supposed to be addressing.

The alliance was beset by prejudicial assumptions about belated, failed, or absent modernization in the Muslim world at large, or in Muslim regions where extremism was most widespread. On one occasion, a secularist intellectual from a North African country explained that the problem with Islamists is that they are "alien to modern thought, *pensée moderne*" (in addition to being recruited from outside the traditional political and cultural elites). Linked to these sentiments was the belief that poverty is the root cause of Islamic radicalism and economic development, therefore, is its best remedy. A steady complement to these progressive, economistic assumptions was the forthright denial that religion has anything to do with hatred or violence. The intended message was, of course, that Islam is not to be generally blamed for the proclamations and deeds of Muslim extremists.

But this message served only to reinforce the presupposition it was meant to undermine: that Islam is characterized by a special relationship to violence, especially to violence against non-Muslims, and especially violence that threatens societies seen as Christian, Western, and modern. This presupposition has deep historical roots; it is a key element in the tradition of Christian and Western Islamophobia. By refusing to place these ideas in the historical contexts that produced them, the Alliance of Civilizations, at its highest organizational level, refused to confront Islamophobia head-on. It chose instead to beat its shadow. That decision was a tribute to Islamophobia and a lost chance to engage seriously with the explosive cocktail of religion and politics in our own time.

Another prodigious obstacle on our path was the very idea of an "alliance of civilizations." Clearly, that label was made in response to the "clash of civilizations." But the substance of the response was never clearly articulated. In effect, a worthwhile effort chained itself to a dichotomizing notion, civilization, a concept loaded with racist and supremacist ideas on one side and painful experiences of colonial subjugation, humiliation, and exploitation on the other. In recent centuries, the subjugated, humiliated, and exploited have often been Muslims. If one pretends that colonialism is water under the bridge, there still remain problems with the very notion of civilization, largely because there is little clarity at the basic level of social and political analysis about what "civilization" is. The unspoken understanding of the Alliance of Civilizations was that the problem with the "clash of civilizations" lay in the "clash." In fact, the problem lies in "civilization," in how we conceptualize the "civilizations" at stake. By focusing on the conflict between the West and the Islamic world, the alliance effectively granted the title of civilization to the Muslim world, implying that, along with Western civilization, it is a political and cultural complex of enduring global significance.[72] In some respects, that was an achievement. But it was an achievement that will guarantee the dragging on of a clash whose long history lives actively in our present.

Notes

1. See Rotter (1986).

2. Cf. Patzelt (1978: 199).

3. Even in Bede's biblical exegesis, where one can find hostile characterizations of Saracens, there is no clear-cut image of Muslims as the focus of Christian hostility. At his harshest, Bede was not rancorous.

4. Eulogius, *Liber apologeticus martyrum* 12, cited in Wolf (2000: 96).

5. Wolf (2000: 92–93).

6. Eulogius, *Liber apologeticus martyrum* 17–19; Alvarus, *Indiculus luminosus* 23–24, cited in Wolf (2000: 98–99).

7. See John to Emperor Charles the Bald, AD 876, in John VIII (1844–64: cols. 696–97). Cf. Becker (1988: 366–67).

8. John to Neapolitans, Salernitans, and Amalfitans, AD 875, in John VIII (1844–64: col. 655).

9. John VIII (1844–64: col. 656).

10. A notorious case was the seizure, in 1085, of the chief mosque of Toledo, the continued use of which had been guaranteed to the Muslims under terms of the town's capitulation to King Alfonso IV. When the king was away, a monk from Cluny, Bernard de Sédirac, in agreement with Alfonso's French wife, entered the mosque with the support of Christian troops "and having purged it of the filth of Muhammad [*spurcitia Mahometi*], set up an altar of the Christian faith, and placed bells in the main tower so that the Christians could be called to worship." *De rebus Hispaniae* VI, p. 24, cited in Smith (1988: 88–89).

11. Southern (1962: 14–15, 28).

12. France (1996: 56).

13. See Mastnak (2002: 79 ff).

14. Letter to Bishop Peter of Huesca, May 11, 1098, in Urban II (1844–64: col. 504).

15. Becker (1988: 348–49).

16. Manselli (1965: 136); Vismara (1974: 13); Cardini (1992: 396).

17. See Landes (1995: 14–15).

18. See Rupp (1939).

19. Piccolomini to Cusa, [supposedly] July 21, 1453; to Nicholas V, [supposedly] July 12, 1453, in Piccolomini (1909–18: 200, 209–10). On the cultureless Turks, eating horse meat, oxen, and vultures, given over to loose living, hating sciences, and persecuting humanist studies, see *Oratio Eneae de Constantinopolitana Clade, & bello contra Turcos* (Piccolomini [1551 (1967)]: 681).

20. To Cusa, July 21, 1453 (Piccolomini [1909–18]: 211).

21. Piccolomini (1909–18: 201; cf. 212).

22. Piccolomini ([1551 (1967)]: 678).

23. I am aware of the Schmittian connotations. The charge of nihilism against Schmitt's politics was first raised by Karl Löwith in his 1935 essay, "Der okkasionelle Dezisionismus von C. Schmitt," reprinted in Löwith (1969).

24. Patrides (1963); Schwoebel (1967: 166); Meuthen (1984: 45); Cardini (1997: 43–44); Göllner (1978).

25. *Türkenkalender* (1873: 22, lines 188–90).

26. See Heath (1986).

27. Churchill (1950: 311).

28. Sully (1757: 5.135–36, 150).

29. Erasmus (1977: 90); and see Erasmus (1986).

30. Erasmus (1986: 52); Erasmus (1934: 384).

31. More (1977: 6, 196–8, 236); cf. More (1969: 224–225).

32. More (1981: 411; cf. 32).

33. Ibid., 407.

34. Ibid., 414–15.

35. Vives (1948: 50, 52).

36. The first quote from Las Casas is cited in Pagden, 1993, p. 79. The second is cited in Carro, 1971, p. 275. For a more detailed discussion and references, see Mastnak (1994).

37. On the Christian and *Mahmetische* Turks, see Luther (1920: 391).

38. Luther (1914: 120–24), (1909a: 161 sq., 173), (1909b: 617), (1909c: 207), (1920: 276, 388–89, 394–95).

39. Luther (1920: 388–89).

40. *Vom Kriege widder die Türcken,* followed in the same year by the *Eine Heerpredigt widder den Türcken;* for the accusation of the popes, see, for example, Luther (1914: 110).

41. Luther (1909b: 620).

42. Lipsius (1598), quoted in Tuck (1993: 62).

43. Botero (1589: I, 8; II, 6; III, 3; VI, 7; IX, 2), (1606: X, 9). On the omnipresence of a legitimate reason for war against the Turks, cf. Gentili (1933: I, 12).

44. *Projet de conquête de l'Égypte,* in Leibniz (1859–75: 5.256–67).

45. Leibniz (1983: 579, 593).

46. Letter to Saint-Pierre, Feb. 7, 1715, in Leibniz (1859–75: 4.326).

47. D'Alembert (1821: 261, 267, 278, 279).

48. "Aneantissement futur. Du Mahometisme & des autres Religions humaines par le progrèz continuel de la Rézon humaine universelle." *Pensées diverses,* in Saint-Pierre (1733–41: 13. 204–205, 210, 218, 219, 237). *Discours contre le Mahometisme,* in Saint-Pierre (1733–41: 5.121). Cf. *Observasions Sur le progrèz continuël de la Raizon Universelle,* in Saint-Pierre (1733–41: 11.282, 284).

49. Saint-Pierre (1733–41: 5.131).

50. Saint-Pierre (1986: 689; cf. 690).

51. Ibid., 693. Cf. *Vue generale des efets merveilleux que produiroit nécessairement en Europe Le Nouveau plan de Gouvernement des Etats,* in Saint-Pierre (1733–41: 6.326–27).

52. *Projet de traité,* in Saint-Pierre (1986: 690). For a more detailed discussion, see Mastnak (1998).

53. *Suplement a l'Abrejé,* in Saint-Pierre (1733–41: 2.69).

54. *Abrejé du Projet,* in Saint-Pierre (1733–41: 1.295).

55. Meyer (1976: 49, 99).

56. Ibid., 82; and Frederick II to Voltaire, February 29, 1773, in Voltaire (1953–65: 84.136).

57. Quoted in Meyer (1976: 49).

58. Volney (1989: 243–45, 248–49), (1825: 440).

59. Volney (1825: 379, 397, 404, 440).

60. Grousset (1939: 384–85).

61. To the degree it may suggest that Western animosity toward the Muslims and their world is primarily and predominantly about Islam, "Islamophobia" is a misleading term. Islam, theologically speaking, has been a negligible issue. In the relations between Muslims and Christians, Islam and Christianity are often used as shorthand for ways of life. Religious symbols are marks used in making cultural and political statements. Theology and religion enter these relations almost exclusively as "political theology."

62. Mastnak (2002).

63. Peter the Venerable (1964b: 231).

64. Peter the Venerable (1964a: 213).

65. Bacon (1962: 629, 633), (1859: 1.116–17).

66. The Saracens "sunt qui impediunt universum." *De loqutione angelorum.* Quoted in Gottron (1912: 50).

67. *De Patris Josephi Turciados libri quinque,* 35 (Dedouvres 1894).

68. Letter to Robert Graves, April 21, 1972 (Patai 1992: 403). In that "very personal preface" to *The Arab Mind* (1973: 1–7), Patai did not use the word Arabophilism.

69. Patai (1992: 403).

70. Prutz (1883 [1964]).

71. For more details, see http://www.unaoc.org.

72. Efforts to put on the map other "civilizations" and parts of the world with less significant numbers of Muslims were blocked.

Works Cited

Alvarus. 1973. "Indiculus luminosus." In *Corpus Scriptorum Muzarabicorum,* ed. J. Gill. Madrid: Instituto Antonio de Nebrija.

Bacon, Roger. 1962. *The Opus Majus.* Trans. R. B. Burke. New York: Russell & Russell.

———. 1859. *Opus tertium.* In *Opera quaedam hactenus inedita.* Ed. J. S. Brewer. Vol. 1. Rolls Series, 15. London: Longman, Green, Longman, and Roberts.

Balzaretti, Ross. 1992. "The Creation of Europe." *History Workshop Journal* 33(1): 181–196.

Becker, Alfons. 1988. *Der Papst, die griechische Christenheit und der Kreuzzug.* Vol. 2 of *Papst Urban II (1088–1099).* Monumenta Germaniae Historica Schriften, 19. Stuttgart: Anton Hiersemann.

Botero, Giovanni. 1589. *Della Ragion di Stato Libri Dieci, Con Tre Libri delle Cause della Grandezza, e Magnificenza delle Città.* Venice: Appresso i Gioliti.

———. 1606. *Della Ragion di Stato Libri Dieci, Con Tre Libri delle Cause della Grandezza, e Magnificenza delle Città.* Venice: Appresso Nicolò Benese.

Cardini, Franco. 1992. *"La guerra santa nella cristianità."* In *"Militia Christi" e Crociata nei secoli XI–XIII*. Miscellanea del Centro di studi medioevali. Milan: Vita e Pensiero.

———. 1997. *Le radici cristiane dell'Europa: Mito, storia, prospettive*. Rimini: Il Cerchio Iniziative Editoriali.

Carro, Venancio O. 1971. "The Spanish Theological-Juridical Renaissance and the Ideology of Barlolomé de las Casas," in *Barlolomé de las Casas in History: Toward an Understanding of the Man and His Works*, ed. J. Friede and B. Keen. DeKalb, Ill.: Northern Illinois University Press.

Churchill, Winston. 1950. *Europe Unite: Speeches 1947 and 1948*. Boston: Houghton Mifflin.

D'Alembert, Jean le Rond. 1821. "Éloge de Saint-Pierre." In *Oeuvres de D'Alembert*. Vol. 3, part 1. Paris: A. Belin.

Dedouvres, Louis. 1894. *De Patris Josephi Turciados libris quinque*. Angers, France: Germain et G. Grassin.

Erasmus of Rotterdam. 1934. *Opvs epistolarvm Des. Erasmi Roterodami*. Ed. P. S. Allen and H. M. Allen. Vol. 8. Oxford: Clarendon.

———. 1977. *Qverela pacis*. In *Opera omnia Desiderii Erasmi Roterodami*, ed. O. Herding. Series IV, vol. 2. Amsterdam: North-Holland.

———. 1986. *Vtilissima consvltatio de bello Tvrcis inferendo, et obiter ennaratvs Psalmvs XXVIII*. Ed. A. G. Weiler. *Opera omnia Desiderii Erasmi Roterodami*. Series V, vol. 3. Amsterdam: North-Holland.

Eulogius. 1973. "Liber apologeticus martyrum." In *Corpus Scriptorum Muzarabicorum*, ed. J. Gill. Madrid: Instituto Antonio de Nebrija.

France, John. 1996. "Les origines de la première croisade: Un nouvel examen." In *Autour de la première croisade*, ed. M. Balard, 43–56. Paris: Publications de la Sorbonne.

Gentili, Alberico. 1933. *De iure belli libri tres*. The Classics of International Law. Oxford: Clarendon.

Göllner, Carl. 1978. *Die Türkenfrage in der öffentlichen Meinung Europas im 16. Jahrhundert*. Bucharest: Editura Academiei Republicii Socialiste România.

Gottron, Adam. 1912. *Ramon Lulls Kreuzzugsideen*. Berlin: Walther Rothschild.

Grousset, René. 1939. *L'épopée des croisades*. Paris: Plon.

Heath, Michael J. 1986. *Crusading Commonplaces: La Noue, Lucinge and Rhetoric against the Turks*. Geneva: Droz.

John VIII, Pope. 1844–64. *Joannis Papae VIII Epistolae et decreta*. Vol. 126 of *Patrologiae cursus completus. Series latina*. Ed. J.-P. Migne. Paris: Migne.

Landes, Richard. 1995. *Relics, Apocalypse, and the Deceits of History: Ademar of Chabannes, 989–1034*. Cambridge, Mass.: Harvard University Press.

Leibniz, Gottfried Wilhelm. 1859–75. *Œuvres de Leibniz*. Ed. L. A. Foucher de Careil. Paris: Firmin Didot Frères.

———. 1963. *Sämtliche Schriften und Briefe*. Series IV, Vol. 1. Berlin: Akademie der Wissenschaften der DDR.

———. 1983. *Sämtliche Schriften und Briefe*. Series IV, Vol. 2. Berlin: Akademie der Wissenschaften der DDR.

Lilienfeld, Jakob Heinrich von. 1767. *Neues Staats-Gebäude: In drey Büchern*. Leipzig: B. C. Breitkopf.

Löwith, Karl. 1969. *Gesammelte Abhandlungen: Zur Kritik der geschichtlichen Ezistenz*. Stuttgart: Kohlhammer.

Luther, Martin. 1909a. *Eine Heerpredigt widder den Türcken*. In *D. Martin Luthers Werke: Kritische Gesamtausgabe*, Vol. 30. Weimar: Bohlau.

———. 1909b. *Vermanunge zum Gebet Wider den Türcken*. In *D. Martin Luthers Werke: Kritische Gesamtausgabe*, Vol. 30, Weimar: Bohlau.

———. 1909c. *Vorwort zu dem Libellus de ritu et moribus Turcorum*. In *D. Martin Luthers Werke: Kritische Gesamtausgabe*, Vol. 30, Weimar: Bolau.

———. 1914. *Vom Kriege widder die Türcken*. In *D. Martin Luthers Werke: Kritische Gesamtausgabe*, Vol. 51, Weimar: Bohlau.

———. 1920. "Verlegung des Alcoran Bruder Richardi." In *D. Martin Luthers Werke: Kritische Gesamtausgabe*. Vol. 53, Weimar: Bohlau.

Manselli, Raoul. 1965. "La res publica cristiana e l'Islam." In *L'Occidente e l'Islam nell'alto medioevo*. Settimane di studio del Centro italiano di studi sull'alto medioevo, 12. Spoleto: Presso la sede del centro.

Mastnak, Tomaž. 1994. "Fictions in Political Thought: Las Casas, Sepúlveda, the Indians, and the Turks." *Filozofski vestnik* 15(2).

———. 1998. "Abbé de Saint-Pierre: European Union and the Turk." *History of Political Thought* 19(4): 570–598.

———. 2002. *Crusading Peace: Christendom, the Muslim World, and Western Political Order*. Berkeley: University of California Press.

Meuthen, Erich. 1984. "Der Fall von Konstantinopel und der lateinischen Westen." In *Der Friede unter den Religionen nach Nikolaus von Kues*, ed. R. Haubst, 35–60. Mainz: Matthias-Grünewald-Verlag.

Meyer, Henry. 1976. *Voltaire on War and Peace. Studies in Voltaire and the Eighteenth Century*, 144. Banbury, UK: Voltaire Foundation.

More, Thomas. 1969. *Responsio ad Lutherum*. Ed. T. Lawler, G. Marc'Hadour, and R. Marins. Vol. 5 of *The Yale Edition of the Complete Works of St. Thomas More* New Haven, Conn.: Yale University Press.

———. 1977. *A Dialogue of Comfort against Tribulation*. Ed. F. Manley. Vol. 4 of *The Yale Edition of the Works of St. Thomas More: Selected Works*. New Haven, Conn.: Yale University Press.

———. 1981. *A Dialogue Concerning Heresies*. Ed. T. Lawler, G. Marc'hadour, and R. Marius. Vol. 6, parts I & II of *The Yale Edition of the Complete Works of St. Thomas More*. New Haven, Conn.: Yale University Press.

Pagden, Anthony. 1993. *European Encounters with the New World: From Renaissance to Romanticism*. New Haven, Conn.: Yale University Press.

Patai, Raphael. 1973. *The Arab Mind*. New York: Charles Scribner's Sons.

———. 1992. *Robert Graves and the Hebrew Myths: A Collaboration*. Detroit: Wayne State University Press.

Patrides, C. A. 1963. "'The Bloody and Cruell Turke': The Background of a Renaissance Commonplace." *Studies in the Renaissance* 10: 126–135.

Patzelt, Erna. 1978. *Die fränkische Kultur und der Islam mit besonderer Berücksichtigung der nordischen Entwicklung: Eine universalhistorische Studie.* Aalen, Germany: Scientia.

Peter the Venerable. 1964a. "Epistola Petri Cluniacensis ad Bernardum Claraevallis." In J. Kritzeck, *Peter the Venerable and Islam.* Princeton, N.J.: Princeton University Press.

———. 1964b. "Liber contra sectam sive haeresim Saracenorum." In J. Kritzeck, *Peter the Venerable and Islam.* Princeton, N.J.: Princeton University Press.

Piccolomini, Aeneas Sylvius. 1909–18. *Der Briefwechsel des Eneas Silvius Piccolomini.* Ed. R. Wolkan. *Fontes rerum austriacarum,* 61 (I/1), 62 (I/2), 67 (II), 68 (III). Vienna: A. Holder.

———. 1551 (1967). *Opera quae extant omnia.* Frankfurt: Minerva.

Prutz, Hans. 1883 (1964). *Kulturgeschichte der Kreuzzüge.* Hildesheim, Germany: G. Olms.

Rotter, Ekkehart. 1986. *Abendland und Sarazenen: Das okzidentale Araberbild und seine Entstehung im Frühmittelalter.* Studien zur Sprache, Geschichte und Kultur des islamischen Orients, 11: 19–36. Berlin: Walter de Gruyter.

Rupp, Jean. 1939. *L'idée de chrétienté dans la pensée pontificale des origines à Innocent III.* Paris: Les presses modernes.

Saint-Pierre, Abbé de. 1733–41. *Ouvrajes de Politique [& de Morale].* Rotterdam: J.D. Beman.

———. 1986. *Projet pour rendre la Paix perpétuelle en Europe.* Paris: Fayard.

Schwoebel, Robert. 1967. *The Shadow of the Crescent: The Renaissance Image of the Turk, 1453–1517.* Nieuwkoop, Netherlands: B. de Graaf.

Smith, Colin. 1988. *Christians and Moors in Spain.* Warminster, UK: Aris & Phillips.

Southern, R. W. 1962. *Western Views of Islam in the Middle Ages.* Cambridge, Mass.: Harvard University Press.

Sully, Duc de. 1757. *Memoirs of Maximilian de Bethune, Duke of Sully, Prime Minister to Henry the Great.* London: Printed for A. Millar.

Tuck, Richard. 1993. *Philosophy and Government, 1572–1651.* Cambridge: Cambridge University Press.

Türkenkalender auf das Jahr 1455. 1873. Ed. A. Bieling. Vienna: Kubasta & Voigt.

Urban II, Pope. 1844–64. *Beati Urbani II Pontificis Romani Epistolae et privilegia.* Vol. 151 of *Patrologiae cursus completus. Series latina.* Ed. J.-P. Migne. Paris: Migne.

Vismara, Giulio. 1974. *Impium foedus: Le origini della "respublica Christiana."* Milan: A. Giuffrè.

Vives, Juan Luis. 1948. *Obras completas.* Ed. Riber. Vol. 2. Madrid: Aquilar.

Volney, C. F. 1825. *Considérations sur la guerre des Turks, en 1788.* Vol. 3 of *Oeuvres de C. F. Volney.* Paris: Parmanties [et] Froment.

———. 1989. *Les Ruines ou Méditation sur les révolution des Empires.* Vol. 1 of *Le Corpus des Oeuvres de philosophie en langue française.* Paris: Fayard.

Voltaire. 1953–65. *Correspondence.* Ed. Th. Besterman. Geneva: Institut et musée Voltaire.

Wolf, Kenneth Baxter. 2000. "Christian Views of Islam in Early Medieval Spain." In *Medieval Christian Perceptions of Islam,* ed. J. V. Tolan, 85–108. New York: Routledge.

2

The Khalil Gibran International Academy: Diasporic Confrontations with an Emerging Islamophobia

Naamah Paley

Reactions to the establishment of the Khalil Gibran International Academy (KGIA), the first New York City public school to teach an Arabic dual curriculum with a focus on Arab history and culture, were intense. Over the summer of 2007, KGIA and its principal, Debbie Almontaser, became lightning rods in local and national Arab American and Jewish communities, drawing considerable media attention. The school was to be public, part of the public space funded by city resources, and as such it was a focus of general concern. Because dual-language and culturally specialized schools have succeeded across the nation, it is important to understand hostile responses to the KGIA, which was targeted for its associations with a language and an identity that, in the minds of many Americans, are stigmatized and highly suspect. Debbie Almontaser, an observant Muslim who wears the hijab, was all too easily associated with negative stereotypes of the "Arab-Middle Eastern-Muslim Other" (Naber 2006: 236), and attacks against KGIA and her leadership can be seen as part of an emerging Islamophobia.

The conflict over KGIA assumed national significance because it unfolded in New York City. Home to one of the world's largest, most influential Jewish communities, New York is an urban setting in which overt Arab identities, expressed publicly through pan-Arab nationalism and support for Palestinian statehood, are discouraged and persistently thwarted. As in other American cities, Arab-Jewish relations in New York are fundamentally shaped by the Arab-Israeli conflict. Both communities locate themselves "here," in the U.S., and "there," in the Middle East, by supporting parties to a foreign conflict that has become a central component of their diasporic identities. As Arabs and Jews renegotiate these identities in American society, they set new guidelines for determining their distinctly American selves, but these selves cannot be entirely divorced from images of a Jewish or Arab Other who is considered a potential threat. KGIA, accordingly, served as a litmus test for New York's Jewish community: whether a Jewish group or leader chose to support or criticize Almontaser and the school gave them a clearly defined place on the spectrum of Jewish organizations. This test was applied with similar results in the Arab American community; for example, collaborating with Jewish organizations made Debbie Almontaser the recipient of vocal criticism from within her own community. On all sides of the contest, people realized that the success of KGIA would be an important opportunity for Arab Americans in New York City to generate positive attention and public support. Understanding why the school attracted mostly negative attention instead will provide critical insight into how Arab and Muslim Americans are denied normative status in the U.S. as the borderless "war on terror" persists.

My Role and Research Methods

I became personally involved with the Khalil Gibran International Academy after reading about it in early 2007 during my junior year abroad in Cairo, Egypt. Since I am interested in both Arabic and education, this school presented an ideal opportunity. From June through August of 2007, I interned with Debbie Almontaser at KGIA, working on a number of initiatives, including the enrollment process. In October, I spoke on Almontaser's behalf at a rally on the steps of City Hall in the aftermath of the summer controversies.[1] My research is drawn from this period, and from interviews I conducted with community and staff members during the following fall and winter. Although I tried to be neutral and fair, I did view myself as a representative of the Jewish community. Funding for my summer came from a Hillel internship, sponsored by the largest American Jewish campus organization, and I worked primarily out of the Jewish Federation office in the external relations department. As KGIA represented a complicated set of issues, I was asked to represent KGIA and defend it to the mainstream Jewish public. In this role, I met with various Jewish leaders who work with the Arab American and Muslim American communities, and I was expected to provide them with a report about the school. While I did not see myself as a spy, I was certainly an insider asked to respond to the controversies and questions at hand. My delicate role allowed me to balance the components of my identity as needed and as benefited me—and the several parties I represented—in varying situations.

Case Study: The Khalil Gibran International Academy

In understanding, all walls shall fall down.
—Khalil Gibran

In February 2007, a number of local and national media outlets based in New York City announced the establishment of the Khalil Gibran International Academy (KGIA). The school was to be led by Debbie Almontaser, a Yemeni American Muslim educator who had worked to build ties with Christian and Jewish communities. The intent was to provide New York City's youth with "the opportunity to expand their horizons and be global citizens."[2] The school was awarded a grant from New Visions for Public Schools and invited to join a small group of community-based schools. KGIA partnered with the Arab American Family Support Center, a social service agency, and began to solicit support from Brooklyn's Arab American population. The New Visions proposal stressed the multicultural perspective of the school: "New York is a microcosm of the world. And, Brooklyn, as one of the most diverse boroughs in the nation and home to one of the oldest Arab communities in America, is the perfect site for KGIA."[3] The namesake of the school, Khalil Gibran, was a renowned Lebanese Christian immigrant, poet, and author of *The Prophet*. Although a Christian Arab is more representative of New York's communal demographics, some leaders from the Muslim Arab community felt that naming the school after a Christian was a defense mechanism designed to avoid the Muslim connotations of an Arab school. Some community members argued that they should not have to defend themselves or name the school after Khalil Gibran. KGIA, a school led by a woman who publicly wears the hijab, should, they believed, represent a milestone for both the Arab American and Muslim American communities. Most community people, however, supported Gibran as a model Arab American and a positive, recognizable face for the school.

As the KGIA gained publicity in April 2007, controversy erupted in response to Almontaser and her efforts. Daniel Pipes, a Jewish neoconservative historian and analyst, began documenting and criticizing KGIA in the right-of-center newspaper the *New York Sun*. Pipes has made himself known, particularly throughout the Jewish community, for his involvement with the Middle East Forum and Campus Watch—both watchdog organizations dedicated to "fighting radical Islam" and "protecting Americans and their allies."[4] In 2007, he also founded Islamo-Fascism Awareness Week, an initiative that reached two hundred American college campuses. In his article "A Madrassa Grows in Brooklyn," Pipes wrote that "Arabic language instruction is inevitably laden with pan-Arabist and Islamist baggage."[5] He claimed that Debbie Almontaser was a 9/11 denier, held anti-American views, and had called President Bush a "nightmare." Pipes and his supporters founded the Stop the Madrassa Coalition, using the Arabic term *madrassa*, which is widely associated among English-speakers with the training of Muslim extremists, to further instill a sense of fear in the public. Almontaser considered this translation when naming the school and decided to use the word "academy" (*akademiyya*) rather than "school" (*madrasa*) for exactly this reason. Critics also identified Almontaser by her Arabic first name, Dhabah, "the better to render her alien . . . adding the phrase 'a.k.a. Debbie,' treating her chosen name as a sort of criminal alias."[6] The coalition website asked Joel Klein, chancellor of New York City's schools, to "keep your promise . . . shut down the Khalil Gibran International Academy. Now."[7] Arab identity and American patriotism were painted as two poles in opposition to one another, an argument that proved convincing to the general public as opposition to the school increased.

On August 6, 2007, a local tabloid, the *New York Post*, accused Almontaser of condoning T-shirts that read "Intifada NYC." The shirts had been produced two years earlier by members of Arab Women Active in Art and Media (AWAAM), a group that had once shared an office space with the Saba Association of American Yemenis, for which Almontaser is a board member.[8] This loose connection led to a media storm. When asked about the meaning of the word *intifada*, Almontaser stated: "The word basically means 'shaking off.' That is the root word if you look it up in Arabic." She said the T-shirts were "pretty much an opportunity for girls to express that they are part of New York City society . . . and shaking off oppression." Following this interview, newspaper headlines included "Intifada Principal," and "What's Arabic for 'Shut It Down.'" It was implied that Almontaser had taken this opportunity to condone, rather than condemn, the Palestinian Intifada, which is *the* contentious point in New York City. The clarifying comment she made during her interview was strategically left out: "I understand it is developing a negative connotation due to the uprising in the Palestinian-Israeli areas. I don't believe the intention is to have any of that kind of [violence] in New York City."[9] With this statement, which was later published in alternate news sources, the Arabic word *intifada* was separated from the Palestinian political activism captured by the Intifada.[10]

After several days, countless articles, and a number of threatening verbal assaults, Almontaser was forced to resign her position as founding principal of KGIA. Randi Weingarten, the president of the United Federation of Teachers, wrote that "the word 'intifada' is something that ought to be denounced, not explained away." She further claimed that Almontaser "was becoming a lightning rod. Instead of debunking the misapprehensions about the school, all she did was confirm them."[11] As I read letters to the editor published in various local and national newspapers and blogs following the initial attacks on Almontaser, supportive statements were extremely rare. Almontaser was quickly replaced by an interim principal, Danielle Salzberg, a Jewish representative from New Visions who had worked with the school in a limited capacity. The media seized the opportunity to write about an allegedly Zionist principal taking over an Arab school. Headlines included "Jew-Turn" and "Hebrew ha-ha." Conflict around KGIA's intentions instantly translated into a Jewish-Arab controversy as an Arab public school seemed brazenly to trespass on Jewish space.[12] Ms. Salzberg was later replaced by Holly Reichert, another non-Muslim and non-Arabic speaker, who remains the school's principal. Throughout the 2007–2008 school year, Almontaser's case gained attention across the city as coalitions formed both in support of and in opposition to her efforts. Activists organized Communities in Support of KGIA (CSKGIA), whose goal was to reinstate Almontaser as KGIA's principal. Many of its leaders, including Almontaser's lawyer and CSKGIA's main organizer, were Jews who believed it was their duty to reclaim the Jewish voice from its increasingly anti-Arab reputation. While their efforts must be recognized, Daniel Pipes did manage to successfully instill fear in both the Jewish and general public of New York City, whose greatest concern was that their tax dollars would be spent on a terrorist training camp disguised as a public school.

The KGIA Community: Partners and Allies

Our community will extend beyond the walls of the school.[13]

Debbie Almontaser has long been in the public eye, as both an Arab and a Muslim, particularly since September 11, 2001. She is a specialist in multicultural education and has been employed by the Department of Education for nearly twenty years. Her efforts have included facilitating workshops on Arab culture and Islam, co-founding the September 11th Curriculum Project, and coordinating Arab American Heritage Week in New York City. She co-designed and developed curricula entitled *(Re)embracing Diversity in NYC Public Schools: Educational Outreach for Muslim Sensitivity* and *Arab Peoples: Past and Present*, both representing efforts to bring the Arab and Muslim voice into the public education system. She belongs to mainstream Arab American organizations like Women in Islam and maintains positive ties to the Jewish community through the Dialogue Project and a number of joint projects with prominent Jewish organizations. In conjunction with her impressive credentials, she also represents a "safe" Arab American community member: a religious Yemeni Muslim raised in America. Her loyalty to the United States was apparent: her son, an Army Reserve officer, served as a rescue worker at "ground zero" in the aftermath of the 9/11 attacks, illustrating his family's commitment to American values and nationalism.

When developing KGIA, Debbie Almontaser was careful to establish a safety network that she believed would protect and support the school. Early suspicions of KGIA centered on the belief that it would send an Islamic message to its students, so Almontaser formed an advisory board of interfaith religious leaders in the spring of 2007 that consisted of rabbis, pastors, and imams. The rabbis emphasized that they knew KGIA was not a religious school and that they did not join the board to encourage interfaith connections. Although Almontaser intended the board to serve as guardians and allies of the school, this strategy ultimately backfired. Critics used the creation of the board as an excuse to investigate board members and hold Almontaser responsible for any of their questionable comments. Stop the Madrassa declared one of the board's imams to be a radical jihadist, citing his mosque's website as proof. Because this imam was a prison chaplain, Stop the Madrassa members claimed that he contributed to "radicalization and recruitment in U.S. prisons," and that, consequently, "we soon will see KGIA students in combat fatigues emblazoned with patches picturing the sword of Islam."[14] They demanded a response from Mayor Bloomberg, questioning why a man of this background, who "attempts to undermine basic American beliefs and traditions," was sitting on KGIA's advisory board.[15] This guilt-by-association tactic was employed throughout the summer to undermine KGIA.

Almontaser and supporters believed that KGIA would not be subject to accusations that it was an extremist *madrassa* if the school was clearly situated within the public realm. In response to mounting anxieties, Chancellor Joel Klein promised that "if any school became a religious school . . . or it became a national school . . . I would shut it down."[16] Almontaser's past experience in the public school system should have guaranteed credibility, but the Department of Education's support provoked concern instead. The most commonly uttered phrase was, "Is this where my tax dollars are going?" Concerned New Yorkers felt that, because the school was public, they held a degree of ownership in it. Suddenly, there was an Arabic or potentially "Islamist" school opening in their neighborhood, on their streets, with their money. Vocal non-Arab and non-Muslim critics feared the label "community-based school," refusing to accept that KGIA belonged on their turf or could ever be part of their community.

Critique and Fear: Defining the "Hatemongers"

> *Just think, instead of jocks, cheerleaders and nerds, there's going*
> *to be the Taliban hanging out on the history hall, Al Qaeda hanging*
> *out by the gym, and Palestinians hanging out in the science labs.*
> *Hamas and Hezbollah studies will be the prerequisite classes for*
> *Iranian physics. Maybe in gym they'll learn how to wire their bomb*
> *vests and they'll convert the football field to a terrorist training camp.*
> —Unidentified blogger in *The New York Times*[17]

Because public schools in other parts of the country, particularly in Virginia's Fairfax County and in Dearborn, Michigan, have long offered Arabic as an accredited foreign language, I began to investigate a critical question: "Why not in New York?"[18] Why, in New York, did this school come under such intense scrutiny? It was widely believed that the school was treading on sensitive ground, on Jewish space. Although not all criticism of KGIA originated among Jews or Zionists, Jewish fear of Arab Americans was a theme constantly reinforced among those who followed the controversy. The actual composition of the Stop the Madrassa Coalition, the campaign against KGIA, remains unclear. Although Daniel Pipes eventually admitted his participation, as did one of his (non-Jewish) colleagues, the remainder of the campaign's advocates never revealed their true names.[19]

The impact of 9/11, too, must be recognized. According to Louis Cristillo, coordinator of the Muslims in New York City Project, "with New York City being Ground Zero, this is all a reflection of 9/11."[20] As a result of terrorist attacks committed by a small group of Arabs, Arab Americans as a collective are now held accountable. Debbie Almontaser experienced this reality; notwithstanding debate within her community about how to commemorate the second anniversary of 9/11, she was active in the planning of both a local candlelight vigil and a candlelight march, although she feared such programming might incite hate crimes.[21] Even with a figure like Almontaser in the leadership of KGIA, Daniel Pipes relentlessly portrayed the school as an extremist breeding ground, stoking fear of terrorism and anti-Israel activity. The latter threats, he believed, are inevitable results of studying Arabic and gaining sympathy for the Arab world. According to James Coffman, as cited by Pipes: "Arabized students show decidedly greater support for the Islamic movement and greater mistrust of the

West."[22] In this view, studying Arabic increases the likelihood that students will become terrorists or join anti-American Islamic movements.

Whatever their motivation, those who attacked Debbie Almontaser and opposed KGIA employed a familiar strategy. David Cole outlines what he believes to be the McCarthyist tactics now being exercised against Arab Americans and Muslim Americans as features of the "war on terror." Organizations like Campus Watch, the David Project, and *FrontPage Magazine,* among others, target new enemies for our era: "Muslims, Arabs and others in the Middle East field who are identified as stepping over an unstated line in criticizing Israel."[23] These organizations, according to Cole (2003: 2), implemented historically McCarthyist techniques such as censoring subversive speech and assuming guilt by association. Pipes was aware of his methods, and he eventually confessed that the "T-shirts' call for a Palestinian Arab-style uprising in the five boroughs, admittedly, had only the most tenuous connection to Ms. Almontaser."[24] Pipes's confession begs the question: Why did critics of KGIA view the school as a threat deserving this method of attack?

Sharing Disputed Space

> *Where space must be shared, conflicts are likely to multiply.*
> —Suzanne Keller, *Community*

The conflict over the establishment of the Khalil Gibran International Academy, a school designed to foster Arab American identity in New York City, arose from a reluctance to share space with a group whose identity is perceived to be oppositional to one's own. The people most likely to feel this way were antagonistic members of the American Jewish community, who feared official endorsement of a narrative of Arab American and Muslim American identity that would overlap with, and infringe on, their previously claimed space. America is essentially a microcosm of the modern world, where "diaspora runs with, and not against, the grain of identity, movement, and reproduction" (Appadurai 1996: 171). Consequently, America serves as a staging ground for diaspora communities to participate in conflicts that are otherwise located abroad. In this process, communities attempt to carve out ownership over actual public, American, non-diasporic spaces and resources; to "superimpose a place on an existing place" (Lees 2006: 194). Edward Said offers his insight into the general, but often Jewish, fear of Arabs staking claims to territory in public space: "If the Arab occupies space enough for attention, it is a negative value. He is seen as a disrupter of Israel's and the West's existence . . ." (2000:

424–25). Diaspora communities in conflict have historically believed that their cause must vanquish that of the opposing group, not only abroad but in the U.S. as well, since the American public can be sympathetic only to one cause, not both.[25] Therefore, a rising Arab identity must mean a falling Jewish identity and vice versa. This assumption was the constant backdrop of the KGIA dispute, as members of each community attempted to assert their ownership and sense of belonging in New York City's complex landscape.

"Who Can We Work With?": A Jewish Perspective

The Jewish community has internally debated its relationship with the American Muslim and Arab communities, particularly since 9/11, but ultimately these debates trace back to the 1948 establishment of the state of Israel. The organized Jewish community, which supports and represents larger populations of American as well as world Jewry, independently determines what threats and benefits might result from various dialogues or joint projects. A 2004 article in *The Jewish Week,* a mainstream and widely distributed newspaper, addressed the complexities of this prevailing conversation. Editor Gary Rosenblatt, in his article "How to Deal with American Muslims," made the following observation: "Whether, and how, U.S. Jews should deal with Muslim groups in this country is a vital issue that needs to be explored and discussed, particularly in the wake of 9-11. And the variety of possible responses—ignore them, confront them, dialogue with them—tells us as much about our own politics, beliefs and level of confidence as it does about the perceived potential threat of a growing Muslim presence in American life."[26]

Rosenblatt weighs the options of interacting with American Muslims, or refusing to engage with them. On the one hand, American Jews should be sympathetic to a "fellow minority group being blamed for the actions of a small group of terrorists from other countries." Jews, too, are well acquainted with scapegoating and the dangers of collective guilt. On the other hand, Muslims "are sympathetic to the Palestinian cause, blame Israel for the conflict in the Mideast, and have targeted Zionism (and in some cases Jews) as the core of world problems." These factors lead to the inevitable question, "Who can we work with?" This issue has been addressed by Harvard scholar Raquel Ukeles, who attempts to resolve the dilemma by confronting the danger of non-communication between coexisting communities. Ukeles argues that the Jewish community "needs to reconsider the criteria it uses to identify credible partners, including redefining 'moderate,' or there will be no one left to talk to." Rosenblatt adds, "We fool ourselves if we think we can work with (at least on domestic issues) and educate only American Muslims who meet our standards of Mideast correctness."

In my own experience, those standards are highly problematic and dangerously exclusive. Most mainstream Jewish organizations, like the Anti-Defamation League and national Jewish federations, do not include in their mission statements specific guidelines that determine who they "are not willing to work with." Rather, they implement a seemingly impossible set of guidelines, which shifts on a case-by-case basis. It is crucial for the Jewish community to distinguish between domestic goals and foreign policy initiatives; yet American Jewish organizations must stand behind Israel in order to maintain mainstream support, which translates into major communal funding. These standards frequently compel the Jewish community to alienate any group that supports the Palestinian cause, which is typically viewed as a threat to Israel's security. There are no mainstream Arab American or American Muslim organizations that categorically condemn Hamas or reject calls for Palestinian statehood in terms meant to satisfy the security interests of Israel. Political positions of this kind, if adopted independently or to appease the American Jewish public, would result in a loss of credibility in the Arab American and/or American Muslim communities.

This difficult situation, faced by major organizations in many American diasporic populations, directly influences relations between the Jewish and Muslim communities. Prominent, mainstream organizations like the Council on American-Islamic Relations (CAIR) are targeted by influential Jewish organizations such as the Anti-Defamation League (ADL), then systematically excluded from dialogue and collaboration with the organized Jewish community and, whenever possible, with the community's interlocutors in the larger society. Links to CAIR, which once honored Debbie Almontaser, were a key component in the case against her and KGIA. Isolating organizations like CAIR, however, thwarts the type of interfaith dialogue recommended by Ukeles. During a 2007 summer meeting I attended with leaders of the Jewish community, a representative from the Jewish Community Relations Council of New York criticized other participants for their attempts to foster dialogue with Arab and Muslim New Yorkers: "You are meeting with nobodies." They were meeting with "nobodies" because their undefined, yet restrictive, organizational guidelines effectively prevented them from working with "somebodies." There is too much danger in talking to the latter group, since the "somebodies," it is widely believed, may well be connected with terrorism. The risk of working with "nobodies," however, is severe in itself, as the Jewish community attempts to share space with others and be prominent yet approachable. This paradox, it appears, is producing a stand-still in dialogue.

"Who Can We Work With?": An Arab Perspective

This debate has parallels in the Arab American community, where it is widely assumed that Jewish organizations that support Israel are inherently opposing the Palestinian struggle for statehood and supporting apartheid, thus begging the question: "Who can we work with?" Linda Sarsour, the director of the Arab American Association, labeled the Anti-Defamation League "the most racist organization in the country"[27] for its pro-Israel policy. Although various collaborations do exist, particularly in social services, a clash between the two populations is echoed in the lack of formal partnerships between mainstream organizations from the "opposing" communities.

Throughout her career, Debbie Almontaser has struggled to appeal to both sides, to have partners both within and outside of the Arab American community. Antoine Faisal from *Aramica,* the widely circulated local Arab American newspaper, attacked Almontaser for ADL's public support of KGIA. Although Almontaser had not agreed to a formal relationship between KGIA and ADL, ADL's defense solicited this response from Faisal:

> Imagine a NYC charter school for African Americans called the Rosa Parks Academy with an emphasis on Black History and culture whose principal was found to have had a long standing relationship with the KKK. Is there anyone who wouldn't be disturbed by this?[28]

Faisal, and the community leaders interviewed in his article, set a distinct standard for who they were not willing to work with: Zionists. While ADL does have many constructive policies, they do support Israel and are therefore perceived by such critics as a Zionist organization that deserves to be isolated.

There were, however, Arab American voices in the discussion that offered alternative points of view. Aref Assaf, from American Arab Forum, courageously responded that drawing boundaries around Zionism was dangerously limiting. Assaf challenged critiques of ADL that fixated on their Zionist framework. "If we object to the support of ADL," he argued,

> should we not also refuse the financial aid the school will receive from the Melinda and Bill Gates Foundation? [on the false assumption that Bill Gates is a Jewish supporter of Israel] ... should we as Muslims not work with the ACLU ... because it endorses gay marriages? If our moral compass is so truly flawless, should we even open a school in America, the main supporter of Israel ... ?[29]

Assaf attempts to redraw the boundaries of "who we can work with" by noting the success of Jewish organizations in making their issues more mainstream by partnering with a greater variety of groups. Yet Assaf realizes that refusing to collaborate with any Jewish organizations in response to pro-Israel policies is dangerous and would "render our issues beyond mainstream America."[30] Arab Americans, like American Jews, must determine the risk level of compromising their loyalties abroad when forming partnerships that will greatly advance their diaspora stature in the United States.

Jewish Extreme versus Jewish Mainstream

> *You shall not oppress the stranger for you know the feelings of*
> *the stranger, having yourselves been strangers in the land of Egypt.*
> —Exodus 23:9

As I followed the KGIA controversy, I was surprised to find that Jews were prominent on all sides of the argument. They were the most vocal opponents of Debbie Almontaser and her most committed supporters. Jews claimed this struggle as their own, often insisting that it was more a dispute between Jews than between Jews and Arabs or Muslims. Support for Almontaser preceding her resignation was taken up by liberal Jews, who are often considered extreme and on the fringe and, as a result, fail to generate mainstream appeal. Although the Coalition in Support of KGIA gained support from the Arab American community and drew representatives from CAIR, the Arab American Anti-Discrimination Committee, renowned scholar Rashid Khalidi, and others, it was Jews who were highly visible and active on both sides. KGIA functioned as a litmus test within the Jewish community, defining the landscape of "who's who" and where they stood.

The two ends of the "why we should or should not work with American Muslims" spectrum can be explored by looking closely at a distinct struggle: that between Daniel Pipes and Rabbi Michael Paley. Paley, who is my father, studied Islam during his graduate studies and has since gained years of experience in communal and interfaith relations. As scholar in residence at UJA–Federation of New York, which is funded by many conservative donors and certainly holds support for Israel high in its organizational mission, Rabbi Paley must be cautious and often draws criticism for his progressive views. He and Pipes are frequently posed as spokesmen for opposing sides, particularly in the aftermath of Almontaser's resignation. One of these oppositions occurred after a Florida synagogue invited a representative from CAIR to give a high-holiday sermon. In the aftermath, according to a *St. Petersburg Times* article,[31] Pipes warned that "increased affluence and enfranchisement of American Muslims . . . will present true danger to American Jews." Paley, in response to the demand that CAIR support Israel, argued that "it should not be the job of CAIR to support Israel . . . CAIR is a Muslim organization." The Muslim speaker agreed, arguing that "some critics will never accept CAIR unless we put Israel first and we're not willing to do that."

This argument pervaded the KGIA case, as outlined in the *Jewish Week* article "Jewish Shootout over Arab School."[32] Advocating a tolerant stance, Paley spoke against the demands made of Arab and Muslim Americans that "they pass an acid test—that Muslims are terrorists until proven innocent," since this means that "none will pass." It will prove dangerous for the Jewish community *not* to accept other immigrant groups, he added, since mistreatment of the foreigner contradicts the scriptural position stated clearly in Exodus. Paley believes that refusing dialogue with or support for Arab and Muslim Americans will undermine the America that has treated Jews so favorably. America could, he believes, be the ideal location for Jews and Arabs to coexist and solve their conflict. Pipes, on the other hand, feels that a school like KGIA "requires scrutiny beyond that of any other group's school." He avidly supported the Bush administration's policy of profiling, maintaining that "if you're looking for terrorism you must give special scrutiny to this community." Pipes believes that securing American borders overrides the need to protect American (and Jewish) values that, in Paley's view, encourage the acceptance of the stranger.

Not in Our Name: Community Misrepresentation in the Public Arena

כל ישראל צרכים זה לזה
All Jews are responsible to each other. . . . One people, as if they are one person.
—Jewish dictum

Reactions to the Khalil Gibran International Academy generated a crisis of representation within the Jewish community. As has always been true of diaspora Jewries, the acts of one can represent the whole. Donna Nevel, a founder of Communities in Support of KGIA, joined this coalition because she felt the attacks on Almontaser were perpetrated "in the name of the Jewish community." This assault, she believes, was a misrepresentation of the Jewish community. The acts of one small cohort of Jews should not, in her view, be mistaken for the voice of an entire community. Nevel believed it was her responsibility "to stand up and say, 'this is not our community. They don't reflect our community. You may think that you're speaking on behalf of our community but this is not what the Jewish community wants.'"[33] Jewish organizations have struggled for years to create a mainstream identity and to claim a positive image for themselves in American society. Paley agreed with Nevel, saying: "If it hadn't been for the Jews attacking, I don't think I would have found it appropriate for me to defend."[34] He struggles to interject Jewish organizational defense only when necessary. Debbie Almontaser adopted a similar "Not in Our Name" stance following 9/11, when she contended that her community was misrepresented by the actions of a few individuals. Almontaser was stigmatized for her response to young students who asked her about Muslim involvement in 9/11: "I don't recognize the people who committed the attacks as either Arabs or Muslims." The remainder of her comment, which the *New York Post* chose not to publish, focused on a personal reputation that was damaged by others and must now be reclaimed: "Those people who did it have stolen my identity as an Arab and have stolen my religion."[35]

Entering the Public Arena

> *If you live here then become an American first*
> *and maintain your personal culture privately.*
> —Comment posted by Marie, a reader of the *New York Sun*[36]

The process of creating a mainstream identity, sometimes viewed as a commodity, provides a minoritized community with a point of access to American society and a visible presence in the national mosaic. Melani McAlister addresses the role of the private cultural world (marriage, home, and family), which she believes is "necessary to constructing the 'inside' of the national community; that 'inside' is then mobilized to represent the nation itself in its public mode" (2001: 12). In other words, there is a need to expose allegedly private identities in the public sphere in order to form a realistic and accurate representation of the community in question (Shryock 2004: 301–303). Providing the public with a positive glimpse into the life of a marginalized community ideally allows it to be seen not as a cultural impurity but rather as an accepted part of American society. This process occurs in the public sphere and is accomplished through such familiar mechanisms as museums, parades, festivals, and monuments.

It is also accomplished in public schools. Arab American researcher Moustafa Bayoumi argued in support of KGIA that "a school institutionalizes the Arabic language and culture within the mainstream framework . . .

institutionalizes it within a society."[37] The Khalil Gibran International Academy, according to Louis Cristillo, is "perfect in the sense that it's really at the forefront of curriculum development of areas that are sorely needed in the New York public school system."[38] Few New York City public schools have Arabic curricula; only two high schools offer Arabic courses, and the Arabic Regents exam was only developed in the last few years. This lack of knowledge about Arabs and Arabic has long been institutionalized in the American public education system. There are massive gaps in information about the Middle East and the Arab world in public school curricula. KGIA was originally conceived as an attempt to fill these gaps with accurate information and to impart critical knowledge of a misunderstood culture and understudied language to a new generation of American public school students, who would impart this knowledge to the general public.

Stop the Madrassa was especially concerned that the curriculum taught at KGIA would be pro-Arab, pro-Muslim, and anti-Israel, and its supporters demanded to inspect the school's teaching materials. They were unable to gain access to KGIA curricula, however, because in the summer of 2007 a curriculum had not yet been adopted. Curricula pertaining to Arabs and Muslims remain underfunded and underdeveloped, both at KGIA and across the nation. Given this lack of materials, Debbie Almontaser selected the Scholastic My Arabic Library for use at KGIA. This teaching resource, contrary to Pipes's assumptions, is intended to represent mainstream American identity and culture to the Arabic-speaking Middle East, rather than the reverse. Scholastic collaborated with the State Department's Middle East Partnership Initiative to translate American children's books and ship them to the Middle East. In 2007, students in Bahrain, Jordan, Lebanon, and Morocco were given access to My Arabic Library. The aim of this initiative, according to Scholastic, is to ensure that "millions of children, many of whom never had access to quality books like these, will now get to experience stories that capture their imaginations and teach them about the world."[39] Ironically, the stated goal is actually to benefit the Middle East by introducing it to American children's literature, not to enrich, or "endanger," students like those attending KGIA by offering them sympathetic information about the Arab world.

The Dangers of Misunderstanding: Public Education as a Solution

Given the complex range of issues that shaped the KGIA debate, it is important to point out that the central objection to the Khalil Gibran International Academy was its status as a public rather than private or charter

school. Controversy arose around whether highlighting Arab identity and
the Arabic language is, in fact, the responsibility of public education. While
promoting culture or language in the public domain through city-funded
schools is not generally prohibited, teaching religion is. Surfing the current
wave of Islamophobia, critics of KGIA suggested the synonymous nature of
Arabic, Islam, and an anti-Western mentality. The popular argument posed
by *New York Times* contributor and Harvard law professor Noah Feldman was
that "Islam will presumably be taught" and that KGIA "is a watered-down,
American version of the British and Canadian models of state-run religious
schools catering to Muslims."[40] Feldman suggested that, due to its religious
nature, KGIA has private religious value rather than public secular value. This
argument is easily critiqued: the sheer fact that perhaps 75 percent of Arab
Americans are *not* Muslim and that less than 20 percent of the Muslim world
speaks Arabic would be information enough to correct Feldman's misunder-
standing.[41] Still, it is hard for most Americans to distinguish between Arab
and Muslim identities. It is also true that the overwhelming majority of Arabs
are Muslims and that Islam, as an aspect of Arab civilization and history, is
not a topic any school dedicated to understanding Arab language and culture
could realistically ignore.

Debbie Almontaser, as a religious Muslim, has worn the hijab for her entire
career with the Department of Education, and her manner of dress reinforced
the common assumption that KGIA would be an Islamic school. While she has
never been prevented from wearing the hijab by her employers, Almontaser
has certainly been targeted for criticism because she wears it. Her decision to
publicize her Muslim identity provoked opposition from those who believed
that such a religious symbol was threatening to the American school system.
Elements of this scenario are reminiscent of *L'affaire du foulard*, in which French
Muslims were banned from wearing the hijab in public schools. In France,
the individual's right to wear the scarf was judged a threat to the integrity of
a public sphere free of religious symbolism (Benhabib 2004: 183). Similarly, to
critics of KGIA, Almontaser's hijab represented her desire to impose her private
identity on the public sphere. Her hijab was emphasized and stigmatized; it
gave critics the opportunity to attack her Muslim identity, even though the
teaching of Islam, as a religion, was not the intention of KGIA. Almontaser
considers herself perfectly capable of distinguishing between her private identity and her public responsibilities. As she has constantly asserted, the school
she envisions would teach about religion, just as all public schools teach about
the major world religions. Learning *about* Islam is appropriate to American
curricula because religion is a major component of American society.

A Borderless War against Indistinguishable Identities

Representations of the Arab and Muslim communities in the United States, as well as abroad, have always been blurry, and they have become particularly confused in light of recent events. The September 11 attacks were carried out by men who were Arab and professed to be Muslim. Since that moment, uncertainty about Arabs and Muslims has grown. The American government has given minimal effort to comprehending the complexities and contradictions that mark these identities. Popular American misconceptions about what defines Arabs and Muslims have proven dangerous, particularly in this moment of conflict. When exacting revenge for the 9/11 attacks, cultural and geopolitical borders were entirely unclear, and the American government determined that the acts of a handful of individuals could in fact be treated as the acts of a nation, a religion, a country, a community. The complex struggles between figures like Osama bin Laden and Saddam Hussein were played down, or remained unrecognized. Pervasive ignorance about Arabs, Arab Americans, and Muslims produced deadly outcomes. In the act of plotting an appropriate response to the 9/11 attacks, the American government imposed an imagined sense of responsibility on two countries, Afghanistan and Iraq, which it promptly invaded and still occupies, at a cost of trillions of dollars and hundreds of thousands of human lives.

Wars waged abroad are particularly complicated for America, a nation composed of numerous immigrant populations and domestic diasporas. The U.S. government has yet to create a consistent policy for the treatment of immigrant communities and individuals whose home countries are under attack. This is due to the (sometimes) awkward fact that American citizens can identify with, and even belong to, other nations and states, a predicament that leads to a critical question: Can immigrants relocate their political imaginations within American borders, or does a substantial part of their loyalty and patriotism remain abroad? Concerns about the dual loyalties of diasporic communities, which can lead to ambivalent attachments to American society (Appadurai 1996: 172), are not illegitimate. As American mono-patriotism becomes an increasingly unrealistic expectation, many diasporic communities do indeed have dual loyalties. Transnational identities, defined by links to multiple places ("here" and "there"), are nourished and reinforced by return trips to immigrant homelands, by interactions with new immigrants, and by solidarities cultivated by community institutions (Cainkar 2002: 6). These patterns of identity reinforcement are found among both secular and religious communities, and they are nowhere more evident than in American Jewish loyalties to Israel. Such feelings are intelligible to most Americans, and one might easily conclude that the anxiety triggered by the prospect of an Arab public school in New York City was fueled by the ideological discomfort caused by the realization that "dual loyalties" are now a common feature of American society and might be legitimately available to all citizens, even when the loyalties in question are Arab and Muslim.

Insisting on Stigma

While a collapse of identities occurred overseas, and Afghans and Iraqis were lumped in a uniform class of Muslim enemies, American civilians worked out a similar tendency to categorize their enemies sloppily at home. Misperceptions about Arabs and Muslims, especially an inability to distinguish between the two, had serious consequences on the domestic front. "Immigrant communities are targeted," writes Nadine Naber, "when the United States goes to war in their homelands; the significance of this process is that it legitimizes the distinction between 'Americans' and a constructed enemy Other/enemy of the nation" (2006: 236). Those perceived to be Arab were held accountable. They were labeled terrorists, called Osama, and asked to apologize for attacks they did not carry out or support. Muslims and Arabs, it was believed, possessed the most dangerous dual loyalty of all: allegiance to Islam and the Arab world. Hyphenated Muslim and Arab American identities were stigmatized and viewed as inconsistent and potentially dangerous. As President Bush repeatedly stated, "You're either with *us* or with *them*." While *them* referred to the terrorists, and not to Arabs and Muslims as a whole, the labels were treated as synonymous and interchangeable.

Determining loyalties is a critical step in defining Otherness and isolating political impurities that threaten American society. Debbie Almontaser was subject to accusations of impurity and disloyalty: she wears the clothing, prays the prayers, and speaks the language of the enemy. The stigmatization of the hijab was shocking for American Muslims, who "felt that their hijab was legitimately part of the American cultural landscape" (Hatem 2005: 44). At the same time, allowing overtly Muslim behavior and Arab identities into the American mainstream was, for many critics of the KGIA, unimaginable. This level of acceptance represented what many Americans feared: that Middle Eastern Muslims are no longer only in the Middle East (McAlister 2001: 261). That "they" might now have their own public school would mean that being Arab and Muslim was simply another way of being American. What opponents of the KGIA seemed to fear most was not the Arab Muslim as alien and Other, but the likelihood that the Arab Muslim might be incorporated into the American Self.

The Khalil Gibran International Academy served as a battleground, and a laboratory, for understanding conflicting definitions of American identity. Fears of KGIA focused on the possibility that it would erode the *us* vs. *them* binary that has been essential to American rhetoric in a "war on terror" that is, at ground level, a war against Arabs and Muslims. For many New Yorkers, KGIA had the potential to serve as a terrorist training cell, an American *madrassa* that would infiltrate our society and propagate dangerous Arab mentalities. It has become clear, however, that the battle is not one of *us* vs. *them* but rather one of *us* vs. *us*. This internal clash represents a long-standing but nevertheless urgent American battle: the struggle to define ourselves. Although situated within the framework of a war against terrorism, the current conflict has resulted in a war of identity centered on a culture under siege. According to Rabbi Paley, "The foreign war is not just a foreign war against real Muslims, who pose no threat to us, but [also a war waged] for the sake of our identity."[42] The domestic struggle of various diasporic communities is one of definition: "Who are we?" This question has shaped the struggle between American Jewish and Arab and Muslim American communities. Many leaders in these communities believe their communal identities will be compromised if a place is carved out for an "opposing" identity, particularly in the public domain. This communal struggle is charged by distrust of "the Other" and persistent attempts to maintain an outdated, parochial understanding of what it means to be American.

America today is a compelling reality for American Jewry in the larger context of Jewish history. America provides a haven for diasporic communities, and if this country upholds its potential and embraces its reality, it can become the first truly global nation. For Jews, a nation constantly in diaspora, America holds unique opportunities. This country can serve as a microcosm in which all overseas entanglements can be confronted. Here, populations struggling in diaspora can learn what it means to be a reinterpretation of a community rooted geographically in another time or place. The global nature of American society enables us to reconsider conflicts abroad on the common ground of a hyphenated American identity. The Khalil Gibran International Academy, which should not have been a school about the Arab-Israeli conflict, became a critical site for confronting, if not necessarily reconsidering, one of the most important overseas conflicts in shared American space. The future of the school is unresolved, and the struggle for Arab and Muslim space in New York, and in the American public sphere, continues. It is a disturbing, potentially enlightening contest over who we, as Americans, can be.

Epilogue

According to the NYC Department of Education, the first year of the Khalil Gibran International Academy was a success. In reality, however, the school was ridden with serious, debilitating problems. In the fall of 2007, the Department of Education transferred a number of special-needs students into the incoming sixth-grade class, well aware that the school was ill equipped to address their behavioral and educational needs. Sean Grogan, KGIA's former science teacher, reported to *The New York Times* that "kids bang on the partitions, yell and scream, curse and swear. It's out of control."[43] One of the school's Arabic teachers informed me that one of the students had called her a "terrorist." By the conclusion of the school year, half of KGIA's staff had been removed and the plan to extend KGIA to a high school had been crushed. Since her resignation, Debbie Almontaser has lost both a court case and an appeal to have her position reinstated.[44]

Notes

1. Arab Women in the Arts and Media website: http://www.awaam.org/uploads/paley 101607.mov.

2. New Visions grant proposal, the Khalil Gibran International Academy; copy in author's possession.

3. Ibid.

4. Middle East Forum home page: http://www.meforum.org. Pipeline home page: http://pipelinenews.org/.

5. Daniel Pipes, "A Madrassa Grows in Brooklyn," *New York Sun*, April 24, 2007. http://www.nysun.com/foreign/madrassa-grows-in-brooklyn/53060/.

6. Samuel Freedman, "Critics Ignored Record of a Muslim Principal," *New York Times*, August 29, 2007. http://www.nytimes.com/2007/08/29/education/29education.html.

7. Stop the Madrassa home page: http://stopthemadrassa.wordpress.com/.

8. Chuck Bennett and Jana Winter, "City Principal Is 'Revolting': Tied to 'Intifada NYC' Shirts," *New York Post*, August 6, 2007. http://www.nypost.com/seven/08062007/news/regionalnews/city_principal_is_revolting_regionalnews_chuck_bennett_and_jana_winter.htm.

9. Andrea Peyser, "Shirting the Issue: 'Sorry' Principal First Defends 'Intifada'-Wear," *New York Post*, August 7, 2007. http://www.nypost.com/seven/08072007/news/columnists/shirting_the_issue_columnists_andrea_peyser.htm.

10. To clarify: "Intifada" literally means the act of shaking off. In this context, it refers to two Palestinian uprisings against the Israeli occupation of the West Bank and Gaza Strip. The First Intifada lasted from 1987 to 1993 and originated in Palestinian civil disobedience, general strikes, and boycotts, although it is widely remembered for the violent, highly publicized act of stone throwing. The Second Intifada, also known as the al-Aqsa Intifada, began in September 2000, arguably in response to Prime Minister Ariel Sharon's visit to the Temple Mount. This Intifada was significantly more violent than the first, with greater publicity and a higher number of casualties. It is yet to officially end although most believe it to be over.

11. Julie Bosman, "Head of City's Arabic School Steps Down under Pressure," *New York Times,* August 11, 2007. http://www.nytimes.com/2007/08/11/nyregion/11school.html.

12. The rise of Zionism and the growing alliance between the United States and Israel has long shaped the Arab American landscape. Many Arab populations, including Lebanese, Palestinians, Jordanians, and Egyptians, have been displaced during wars with Israel. From its 1948 independence, to the 1967 Six-Day War, the 1973 war, the 1982 invasion of Lebanon, and the Gulf wars, Israel has deeply affected the region. As Arab Americans respond to this reality, American Jews have consistently viewed their efforts with suspicion. Powerful pro-Israel lobbies, like the American Israel Public Affairs Committee, currently overpower the practically invisible pro-Palestinian lobby.

13. New Visions grant proposal, the Khalil Gibran International Academy.

14. "There's Something Fishy about KGIA 'Advisory Board,'" online posting, October 10, 2007. http://stopthemadrassa.wordpress.com/2007/10/10/theres-something-fishy-about -the-kgia-advisory-board.

15. Ibid.

16. NY1 News, "Arabic Language School Struggles to Find a Home," May 4, 2007. http:// www.ny1.com/default.aspx?ArID=69409&SecID=1000.

17. Samuel Freedman, "Critics Ignored Record of a Muslim Principal," *New York Times,* August 29, 2007. http://www.nytimes.com/2007/08/29/education/29education.html.

18. Helen Hatab Samhan, "Who Are Arab Americans?" Arab American Institute Foundation. http://www.aaiusa.org/foundation/358/arab-americans.

19. Daniel Pipes, "New Approach Needed for Arab School," *New York Sun,* August 15 2007. http://www.nysun.com/new-york/new-approach-needed-for-arab-school/60542/.

20. Louis Cristillo, personal interview, January 24, 2008.

21. Daniel J. Wakin, "For Muslims, an Uneasy Anniversary; Urge to Speak Out Conflicts with Low-Profile Instincts," *New York Times,* August 19, 2002. http://www.nytimes .com/2002/08/19/nyregion/for-muslims-uneasy-anniversary-urge-speak-conflicts-with -low-profile-instincts.html?sec=&spon=&pagewanted=1.

22. Daniel Pipes, "A Madrassa Grows in Brooklyn," *New York Sun,* April 24, 2007. http:// www.nysun.com/foreign/madrassa-grows-in-brooklyn/53060/.

23. Larry Cohler-Esses, "The New McCarthyism," *The Nation,* November 12, 2007. http://www.thenation.com/doc/20071112/cohler-esses.

24. Daniel Pipes, "New Approach Needed for Arab School," *New York Sun,* August 15, 2007. http://www.nysun.com/new-york/new-approach-needed-for-arab-school/60542/.

25. Of course, not all American Jews, Arabs, or Muslims develop their identities in relation to homeland politics or overseas conflicts. My argument will deal with those who do.

26. Gary Rosenblatt, "How to Deal with American Muslims," *Jewish Week*, September 10, 2004. Online at http://www.israelforum.com/board/showthread.php?t=6933.

27. Antoine Faisal, "Zionist Organization Supports Gibran School Principal," *Aramica*, June 29–July 11, 2007. http://www.viewda.com/webpaper/aramica/.

28. Ibid.

29. Aref Assaf, "Questioning Motives?" *Arab American Forum*, July 18, 2007. http://www.americanarabforum.org/questioning_motives.htm.

30. Ibid.

31. Susan Taylor Martin, "With CAIR, Compromise Complicated," *St. Petersburg Times*, 23 September 2007. http://www.sptimes.com/2007/09/23/Worldandnation/With_CAIR __compromise.shtml.

32. Larry Cohler-Esses, "Jewish Shootout over Arab School," *Jewish Week*, August 17, 2007. http://www.thejewishweek.com/news/newscontent.php3?artid=14422.

33. Donna Nevel, personal interview, January 15, 2008.

34. Rabbi Michael Paley, personal interview, January 15, 2008.

35. Larry Cohler-Esses, "Jewish Shootout over Arab School," *Jewish Week*, August 17, 2007. http://www.thejewishweek.com/news/newscontent.php3?artid=14422.

36. Daniel Pipes, "The Real Arab School Fear," *New York Sun*, May 22, 2007: http://www .nysun.com/new-york/real-arab-school-fear/54935/. "Marie," Reader Comment on "The Real Arab School Fear," online posting, July 26, 2007: http://www.nysun.com/comments/ 33284.

37. Moustafa Bayoumi, personal interview, January 24, 2008.

38. Louis Cristillo, personal interview, January 16, 2008.

39. Scholastic website: http://www.scholastic.com/aboutscholastic/news/press_04172007 _CP.htm.

40. Noah Feldman, "Universal Faith," *New York Times Magazine*, August 26, 2007. http://www.nytimes.com/2007/08/26/magazine/26wwln-lede-t.html.

41. Factbook home page: http://www.factbook.net/muslim_pop.php.

42. Rabbi Michael Paley, personal interview, January 15, 2008.

43. Andrea Elliot and Samuel Freedman, "Critics Cost Muslim Educator Her Dream School," *New York Times*, April 28, 2008. http://www.nytimes.com/2008/04/28/nyregion/ 28school.html?ex=1210046400&en=eb31e0ad46ef2191&ei=5070&emc=eta1.

44. Associated Press, "NY Appeals Court Rejects Claim by Arab School Principal," March 20, 2008.

Works Cited

Appadurai, Arjun. 1996. *Modernity at Large: Cultural Dimensions of Globalization*. Minneapolis: University of Minnesota Press.

Benhabib, Seyla. 2004. *The Rights of Others: Aliens, Residents, and Citizens*. Cambridge: Cambridge University Press.

Cainkar, Louise. 2002. "No Longer Invisible: Arab and Muslim Exclusion after September 11." *Middle East Report* 224 (Fall). http://www.merip.org/mer/mer224/224_cainkar .html.

Cole, David. 2003. "The New McCarthyism: Repeating History in the War on Terrorism." *Harvard Civil Rights–Civil Liberties Law Review* 38(1): 1–30.

Hatem, Mervat F. 2005. "Arab Americans and Arab American Feminisms after September 11, 2001: Meeting the External and Internal Challenges Facing Our Communities." *The MIT Electronic Journal of Middle East Studies* 5: 37–49.

Keller, Suzanne. 2003. *Community: Pursuing the Dream, Living the Reality*. Princeton, N.J.: Princeton University Press.

Lees, Susan H. 2006. "Conflicting Concepts of Community." In *The Seductions of Community: Emancipations, Oppressions, Quandaries*, ed. Gerald Creed, 175–98. Santa Fe, N.Mex.: School of American Research Press.

McAlister, Melani. 2001. *Epic Encounters: Culture, Media, and U.S. Interests in the Middle East since 1945*. Berkeley: University of California Press.

Naber, Nadine. 2006. "The Rules of Forced Engagement: Race, Gender, and the Culture of Fear among Arab Immigrants in San Francisco Post-9/11." *Cultural Dynamics* 18(3): 235–67.

Said, Edward W. 2000. "Interview." In *The Edward Said Reader,* ed. Moustafa Bayoumi and Andrew Rubin. 424–25. New York: Vintage.

Shryock, Andrew. 2004. "In the Double Remoteness of Arab Detroit." In *Off Stage/On Display: Intimacy and Ethnography in the Age of Public Culture*, ed. Andrew Shryock, 279–314. Stanford, Calif.: Stanford University Press.

Part Two Modern (Self) Criticism

3

The God That Failed: The Neo-Orientalism of Today's Muslim Commentators

Moustafa Bayoumi

Thirty years ago, Edward Said published *Orientalism,* the highly influential study challenging the authority of Western representations of the "Orient" through the twin prisms of knowledge and power. Said identified Orientalism as a type of discourse which possesses "a will or intention to understand" what was non-European, and "in some cases to control and manipulate what was manifestly different" (1978: 12). The study of the Orient, moreover, operated not as an innocent intellectual pursuit but functioned as a handmaiden to empire. The Orientalist always spoke for the Orient, and in so doing, developed a style for "dominating, restructuring, and having authority" (Said 1978: 3) over both an object of study and a region of the world.

The Orientalist, according to Said, was a sort of translator—often literally so—of the Orient to the Occident but was always translating one culture for another from the detached perspective of a learned Westerner. This distance endowed the Orientalist with his or her "flexible positional superiority" (1978: 7), so that

> the relation between the Orientalist and Orient was essentially hermeneutical: standing before a distant, barely intelligible civilization or cultural monument, the Orientalist scholar reduced the obscurity by translating, sympathetically portraying, inwardly grasping the hard-to-reach object. Yet the Orientalist remained outside the Orient, which, however much it was made to appear intelligible, remained beyond the Occident. (1978: 222)

It is this distance—in part physical, but more fundamentally ontological—that preserved the essential framework of an "us" and a "them." As we shall see, distance becomes more difficult to maintain in a globalizing age.

Said also shows us how, in the Orientalist canon, "Islam" accounts for the sum total of any Muslim's experience. From Islam comes everything and to Islam goes everything, and Orientalism's aim is to drive this point home with a repeated and relentless monotony. "It is evident that anything is possible to the Oriental," writes British Orientalist Duncan Macdonald, because the "supernatural is so near that it may touch him at any moment" (quoted in Said 1978: 277). Thus, a recurring theme in Orientalist work is that "Islam" is the regulator of life from "top to bottom" (Said 1981: xvi), a motif Said characterizes as not just intellectually lazy but as a model of intellectual production that would be inapplicable to the serious study of Western culture. There the humanities and social sciences engage in "complex theories, enormously variegated analyses of social structures, histories, cultural foundations, and sophisticated languages of investigation" (Said 1981: xvi), but none of that is found in the Orientalist world of "Islam." In short, it is not politics that produces (varieties of) Islam in history. Instead, "Islam" produces politics.

It is almost facile to point out that Orientalism, like imperialism, never seems to go out of style. In fact, in the age of terror, it has reemerged with a vengeance. *New York Times* correspondents—e.g., Robert Worth (2005)—prepare themselves for war reporting in Iraq by reading the old Orientalist Bernard Lewis, who himself has had virtually unparalleled access to the corridors of power in the Bush era. The old trope of "Islamic imperialism" is resuscitated in Efraim Karsh's (2006) book by the same name. *The Arab Mind* (Patai 2002 [1973]), trash scholarship from a generation ago, is dusted off, reissued, and sent into wide circulation in the United States military; it was cited recently in the *New York Times* as a reference book in the library of a counterinsurgency colonel in Iraq (Gordon 2007).

But there is a (somewhat) new twist on an old doctrine, and it is worth paying it some attention. Today, contemporary multiculturalism melds with old-style Orientalism in the writings of Ayaan Hirsi Ali, Irshad Manji, and Reza Aslan, three commentators who self-describe either as Muslim (Aslan), ex-Muslim (Hirsi Ali), or barely Muslim (Manji). Each also claims to reveal the true nature of Islam to Western audiences, promising an insider message of telling it to you like it is! (Hint: Everything Muslims do *is* motivated by Islam.) The fact that these explainers are themselves Western Muslims in some sense collapses the Orientalist distance between East and West; in other senses it does not, for there would be no need for explainers if there were no wide differences between peoples.

Ayaan Hirsi Ali was born in war-torn Somalia, which she fled as a child, eventually winning asylum in the Netherlands, where she later rose to prominence as a legislator known for her anti-immigrant views. She is the author of several works, including the screenplay for *Submission,* a short film about the treatment of women in Islam by Theo van Gogh (for which she provided the voiceover narration and for which van Gogh would later be assassinated by Mohammed Bouyeri). She has published two books, one a collection of essays called *The Caged Virgin: An Emancipation Proclamation for Women and Islam* (2006), and the other an autobiography titled *Infidel* (2007). After questions arose regarding the truthfulness of her statements regarding her own immigration petition, Hirsi Ali left the Netherlands and relocated to the United States. She quickly received permanent residency, which was announced by the U.S. government through a press release (hardly a common practice, to say the least), and she began working at the American Enterprise Institute, a conservative think tank. Irshad Manji was born in Uganda under Idi Amin's tyrannical rule. She and her family fled the East African dictatorship when Manji was four years old, settling in Vancouver, Canada, where she was raised. Manji is the author of *The Trouble with Islam: A Muslim's Call for Reform in Her Faith* (2003), repackaged as *The Trouble with Islam Today* for the paperback version. Reza Aslan was born in Iran in 1972. He and his family left Iran after the revolution in 1979, when Aslan was about seven years old, settling in the United States. Aslan is the author of *No god but God: The Origins, Evolution, and Future of Islam* (2005).

The very existence of these explainers indicates the substantial presence of Muslims in the West, and each of their books either implicitly or explicitly raises the specter of misguided or dangerous Muslims living in our midst. The force of their message in other words is a mission: "Islam" can (or will naturally) be converted from its current treachery into a benign and more palatable force for the Western world. I offer that this is simply a ridiculous message, and that to focus on "Islam" is to entertain a distraction that takes us away from attending to the many serious political issues of our time.

Scholars may have little use for the autobiographical musings of Hirsi Ali or the puerile polemics of Manji. Nevertheless, the fact remains that Manji, Hirsi Ali, and Aslan have become some of today's most prominent explainers of "Islam." According to a search on BookScan (http://en-us.nielsen.com/tab/industries/media/entertainment, performed on October 5, 2007), Hirsi Ali's *Infidel* has sold more than 120,000 copies in hardcover. Manji has sold more than 60,000 total copies of *The Trouble with Islam,* and Aslan's *No god but God* comes in at over 70,000 sales. Moreover, each author is accorded significant media exposure and is credentialed by various institutions and think tanks of higher learning and the power elite, from Yale University (where Manji was a fellow) to the conservative American Enterprise Institute (where Hirsi Ali is a fellow) to CBS News (where Aslan is a consultant). There should be no question that their influence is significant. Their offerings about "Islam," however, raise doubts, for these are the kind of explanations that demand explanation.

The idea of Orientals talking to Western audiences in a Western medium has its predecessors. Fouad Ajami, the Lebanese American historian, chronicler of Arab failures, and close confidant of several members of the Bush administration, immediately comes to mind. According to Adam Shatz, a senior editor at the *London Review of Books*, "Ajami's unique role in American political life has been to unpack the unfathomable mysteries of the Arab and Muslim world and to help sell America's wars in the region" (2003: 15). But in the cases of Hirsi Ali and Manji, who compose narratives centered on their own religious experiences, one could page back to the conversion narratives found in early editions of *The Muslim World*, a journal that began publishing in 1911, for precursors. There we find such narratives by Muslims as "How Christ Won My Heart" (1916), written by "an Indian Convert" in Lahore. We can read "A Mohammedan Imam's Discovery of Christ" (Barton 1916), or "The Story of My Conversion," written by one J. A. Bakhsh in 1926. These brief stories narrate the struggle to proclaim one's belief in Christ in the face of Muslim obscurantism in the Muslim world, and they come with all the good news that the gospel is spreading in Muslim territory. Comparing these essays with Hirsi Ali's and Manji's texts holds insofar as both sets of narratives describe the fundamentally closed world of Islam, but the similarity basically ends there. For one thing, the distance between the Muslim and Christian worlds is still fundamentally alive in the old narratives, as one or two converts along the missionary way may bode well for the power of the gospel, but do not reveal a fully formed social movement. Moreover, the early narratives are essentially about the righteousness of Christianity in the world. Today's Muslim commentators speak from their authority as Muslims to talk not about the glories of Christianity but about the failings of Islam.

And the failures are many. Hirsi Ali, Manji, and Aslan all point to a clearly articulated set of problems that can be summarized as follows: "Islam" is or has become a totalizing system that lags behind the wheel of progress, defies individuality, and blindly oppresses its followers. Where they differ is in their views of how this happened, when it happened, and if there is any opportunity to emancipate Islam from itself.

Manji and Aslan take on the old cliché of "the closing of the gates of ijtihad." Ijtihad, of course, refers to the Islamic juridical principle of independent reasoning within religious law. Ijtihad has a long history within Islam and

Islamic jurisprudence, and many commentators (Manji and Aslan among them) have argued that the practice of ijtihad was essentially snuffed out in the ninth or tenth century C.E./A.D. This idea is commonly referred to as "the closing of the gates of ijtihad" in favor of irrational obedience to religious authority, and this closed door, in Manji's and Aslan's hands, explains the current intellectual, moral, and political stultification of "Islam." Aslan, for example, writes that "the Traditionalist Ulama, who at that time dominated nearly all the major schools of law, outlawed [ijtihad] as a legitimate tool of exegesis . . . signal[ing] the beginning of the end for those who held that religious truth . . . could be discovered through human reason" (2005: 165). Manji, too, notes that "Baghdad oversaw the closing of the . . . gates of ijtihad and therefore the tradition of independent thought," which led to a "freez[ing] of debate within Islam" so that "we in the twenty-first century live with the consequences of this thousand-year-old strategy to keep the [Islamic] empire from imploding" (2003: 59).

Furthermore, all three commentators—Manji, Aslan, and Hirsi Ali—point to the problems of hadith transmission (the system by which the sayings of the Prophet Muhammad are passed down through the ages) to argue that Islam has been forever beset by human fallibility, and the Ulama have been able to manipulate their believers into what modern science can now reveal as blind systems of oppression.

The problem with drawing attention to the inherent limitations of hadith transmission and the closure of the gates of ijtihad, two common preoccupations among many Orientalist schools, is that they are both non-issues. In 1984, Wael B. Hallaq asked the question, "Was the gate of ijtihad closed?" in an important article with that query as its title, answering that "a systematic and chronological study of the original legal sources reveals that these views on the history of ijtihad after the second/eighth century are entirely baseless and inaccurate" (1984: 4). (Many others who read inside the tradition, from Albert Hourani to Said Ramadan, reach the same conclusions.) Hallaq composed another retort to the perennial issue of hadith transmission in another essay, "The Authenticity of Prophetic Hâdith: A Pseudo-Problem" (1999). In brief, Hallaq here argues that since the science of hadith, a pursuit within Islamic jurisprudence, contains within it the means to adjudicate "strong" from "weak" ahadith, the Western discovery of hadith forgery is largely, in his word, "pointless."

We can make a point, however, by noting the reliance of these contemporary travelers in Islam on such explanations. Manji's and Aslan's texts go to considerable lengths to pinpoint a period of Islamic glory (for Aslan, it is the period of the Prophet; for Manji it is al-Andalus—Islamic Spain) in counterpoint to today's distress. Hirsi Ali, on the other hand, ultimately finds nothing redeemable in Islam but argues that Muslims "don't have to take six hundred years to go through a reformation" and need to "examine [their faith] critically, and to think about the degree to which that faith is itself at the root of oppression" (2007: 350). All three are invested, in other words, in drawing a singular narrative account of Islam, where the faith is both a singular system and a singular force in the world, and they rely on the production of a Grand Narrative to achieve their goals. But if post-structuralism has taught us anything it should be skepticism of all Grand Narratives, since Grand Narratives by design are propelled by such singular causes and effects that move their story forward in world historical time.

In fact, many Salafi literalists—those who reject the major schools of Islamic law and instead argue for a direct reading of the Quran and sunnah (the sayings and actions of the Prophet Muhammad)—operate similarly, though out of opposite social circumstances. In *Islam: The Religion of the Future* (1984), for example, the Egyptian Islamist Sayyid Qutb offers a world historical narrative about the rise and fall of civilizations due to religion and human nature. After describing the rise and fall of capitalism and communist society, Qutb writes that "all these [capitalist and communist] civilizations were cut off from the original source without which social orders, principles and values cannot survive: the source of belief issuing from God which gives comprehensive interpretation to existence, to the status of man and his objectives on earth. Hence, they [the Euro-American] were basically temporary civilizations, without roots attached to the depths of human nature" (1984: 63). In Qutb's account, human proximity to or distance from Islam explains history.

I should make it clear that I am not opposed to scholastic treatments of faith systems, or to examining them through history or even within a comparative framework. But that is not what is happening here. The problem arises not when a faith system is placed in history but when it is used to *explain* history. Thus arises the Grand Narrative. And with Aslan, Manji, and Hirsi Ali, the Grand Narratives they posit all describe a straightforward binary of a pre-modern Islam that has erected barriers for Muslims, hindering them from entering modernity. Moreover, these barriers—a rigid Ulama, intellectual sleights of hand like "closing the gates of ijtihad" and fabricating *ahadith*, or even the very faith itself—account for the political behavior of Muslims throughout the world and in world historical time.

Each of these three texts relies on its own Grand Narrative to prove its point, and it is worth examining what kinds of threads underpin their Grand

Narratives to give them force to Western readers. Turning first to Hirsi Ali, we find a detail-driven memoir of a clearly turbulent life that involves survival in war-torn Somalia, flight to Saudi Arabia, refugee hardship in Kenya, oppression through female circumcision and forced marriage, and the remaking of a new life in the Netherlands. It is in many ways a compelling read. But perhaps the first thing to notice from the point of view of narrative is why we are drawn to the story. Part of the reason may lie in the structure of the work, which in fact replicates the American slave narrative in significant ways. Frederick Douglass titles the account of his life *My Bondage and My Freedom;* Hirsi Ali divides her story into "My Childhood" and "My Freedom." And like the slave narrative, hers is also one about achieving true consciousness under a system of oppression. In the slave narrative, the discovery of consciousness is generically inscribed in the act of learning how to write. With Hirsi Ali, it comes with going to school in the Netherlands.

Consider how she describes the vocational college preparatory classes that she was finally able to take. There, she tells us, she studied history voraciously, and the performance of naïveté is instructive of the move from blindness to vision, not just in language but also in political thinking. "That history book taught me Dutch," she writes. "The civics class, on the other hand, was full of terms I didn't understand, like *municipality* and *upper chamber*. I scraped through it. I failed the Dutch class by one point: I still couldn't write proper grammar. But because I had my Dutch equivalency exam, they let me enroll in Driebergen Vocational College anyway. By the skin of my teeth, I had made it" (2007: 229). Education and the Dutch language may bring consciousness to Hirsi Ali, but they also enable simplistic comparisons. "In February 1995," she writes, "there were huge floods across Holland. When Somalis are faced with catastrophic weather, drought and flooding, they all get together and pray. Natural disasters are a sign from God, to show humans they are misbehaving on earth. But the Dutch blamed their government for failing to maintain the dikes properly. I didn't see anybody praying" (2007: 239). When it comes to her education, she writes, "it seemed as if . . . everything I read challenged me as a Muslim. Drinking wine and wearing trousers were nothing compared to reading the history of ideas" (2007: 239).

The obscurant and anti-intellectual world of Islam functions as the slave system in Hirsi Ali's universe, and Muslims are guilty of enslaving themselves. Hirsi Ali's narrative makes this case repeatedly, and she liberally uses skin color to argue her point. Later, she begins work as a translator in the Dutch social welfare sector, and this experience further hardens her to the Muslims in her midst. "When I went to awful places—the police stations, the prisons, the abortion clinics and penal courts, the unemployment offices and the shelters for battered women—I began to notice how many dark faces looked back at me. It was not something you could avoid noticing, coming straight in from creamy-blond Leiden. I began to wonder why so many immigrants—so many Muslims—were there" (2007: 243). Later, she answers her question. "If Muslim immigrants lagged so far behind even other immigrant groups, then wasn't it possible," she asks, "that one of the reasons could be Islam? Islam influences every aspect of believers' lives" (2007: 279). Meanwhile, "by declaring our Prophet infallible and not permitting ourselves to question him, we Muslims had set up a static tyranny . . . we suppressed the freedom to think and to act as we chose. . . . We were not just servants of Allah, we were slaves" (2007: 272).

In the prototypical slave narrative, the former slave finds redemption in True Christianity. But Hirsi Ali's salvation from slavery, updated for today, comes not through Christianity but through atheism. As the Bible has the power to move the spirit in the slave narrative, *The Atheist Manifesto*, loaned to her by her boyfriend, becomes Hirsi Ali's path to emancipation (2007: 280). But the emancipation she details is not hers alone, for what would it matter if one Muslim gives up her faith? Hers is instead a broad prescription for all her co-religionists, and by the end of her narrative it is clear that she is lecturing all the Muslims of the world. If they are to enter modernity, they must give up God within their creed, not just individually but theologically. According to Hirsi Ali, Islam's salvation is atheism.

Hirsi Ali's text is actually rich in detail about different social movements and political strife. It gives us large amounts of context, making it in fact a text of lost promise. The same cannot be said of Irshad Manji's *The Trouble with Islam* (2003), a polemic rife with willful distortions, patent inaccuracies, and self-aggrandizing sanctimony. I will not bother to list these—there are far too many to treat this as a serious work worthy of such scrutiny—but we can explore its narrative structure in a fashion similar to the way we explored Hirsi Ali's memoir.

Manji's is an epistolary text, full of Thomas Friedman–like platitudes and born out of disillusionment. "I have to be honest with you," she begins. "Islam is on very thin ice with me" (2003: 1). She proceeds to catalogue the manner in which she was schooled in a "madrassa" in Richmond, British Columbia, and how the experience traumatized her into action later in life. In her junior high school, she tells us, "dignity of the individual prevailed," but in her "madrassa," she "entered . . . wearing a white polyester chador and departed several hours later with [her] hair flattened and her spirit deflated" (2003: 11). "Islam" is the cause of this oppression, we are lectured again and again, just as Muslims are the cause of every tragedy she can muster. "The Muslims of East Africa treated blacks like slaves," she says (2003: 5). (And what about the Hindus of East Africa?) Muslims are responsible for the honor killings of Pakistan, the lack of independent women travelers in Malaysia, ethnic strife in Nigeria, and the Turkish nationalist genocide of Armenians of 1915. "Muslims did this!" she keeps intoning, as if every Muslim is individually responsible for the action of every other nominally Muslim person in the entire world and throughout time.

At the heart of Manji's polemic is the way in which Muslim and/or Palestinian "culture" squelches the individual (2003: 158). She even draws parallels between the Prophet and bin Laden over the course of several pages, arguing that the Prophet "won decisive military victories through such primitive tactics as digging a ditch around his settlement, catching his opponents unawares, and crippling their combat-ready thoroughbreds," and then offering that "bin Laden's cavalry used box-cutters to attack a superpower" (2003: 149).

Such emotional blackmail is Manji's style: she goes to great lengths to posit Islam as a faith locked outside the gates of modernity due to its tyrannical anti-intellectualism. While the West is proudly freethinking, and Jews are the most freethinking of Westerners, for Manji, "mainstream Muslims . . . suppress their brainpower [with] the stated aim of the no-thinking rule" (2003: 59). She gets more specific. The Palestinians, in Manji's view, function as the ultimate expression of the failures of Islam, and the middle of her book is turned over to a narration of a six-day trip—paid for by a Canadian Jewish group—to Israel and the occupied territories. In Jerusalem, she encounters difficulty entering the Al-Aqsa compound but freely visits the Wailing Wall. There, she writes, "I borrow a pencil and scrawl a request to God, then weave through the crowd to approach the wall. As I spend time in search of an unused crack that will clasp my prayer, I realize I'm holding up the Jews behind me. Still, I don't feel like an interloper [as the Palestinians have made her feel]. I feel at home. More viscerally than ever, I know who my family is" (2003: 85).

For Manji, Judaism stands as the ultimate expression of modernity and the culmination of the West. She presents Judaism as broadminded, universal, and liberal to the core; this is especially evident in her narrative on the state of Israel. Judaism and Israel function as the antitheses to Islam, and as models to aspire to. She uses cultural-religious terms—Islam and Judaism—

but it is really politics that drives her framework. Manji refuses to grant the Palestinians even basic rights. Instead, she imperiously lectures them about how they deserve their fate, due solely to the faults of their Muslim culture. In this bizarre narrative, where Islam is "irredeemably rigid" (2003: 33) and "brain-dead" (2003: 31), Judaism, in fact, even becomes the true Islam. She asks, "How many of us know the degree to which Islam is a 'gift of the Jews'?" (2003: 21). And thus her self-label as a "Muslim Refusenik" takes on another dimension. "That doesn't mean I refuse to be a Muslim," she writes, explaining why she calls herself a refusenik. "It simply means I refuse to join an army of automatons in the name of Allah. I take this phrase," she continues, "from the original refuseniks—Soviet Jews who championed religious and personal freedom. Their communist masters refused to let them emigrate to Israel. For their attempts to leave the Soviet Union, many refuseniks paid with hard labor and, sometimes, with their lives" (2003: 3). For Irshad Manji, "Islam" can enter modernity. It just has to become Jewish.

Turning to Reza Aslan's *No god but God* (2005), we find a more complicated narrative, but one that nonetheless operates on a grand scale, describing how Islam is well on the road to replicating Christianity. Aslan's book is full of the performance of partisan scholarship (he proudly accepts that he is writing an "apology" for Islam), and, insofar as it is a book about Islam as a faith, it is relatively unproblematic. (And I should add that Aslan's text is immeasurably more nuanced than Hirsi Ali's and Manji's, and that some of his public interventions are helpful. But this need not mean his book is beyond criticism.) The first half of the book travels over familiar territory. Here Aslan narrates the early days of Islam with control and sympathy, describing the religion's emergence within the social context of the Arabian peninsula of that era.

More fundamental problems soon arise, however, and from two different directions. The first is the use of what Aslan calls the "story" of Islam to explain the subsequent history and politics of the Middle East and South Asia. (If this is "Islam's story" then where is Indonesia or Mali or Albania?) The second is the central conceit of the book, namely that Islam—like Christianity—is going through a reformation.

In fact, Aslan's book reads like a revisionist history of the Iranian revolution. The initial message of Islam was freedom and liberty, he tells us, but that message has, since the early days of the revolutionary message of egalitarianism, been hijacked by the clerics.

Throughout Islamic history, as Muslim dynasties tumbled over each other, Muslim kings were crowned and dethroned, and Islamic parliaments elected and dissolved, only the Ulama, in their capacity as the link to the traditions of the past, have managed to retain their self-imposed role as the leaders of Muslim society. As a result, over the past fifteen centuries, Islam as we know it has been almost exclusively defined by an extremely small, rigid, and often profoundly traditionalist group of men who, for better or worse, consider themselves to be the unyielding pillars upon which the religious, social, and political foundations of the religion rest. (2005: 139)

The arrogance of this approach, summarizing the sweep of fifteen hundred years of human history within a few words, is at bottom breathtakingly simple. (Not to say historically untenable—what about popular Islam, for one thing?) The idea of a clergy tyrannically holding sway over the masses of people flies in the face of the complex and variegated ways authority and state power have functioned throughout the history of the Muslim world.

But besides sounding very much like contemporary Iran, Aslan's view of a singular Ulama deciding the worldly fates of believers sounds a lot like the history of Christianity in Europe. In fact, in virtually every section one turns to in Aslan's book, the comparison to Christianity is drawn. Sometimes it is explicit, so the brief nine-year reign of the Abbasid caliph Mu'tasim is known only for its "inquisition" (2005: 140). Or when Aslan describes the umma, he writes that "put simply [the umma] is the Church in Islam" (2005: 146). Sufis are compared to Teresa of Avila, and are placed in opposition to the clerical order of the Ulama. Moreover, we are told that "Sufis" believe that "God's very essence—God's substance—is love. Love is the agent of creation" and that they "understood Muhammad in the same way that many Christian Gnostics understood Jesus: as the eternal *logos*" (2005: 215). Sufis and the Indian reformer Sayyid Ahmed Khan are, unsurprisingly, the good guys in this narrative, peacefully opposed to the black-robed Ulama.

For a moment, consider Sufism with more than pacific new-age appreciation. Many of the often quite violent and often very hierarchical anti-colonial struggles the Arab world witnessed—ranging from the Mahdi movement in Sudan to Abdel Kader in Algeria—were Sufi-led or -inspired, and they certainly complicate Aslan's narrative. The text does acknowledge Shah Wali Allah's political Sufism, but only to transition to political Islam (2005: 218–19) and not to investigate the premise that Sufism could be more than private mysticism. Aslan's examination of political Islam itself is preceded by a brief discussion of colonialism, which is put this way: "European ideals of secularism, pluralism, individual liberties, human rights, and, to a far lesser degree, democracy—that wonderful legacy of the Enlightenment that had taken hundreds of years to evolve in Europe—were pressed upon the colonized lands with no attempts to render them in terms the indigenous population would either recognize or understand" (2005: 222–23), as if the ravages of colonialism are due to the arrested development of the colonized themselves.

These consistently drawn parallels between "East" and "West" structure Aslan's story. Of course, there is nothing wrong with analogy or drawing historical correspondences as a heuristic device. But a problem arises when analogy overwhelms the analysis to the point of emulation. In Aslan's narrative, it is as if "Islam" must follow the same world historical script as Christianity. Under such a weight, Islam will always fail, for the simple fact that Islam is not Christianity.

More troubling still is the manner in which politics is subsumed to the narrative of Islam, and from the opening pages of the book—a narration of how Aslan mediated and translated a sudden altercation between American missionaries and an irate Muslim conductor on a train in Morocco—to the ending, which refutes the "clash of civilizations thesis" in its analysis of the September 11 terrorist attacks, we are told that this is a book that will explain not just a faith system but the paroxysms of the world. The violence of our age is due to a struggle over leadership, Aslan concludes, exactly as in the Christian past. "All great religions grapple over [authority]," he writes (so "lesser" religions don't?), "some more fiercely than others. One need only recall Europe's massively destructive Thirty Years' War . . . to recognize the ferocity with which interreligious conflicts have been fought in Christian history. In many ways, the Thirty Years' War signaled the end of the Reformation . . . and [led] ultimately to the doctrinal relativism of the Enlightenment. This remarkable evolution in Christianity . . . took fifteen vicious, bloody, and oc-casionally apocalyptic centuries. . . . And Islam has finally begun its fifteenth century" (2005: 248).

In Aslan's narrative, one that is putatively about the world, responsibility becomes easy to assess. The "story" of Islam, with its incomplete reformation, is the sole cause of today's violence. "What is taking place now in the Muslim world is an internal conflict between Muslims," he writes, "not an external battle between Islam and the West. The West," he continues, "is merely a bystander" (2005: 248).

This is a false dichotomy if ever there was one—to be forced to choose be-tween a civilizational clash and an internal, civilizational civil war—for why can't it be neither? But the idea that the West is "merely a bystander" and, by extension, that "Islam" is a victimizer of the West ends Aslan's narrative. Moreover, it is the central thread that connects Aslan to Hirsi Ali to Irshad Manji. But surely this is ridiculous. The process of assigning political responsibility means assessing who, individually, does what to whom. It means grappling with the historical details of particular wars, state-building projects, specific colonial and postcolonial policies, the rise of secular nationalism, regionalism, military pacts, control over resources, globalization, and everything else. The narratives of Aslan, Hirsi Ali, and Irshad Manji, on the other hand, reduce politics to the spurious fact that Muslims are agents of Islam and only of Islam throughout the pages of history. Such epic civilizational narratives as these talk the language of political responsibility while obfuscating the same. To Western audiences, however, this is an oddly comforting story. It means that the world, meaning now the Western world, has been invaded by "Islam," an Islam that for centuries has been on the march to defeat individuality at every turn, is anti-modern to the core, and has a totalitarian-like Comintern at its heart called "the Ulama." The truth of the proposition is made all the more "truthful" when it issues from the lips of Western Muslims. And the solution, if one can be found, is simplistically plotted as a stripped-down ijtihad, for ijtihad brings with it reformation, liberalism, and individuality.

Orientalism provides the means by which these narratives succeed, for it enables precisely this kind of wholesale summary of the complexity of human experience. It is Orientalism that endows one with the authority to proclaim the wish that "Islam" would become or emulate atheism, Judaism, or Christianity (or, in the case of Thomas Friedman, that Islam would finally just become Hinduism). But Orientalism does not account for the overarching structure of these three stories. In their repeated insistence on a system of tyranny defeating human liberty, these stories fundamentally replicate another narrative in our recent history, one similarly made more concrete by the collapsing of distance, since it is ex–fellow travelers who tell them. I am referring to familiar Cold War narratives published in the middle of the twentieth century, and particularly the confessional tales composed by ex-Communists.

In 1949, Richard Crossman edited an influential series of essays with the title *The God That Failed*. Reprinted through the 1960s and, as Frances Stonor Saunders shows, supported by the Congress for Cultural Freedom, a wing of the Central Intelligence Agency, *The God That Failed* features essays by André Gide, Richard Wright, Stephen Spender, Ignazio Silone, Arthur Koestler, and others who describe their excited journeys into Communism and their disillusioned return. The narratives in the book share a good many characteristics, most notably that Communism defeats every ounce of individuality, mainly by its collective belief that—as Arthur Koestler put it—Communism is "the incarnation of the will of History itself" (1949: 58). Similarly, Ignazio Silone characterizes the history of the Communist International (sounding very much like these accounts of Islam) as "a history of schisms, a history of intrigues and arrogance . . . toward every independent expression of opinion" (1949: 89). In *The God That Failed,* Communism is a bullying, anti-human pursuit recklessly imposing its idea of Truth on the world through brutality (Wright) and murder (Spender).

It is far less important to adjudicate the truth of these claims than it is to connect old rhetorics of persuasion and argument to newer rhetorics, allowing us to see how certain tropes function in our society, how they are consistent, and how they differ. With this in mind, one crucial comparison arises. The failures of Communism spelled out in *The God That Failed* are likened to the failures of organized religion; the acolyte of Lenin was seen as being the same as the Catholic neophyte. "The strength of the Catholic Church," writes Crossman in his introduction, "has always been that it demands the sacrifice of [spiritual] freedom uncompromisingly, and condemns spiritual pride as a deadly sin. The Communist novice, subjecting his soul to the canon law of the Kremlin, felt something of the release which Catholicism brings to the intellectual, wearied and worried by the privilege of freedom" (1949: 6). Communism, like organized religion (especially Catholicism), flees from freedom and defeats the individual. The existence of this old narrative endows contemporary tales of "Islam" with the "truthfulness" on which they rest, because "our" violence, in this mythology, promotes liberty, while "their" violence is forever atavistic.

In *The God That Failed,* Communism loses because it turns ideology into religion. In the hands of Ayaan Hirsi Ali, Irshad Manji, and Reza Aslan, "Islam" fails because it has transformed religion into ideology.

Works Cited

An Indian Convert. 1916. "How Christ Won My Heart." *The Muslim World* 6(1): 79–81.

Aslan, Reza. 2005. *No god but God: The Origins, Evolution, and Future of Islam.* New York: Random House.

Bakhsh, J. A. 1926. "The Story of My Conversion." *The Muslim World* 16(1): 79–84.

Barton, James L. 1916. "A Mohammedan Imam's Discovery of Christ." *The Muslim World* 6(4): 389–93.

Crossman, Richard, ed. 1949. *The God That Failed.* New York: Bantam Books.

Gordon, Michael R. 2007. "The Former-Insurgent Counterinsurgency." *New York Times Magazine.* September 2.

Hallaq, Wael B. 1999. "The Authenticity of Prophetic *Hâdith:* A Pseudo-Problem." *Studia Islamica* 89: 75–90.

———. 1984. "Was the Gate of Ijtihad Closed?" *International Journal of Middle East Studies* 16(1): 3–41.

Hirsi Ali, Ayaan. 2006. *The Caged Virgin: An Emancipation Proclamation for Women and Islam*. New York: Free Press.

———. 2007. *Infidel*. New York: Free Press.

Karsh, Ephraim. 2006. *Islamic Imperialism: A History*. New Haven, Conn.: Yale University Press.

Manji, Irshad. 2003. *The Trouble with Islam: A Muslim's Call for Reform in Her Faith*. New York: St. Martin's Press.

Patai, Raphael. 2002 [1973]. *The Arab Mind*. Long Island City, N.Y.: Hatherleigh Press.

Qutb, Sayyid. 1984. *Islam: The Religion of the Future*. Riyadh: International Islamic Federation of Student Organizations.

Said, Edward W. 1981. *Covering Islam*. New York: Pantheon.

———. 1978. *Orientalism*. New York: Vintage.

Saunders, Frances Stonor. 2001. *The Cultural Cold War: The CIA and the World of Arts and Letters*. New York: New Press.

Shatz, Adam. 2003. "The Native Informant." *The Nation* (April 28): 15–24.

U.S. Citizenship and Immigration Services. 2007. "Noted Author Ayaan Hirsi Ali Receives Her Green Card, Becomes Permanent Resident during Special DC Ceremony." Press Release. http://www.uscis.gov/files/pressrelease/HirsiAliRlease25Sep07.pdf.

Worth, Robert F. 2005. "The Reporter's Arab Library." *New York Times Book Review*. October 30.

4

Gendering Islamophobia and Islamophilia: The Case of Shi'i Muslim Women in Lebanon

Lara Deeb

In the ten years that I have been conducting field research in the southern suburb of Beirut, there has been a drastic shift in the geopolitical climate in relation to my interlocutors, many of whom are supporters of the Lebanese Shi'i political party, Hizbullah. In the late 1990s, the party was described by major U.S. media outlets as a "guerrilla" movement or a "militia," and at least one U.S. news magazine ran a spread focusing on Hizbullah's social welfare provision networks and entrance into mainstream Lebanese politics.[1] In the post-9/11 world, Hizbullah has returned to "terrorist" status in these same media and in the rhetoric of U.S. officials. This shift is symptomatic of what is often described as a growing "Islamophobia," a term used by journalists, politicians, scholars, and the Organization of the Islamic Conference. Yet what is meant by this term differs almost as widely as those who invoke it.[2] Everything from cartoons depicting the Prophet Muhammad to racist fears of unemployed Muslim youth to the ever-present nomenclature of "terrorism" is subsumed in this fluid category of discrimination.

In contrast to the European context, with its focus on the hijab, most Islamophobic discourses in the United States focus on images of Muslim men and hinge on associations between masculinity and violence.[3] Below, I will complicate this image in three ways. First, by bringing a transnational feminist analytic lens to bear on these images and discourses, I reinsert Muslim women into the picture, highlighting the importance of ideas about "civilization" and civilizational status—as constructed through women's roles and bodies—to the construction of anti-Islam and anti-Muslim rhetoric. Second, by considering the perspectives of Hizbullah gender activists, I examine how an awareness of transnational discourses that portray Muslims as universally

94

oppressive to women has contributed to the popularity of a specific sort of Islamophilic discourse within the pious Shiʻi Muslim community in Lebanon. Discourses originating in the U.S. and Europe that depict Islam as the root of all evil reverberate in Lebanon and produce oppositional responses that invert this equation, making Islam the sole source of good. Finally, the example of Hizbullah in Lebanon adds yet another layer of complexity to conversations about Islamophobia. It is impossible to talk about Lebanon today without talking about sectarianism and the rise of specifically "Shiʻa-phobic" discourses. The latter are particular to Lebanon, but they share numerous features with strains of Islamophobic thought now common in Israel, Europe, and North America.

Gender, Islam, and Civilizational Status in al-Dahiya

The southern suburb of Beirut, referred to in Lebanon simply as *al-Dahiya*— literally, "the suburb"—is composed of a series of neighborhoods whose population today is mostly Shiʻi Muslim. This area of the city is known in the United States and among many Lebanese as "the Hizbullah stronghold." The appellation is exaggerated: Hizbullah *is* the most popular and powerful political party in the area, but by no means are the southern suburbs and the party coterminous. *Al-Dahiya* is also the area of the capital where entire neighborhoods were destroyed in Israeli bombardment during the July 2006 war. Even when wars are not being actively waged, the Shiʻi community that resides here has lived in a situation of chronic military conflict for decades; it is the community that bore the brunt of the twenty-two-year Israeli occupation and carried most of the burden of the resistance that brought that occupation to an end in 2000.

Among pious Shiʻi Muslims living in *al-Dahiya*,[4] certain expressions and cultivations of piety have converged in recent decades with particular definitions and expressions of modernity. By "modern" or "modernity," I mean to connote a value-laden, context-derived concept. In this particular case, the concept can be reduced to notions of progress in both the spiritual and material realms.[5] But there is another relevant usage: frequently, people use "modern" almost interchangeably with "civilized" to indicate their placement along a "civilized"–"barbaric" continuum. Emphasis on the term "civilized," usually phrased in Arabic as "we have civilization" (*ʻindna hadara*), is crucial. In addition to evoking the "clash of civilizations" thesis and rhetoric, it prompts questions about who has the authority to define "civilized status" and what signifiers can be used to do so.

Of the many criticisms of the "clash of civilizations" thesis, which underlies the binary distinction between Islam and the West, I want to highlight a feminist critique made by Minoo Moallem (2005), Therese Saliba (2002), and Lila Abu-Lughod (1998), among others, which examines how civilizational discourses are dependent on gendered assumptions.[6] Often grounded in histories of colonialism or nationalist movements, this critique underscores the ways in which women are used, in the manner of a barometer, to determine a society's "civilizational status." Gender is implicated here for a number of reasons, including the symbolic relationship between woman and nation, ideologies that emphasize women's role in producing and reproducing communities, and a "discourse of protection" that creates alliances between white men and women and legitimates their positions as protectors of "free women" (Moallem 2005). These alliances and implications are familiar to us from postcolonial studies, but they are also important thematically in contemporary forms of neoimperialism in the Middle East.

Civilizational status is typically gauged along two dimensions. Women's status may be understood to signify the level of developmental progress a nation has achieved, as in the writings of Egyptian reformer Qasim Amin on women's education (2000 [1899]), or in the historical politics of forced unveiling in state modernization programs in Turkey and Iran. Women's status can also signify the preservation of national culture in the face of colonialism, as in the reversal of veiling policies in Iran during and after the Islamic Revolution, or the association of women with private, domestic culture in the nationalist movement in Bengal (Chatterjee 1993). In examples of the first type, civilizational status is measured by movement away from a state of "backwardness" or "barbarism." In the second, an age-old civilization is seen to be under attack from certain aspects of modernization, driven by colonialism, and civilizational status is measured by the ability to preserve traditions that are considered culturally distinctive. In both cases, however, it is the treatment of women's bodies that determines the relative position of a culture or society as civilized (cf. Jarmakani 2008). And in both cases, transnational discourses are critical to the placement of women's bodies, and the evaluation of their status, at the borders between civilizational and moral constructs.[7]

The belief that it is crucial not only to demonstrate the modernity and civilized status of Islam, but to do so by demonstrating the modernity and civilized status of Muslim women is a dominant theme that has emerged again and again in my conversations with pious Shi'i Muslims—men and women— in Lebanon over the past ten years. For example, in December 1999, toward the beginning of an extended period of field research in *al-Dahiya*, Widad,[8] the president of an Islamic women's organization where I had recently begun volunteering, asked Aziza, my closest friend in the community, about me. As a researcher from the United States, I was used to encountering suspicion; however, as Aziza related their conversation to me, it became clear that this moment was different. Rather than trying to assess whether I had any ties to espionage or the U.S. government, Widad was trying instead to determine whether I was talking to the "right" people in her community. She wanted to know which other organizations I had gone to and what sort of information I had been receiving about Islam and Muslim women. Widad concluded the conversation by emphasizing that she "welcomed the opportunity to show Lara the way that Islam is civilized and how modern our women are."

Widad's concerns are equally present ten years later. Indeed, as there has been a resurgence of discourses that equate specific forms of Islam with absolute Otherness and call upon women's bodies and practices to mark this imagined boundary between "us" and "them," there has been an accompanying amplification of the representational concerns of my Lebanese Shiʻi interlocutors. In short, contemporary Islamophobic discourses are often built on gendered assumptions and ideas about the status of Muslim women. The pious Shiʻi women with whom I worked in *al-Dahiya* simultaneously articulated this sense of being responsible for representing their community's civilized status *and* reproduced the civilizational binarisms upon which their role as signifier rested. In *al-Dahiya*, the codependence of ideas about being pious and ideas about being modern has emerged in a gendered way. It is women who are primarily responsible for demonstrating and inhabiting a moral position related to *both* states (piety and modernity) in the contemporary world. Furthermore, to be considered fully "civilized" or "modern" within the community, one has to demonstrate these qualities in both the material and spiritual registers.

This responsibility entails a reversal of the rhetoric that constructs Muslim women as universally oppressed by Islam, favoring instead a response that posits Islam as the only context in which women can truly be free from oppression. In part, this model for Muslim womanhood was constructed as a direct, conscious response to Islamophobic images emanating both from the U.S. and from other communities in Lebanon. While it may seem counterintuitive to describe this response as Islamophilic (because the community that cultivates it is already Muslim), this descriptor crucially emphasizes the reactive impulses at work. The images of Islam and Muslims produced by Hizbullah activists are meant to be positive and corrective; they take the hostile views of others into account, counteracting them in ways that are reshaping everyday belief and practice.

Consciously Countering Stereotypes through Muslim Visibility

In its contemporary formations—as in many of its colonial ones—the question of Muslim women's status has often focused on two related areas: the headscarf and women's public participation.[9] In *al-Dahiya,* it is the latter—women's participation in the public arena—that is the principal concern. Indeed, the public visibility of Shi'i women marked as pious, generally by their dress but also by comportment and activity, has increased substantially in *al-Dahiya* since the 1970s. The most common and commonly noted aspect of this participation is women's volunteer work for Islamic social welfare organizations, where they do everything from providing for the basic needs of poor families to leading educational seminars on topics ranging from hygiene to Quranic interpretation to how best to approach the religious court system. Women also enter public life by running for local political office, working in media, and being elected to party committees, in addition to their growing involvement in fields ranging from medicine to education. They also participate visibly in communal religious life, especially during Ashura.

Women's increased participation in public life in these neighborhoods of Beirut is related to two major changes in the Lebanese Shi'i community over the past several decades. The first is the development of an organizational network through which various forms of work, education, and activism can take place. This network represents the institutionalization of a Lebanese Shi'i Islamic mobilization that began in the 1970s and today is represented most prominently—though not exclusively—by Hizbullah. The second change is the concurrent development of a "new" model of ideal moral womanhood for pious Lebanese Shi'i women, described by one of my interlocutors as "outspoken, Muslim, committed, and educated." In this model, a woman's piety and her participation in community life are understood as linked, and they are evaluated in terms of three factors: her contribution to the common good, the cultivation of her own piety through public activity, and the demonstration of the modern or civilized status of herself and her community to the outside world.

Women's role as barometer of the community's status is not the only important factor in this dynamic. The "new" model of moral womanhood is also related to the political mobilization of Lebanese Shi'i Muslims as Shi'i, urbanization, greater educational opportunities for Lebanese women of all confessional communities, return migration, women's education in *hawzas* (religious seminaries) and greater participation in religious life, and the relatively gender-progressive interpretations of the popular Lebanese *marja' al-taqlid*, Sayyid Muhammad Hussein Fadlallah.[10]

However, a transnational discursive context in which Islam is depicted as inherently oppressive to women plays a key role in shaping this alternative gender ideology as an Islamophilic response, providing it with an added sense of reactive urgency. Many women like Widad felt pressure to respond to those stereotypes and drew upon new models of moral womanhood in order to do so. As one community activist put it, "We see these terrible images of Muslim women, images that say that we are very oppressed and backward. It is important that we show people that this is incorrect, to show that we can be committed to our religion and be cultured (*muthaqqaf*) at the same time." When I asked her where she saw these images, she said: "They are everywhere. Look at the news. Look at CNN. Even here in Lebanon, have you ever seen LBC?[11] You will never find a woman like me there."

A Hizbullah Seminar

The process by which oppositional gender discourses emerge can be seen in the example of a seminar about women's public participation held by the Hizbullah Women's Committee in 2000. Such seminars were common venues for discussions about women's activism and often worked both to encourage and to facilitate it. For example, a series of discussions prior to this one had led to Hizbullah deciding to run a woman on its parliamentary electoral slate, though that decision was later revoked for reasons related mostly to the contingencies of Lebanese politics.

This particular seminar was led by Nayla, an engineer who had recently left her job at an architectural firm in order to devote more of her time to working directly in politics. At the time, she was the president of the party's Women's Committee. The twenty participants ranged from women in their forties and fifties who held only high school diplomas, to college graduates in their twenties and thirties, and a few undergraduate students. In general, they were active in their community, sometimes in opposition to their families' or husbands' wishes, and they shared the view that one of the tasks of their activism was to work to change that opposition.

Nayla opened the seminar by speaking about the different types of struggle—*jihad*—women should take part in, including military, social, and cultural struggles. She defined "cultural struggles" as being able to learn about and discuss gender norms from "other societies." Consistently, she returned to textual citations from the Quran and hadith, as well as from the *ijtihad*, or interpretation, of various Shiʻi scholars, especially Ayatullah Ruhullah Khomeini and Fadlallah. After about twenty minutes, she opened the seminar to general discussion. Over the next hour and a half, the conversation tacked in myriad ways, including among its many topics possible strategies for facilitating women's greater role in electoral politics; patriarchy in Lebanese society and how to teach men to take on more work in the domestic sphere; the need to change laws in Lebanon on issues like childcare, maternity leave, and citizenship; and the recent increase in the interest of international journalists in their work.[12]

Throughout, participants drew on transnational examples to make their points. For instance, women's participation in the Algerian anti-colonial resistance came up as a classic example from which a lesson was to be learned. A student at the Lebanese University who had been reading about how Algerian women had been "sent home" after the revolution brought this up as a cautionary note, asking what could be done to prevent such a reaction against women's public role in Lebanon in the event of a just peace with Israel.[13] Iran was also raised as an example, one to which women in this Lebanese community have complex and varied relationships. On this occasion, most women agreed that the contemporary situation in Iran was "better" than what happened in Algeria, but "not good enough" in terms of women's participation in society. This mixed response to Iran is particularly interesting in light of assumptions that Hizbullah merely duplicates Iranian policies or goals, and points both to the limitations of that relationship and to the diversity of views that do exist among the party's constituents. Most relevant to my purposes here are the ways in which transnational discourses about gender norms figured in ideas about the West's views of Muslim women and ideas about Western women. In this regard the seminar discussion shows both how binary civilizational discourses are drawn upon *and* the points at which those binary distinctions collapse.

Many participants commented on the interest Western journalists took in "Hizbullah women." Several of them had been interviewed by foreign reporters, and they observed that these reporters, as one woman put it, "all want to see if Islam is modern. So what do they do? They look at the women." Others noted that this was because people coming from the West all think that Muslim women are "backward and oppressed" (*mutakhallif wa mazlum*). In challenging these negative images, Nayla and the other seminar participants called upon the model of ideal Muslim womanhood I described earlier, and several women emphasized its "newness." As one of the college students put it: "We have no examples, because the examples we have are either of oppressed women or of

Western women. Instead, we have to set a new example for the world."

At this point, one of the older women in the group stepped in and corrected the student sharply, saying, "But don't forget, we have Sayyida Zaynab [sister of Imam Husayn] and all the women of the Prophet's family (*ahl al-bayt*)." Following a silence that seemed longer than it probably was, Nayla cited the beauty of *ijtihad* in Shi'i Islam, making the common observation that *ijtihad* was what made it possible to adapt models like Zaynab's to contemporary society. While she was partly trying to smooth over a minor disagreement that signaled both generational and educational differences, she was also suggesting that these were not mutually exclusive perspectives. Indeed, at the close of the seminar, "setting a new example" for both their peers and the world was highlighted as one of the tasks participants would take with them. But this new example was one inspired by models like Zaynab and located in a belief that Islam provides the only real space for women's freedom from oppression. Furthermore, this "new example" was to be set by their visibility in the public sphere specifically as *pious Muslim* women.

This seemingly straightforward "Islam is the solution" response was further complicated by the discussion the participants had about "the liberated Western woman," a construct that is often just as monolithic as that of "the oppressed Muslim woman." Perhaps the most commonly cited instance of this construct is the "Westoxicated" woman, a figure that saturated revolutionary discourse in the Iranian context.[14] On the one hand, participants in the Hizbullah seminar echoed elements of a notion of "Westoxication," highlighting especially the ideas that the West stands for rampant consumerism, the objectification of women, and the isolation of individuals from their family or social contexts—all tendencies that lead to a deterioration of moral values. Yet on the other hand, several women in the group presented a more ambivalent relationship to the "Western woman." When one participant noted the difficulties women face in working outside the home in Lebanon, including societal expectations that they should privilege the domestic realm, pressure from spouses, and the gossip of neighbors and relatives, she concluded, "In the West, women don't have this problem." Another woman concurred, and noted that "in the West, all parts of society are working, women and men are standing together. Here, we are a society that is missing half of our potential. They work with two teams, we have only half of that."[15]

Before moving on, I should emphasize two unarticulated moves that the combination of these various images of Islam and the West made possible. First, in these seminar discussions, the opposite of the West was never Islam per se, but "Eastern society," a monolithic construct that figured as the source of patriarchal oppression. Second, these binarized constructions served also to mask complex histories of feminist movements and gender activism in Muslim societies, including Lebanon, that are not simply impositions or contaminations from the West.

Outside the Hizbullah seminar, too, pious Shi'i women frequently expressed an acute understanding of the importance of women's status to perceptions of the level of civilization characteristic of a people or place. For example, in a conversation about local responses to the women-run organization where she worked, an activist told me that she hoped the organization would provide evidence of women's public capabilities. On other occasions, it was local responses with which women were concerned. A different volunteer with the same organization told me about the nursery they ran, saying, "Our nursery is being spoken of as the best nursery in all of Beirut, not even only *al-Dahiya*. People from all over walk in to see, and they are surprised. They say, 'Wow, these are Muslims, but they understand; they are educated; they have awareness.'" Her use of the phrase "Muslim, but" is indicative of the extent to which she and other volunteers have encountered and confronted negative stereotypes about their religious community in local Lebanese discourses. Local and transnational discourses are not unrelated, and each works in conjunction with the other in various ways. For some of my interlocutors, "the West" was itself represented by other communities in Lebanon. And in Lebanon, there is a *particular* negative stereotype associated with Shi'ism and *al-Dahiya*, to which I will return below.

Since 2001, the general sense in *al-Dahiya* is that both the public visibility of pious women and the imperative to actively address the negative stereotypes that are part of Islamophobia have increased. During a conversation I had with Nayla in 2007, she said that she had decided to stop granting interviews to anyone who was interested in talking about "Hizbullah women," though she continued to communicate with a few journalists via e-mail. She had numerous reasons for this stance, including changes in her work schedule and responsibilities within the party and her desire to be viewed as a political figure regardless of her sex. She also complained that the questions she was asked had become repetitive and were often too simplistic, and she expressed new suspicions that the interviewers themselves "already knew what they were looking for" or were uninterested in genuine dialogue. Despite her newfound reluctance to deal directly with journalists, Nayla said that she still thought it was very important to use the media as much as possible to confront stereotypical images. She then showed me clips of an al-Jazeera English special on "Hizbullah women" in which she had recently taken part.

Complicating Contemporary, Gendered, Islamophobic Discourses

Lebanese Shi'i women's engagements with transnational discourses about Muslim women are a contemporary example of how ideas about women and gender norms are used to establish boundaries between binarized civilizational constructs, Islamophobic and Islamophilic ones alike. One question that arises, given the long history of such discourses, is what, if anything, is different about contemporary discourses that rest in part on gendered distinctions.

One possibility is that the circulation of discourses itself differs. While transnational discourses about Islam and Muslim women are clearly not new, contemporary circulations are heavily mediated, adding new circuits of knowledge production to engagements with gender and other discourses. Electronic media and satellite television in particular contribute to the production of different kinds of public spheres, and new relationships to information and ideas.[16] Shi'i Lebanese women respond in part to images of Muslim women they see on CNN International and the BBC, and they confront those images in part through their work with al-Manar—Hizbullah's television station—and al-Jazeera. Over the past two decades, Hizbullah itself has built a sophisticated, media-savvy information production and distribution network that selectively targets various Lebanese and international audiences. It has employed numerous pious women who were unable to find employment in media in other parts of Beirut due to anti-Muslim discrimination.

The second potential difference may stem from the varying contingencies of European colonialisms versus U.S. neoimperialism in its multiple phases.[17] One of the most common images of Muslim women purveyed in relation to specifically *U.S.* power is that of the oppressed woman in need of liberation by the U.S. military, a figure that emerged most strikingly in the Bush administration's rhetoric justifying the U.S. invasion of Afghanistan. In a radio address on November 17, 2001, First Lady Laura Bush cast the invasion as a mission to bring civilization to Afghan women, thereby "saving" them from both the Taliban and their burkas.[18] "Afghan women," she claimed, "know what the rest of the world is discovering: The brutal oppression of women is the central goal of the terrorists" (quoted in Abu-Lughod 2002). This observation placed the U.S. military in the role of protector and liberator of women, despite U.S. support for the regime in Afghanistan prior to September 11.

We can also look to recent trends in popular literature purporting to "expose" the status of women in Muslim communities, including works by Ayaan Hirsi Ali and Irshad Manji (see chapter 3), and Azar Nafisi. Even David

Horowitz's conservative, hatemongering Terrorism Awareness Project high-lights "the status of Muslim women" in its efforts. In the fall of 2007 academic inboxes were flooded with e-mails warning scholars of the "Islamo-Fascism Awareness Week" that the organization was promoting. Among the suggested events for conservative student organizations to sponsor were a "teach-in on the oppression of women in Islam" and "sit-ins in Women's Studies depart-ments to protest their silence about the oppression of women in Islam." Several women's studies departments across the U.S. were bombarded with requests from students who appeared to be foot soldiers in this campaign, demanding departmental statements on "Muslim women's oppression."

In the Lebanese case, the U.S. government's complicity in the 2006 Israeli attack on Lebanon was not justified with explicit mentions of Muslim women or Islam as such. However, a civilizational discourse in which Muslim women play a key representative role remains a major subtext in the dynamics by which U.S. power is negotiated in Lebanon and elsewhere. This type of gender con-struction legitimates military adventure by dividing the world along a binary axis and granting those deemed "civilized" the right to "bring" civilization to those who are not so deemed by whatever means necessary, in the role of male savior. Armed opposition to U.S. (or in this case, Israeli) military intervention is then portrayed as terrorists hiding behind "helpless women and children," which again reinforces the idea that certain women require rescue from their own (Muslim) men.

This imagery is critical to the context in which Shi'i women's public par-ticipation is viewed as proof of their community's status. When I asked Nayla why she thought there was so much interest among journalists and others in Hizbullah women, she answered that this was related in part to a general in-terest in the party, in part to a sense that Hizbullah women were more visibly active than women in other Islamic movements, and in part because "even the spies and/or informers (*mukhabarat*) are working on this topic, because usually when they want to attack any group, they study its details and espe-cially about its women." Lest Nayla's fears seem conspiratorial, consider a May 31, 2007, article in the *Jerusalem Post* that I received in my e-mail from two other women in *al-Dahiya*, as well as two colleagues in the U.S. The article, "Empowered Women Could Combat Islamic Extremism," described a confer-ence "on the empowerment of Arab women at the Hebrew University's Shasha Center for Strategic and Policy Studies," a center directed by Ephraim Halevy, "a former head of the Mossad and the National Security Council." Attendees at this conference "examined the traditions within Muslim society that prevent women from obtaining work and education outside the home and what the

Israeli government could do in this area." Not only does this example lend credence to Nayla's fears, but it also demonstrates how such ideas circulate, pointing to continuities between historical and contemporary colonial gender discourses.

Shi'a-phobia

Thinking about Lebanon in relation to discussions of Islamophobia opens up another layer of complexity within these contemporary political-discursive dynamics. One of the effects of the July 2006 war was to polarize a rift between Hizbullah and the majority in the Lebanese government that had been gradually growing since the assassination of Lebanese prime minister Rafiq Hariri in 2005. After the 2006 war, this rift continued to deepen, triggering strikes and protests, the withdrawal of Hizbullah and allied ministers from government, conflict over presidential and parliamentary elections, and brief periods of internal violence. Throughout this period, a discourse of what might be called "Shi'a-phobia" has been revitalized in Lebanon.

This Sunni-Shi'i rift in Lebanon has been explained in the U.S. press, as has the violence in Iraq, as the inevitable result of age-old sectarian conflicts. But these conflicts are political and economic, with differences laid onto the lines of religious identity; they are not conflicts about religious difference per se.[19] Furthermore, this particular sectarian fault line is relatively new to Lebanese politics, and it runs through a wide variety of issues, including support for Hizbullah's military resistance wing, arms held by nearly every political party in the country, economic policies, corruption, and political representation. Perhaps the most crucial aspect of this conflict is over alliance with or opposition to U.S. economic, political, and military policies in the Middle East. Here the binary distinction between "us" and "them" is applied to the government majority and its allies, who are carefully aligned with the United States and Saudi Arabia against Hizbullah and other opposition parties, who are in turn aligned with Syria and Iran. Once again, civilizational rhetoric is used to draw the lines, with both sides in the internal Lebanese conflict claiming moral high ground by asserting their "civilized" status.[20] The picture is complicated further when one steps out of Lebanon and considers responses in the Arab world to Hizbullah during the July 2006 war. A divide emerged between Sunni Arab governments allied with the U.S. (Saudi Arabia, Jordan), who were eager to distance themselves from Hizbullah, and popular sentiment within the same countries, where Hizbullah secretary general Sayyid Hasan Nasrallah attained rock star status.

Within Lebanon, assumptions and stereotypes about Shiʻi Islam have echoed many of the tropes found in other Islamophobic discourses, most prominently in accusations of terrorism, despite the Lebanese army's 2007 battle with a Sunni Islamist group in the north of the country (Fath al-Islam). Fears of a "Shiʻa takeover" of Lebanon have become a sentiment all too commonly expressed among supporters of the majority in government, whether Sunni or Christian.[21] Lebanese Shiʻi Muslims are accused of "really being Iranians," not only in terms of imagined loyalties but literally in terms of race. In 2007, dinnertime commentary in the households of government-majority supporters characterized the Hizbullah-led sit-in in downtown Beirut with a plethora of references to "dirt" and "smells" brought into the area and the "contamination" of what had been an upper-class space of business and leisure. Obviously, such commentary is also a reflection of class differences between supporters of the government majority and members of the opposition.

Once again, much of this discourse is built on gendered stereotypes. "They brainwash their women" was a common refrain. "That's how they get them to all wear those abayas." "Abayas are Iranian dress anyway; why are they wearing them here? See, they're not Arab." Or, as a Sunni-identified acquaintance said to me, "They will force everyone to veil, you'll see." Similar statements, especially around forced veiling, can be found in the "Statement Calling on Feminists to End Their Silence on the Oppression of Women in Islam," written by David Horowitz's Terrorism Awareness Project (2007), which locates the beginnings of what he calls Islamo-Fascism in the Islamic revolution in Iran. In both Lebanon and the U.S., the idea that Islam is inherently oppressive to women is centered in part on political conflict between the U.S. and Iran. Just as we see gendered anti-Islam discourses emerging in the U.S. today around the "specter" of Iran, statements about Shiʻi Muslims, in particular in Lebanon, are similarly inflected and focused.

This is underscored further by the fact that anti-Shiʻi discourses have not been met thus far with specifically Sunni-phobic discourses in Lebanon, at least not in the public arena. Instead, the rhetoric of Shiʻi Lebanese leaders tends to emphasize coexistence and the importance of Islamic unity in the face of U.S. imperialism, and tends to present conflict between Sunni and Shiʻi in Lebanon as instigated by the U.S. On the ground, things look slightly different. In *al-Dahiya*, many young women have stopped visiting an all-women's beach in the (historically Sunni) "other part" of the city, finding new fault with it, claiming it is not really *sharʻi* (in keeping with Islamic law), and insisting that only the beach monitored by Fadlallah's office is appropriate for Muslims.

This avoidance suggests that a sectarian spatial divide has reemerged in Beirut, and that the rationale for this distinction emphasizes the young women's own standards of piety, without casting the Sunni beach in particularly derogatory terms. I encountered two exceptions to this in 2007, both occasions when Shi'i acquaintances wryly cited the Prophet's wife Aisha (who led a battle against Imam Ali) as an example of why Sunni Lebanese politician Bahia Hariri should not be allotted so much power.[22]

In all these examples, we see gendered assumptions underlying Islamophobic, Shi'a-phobic, and Islamophilic discourses. Indeed, I would suggest that a gendered reading of these discourses is necessary to understanding the complexity of their reemergence and deployment in the contemporary political moment. Both Hizbullah women's engagements with transnational discourses and the current political fracturing of Lebanon highlight several ways in which pro- and anti-Muslim constructs depend on a binary civilizational construct that can be shaped and deployed by various actors, often in ways that reflect political differences unrelated to religion. Through their circulations, ideas and policies originating in the West influence how Islam is drawn upon and put to use by Shi'i Muslims in Lebanon and how those responses are viewed by other Lebanese. Hizbullah women's relationships to prevailing ideas about Muslim and Western women also underscore how the simplistic binaries on which these concepts are built often collapse, betraying far more complex political contingencies and relationships, and unearthing some of the possibilities that lie in the gray spaces between.

Notes

Portions of this article appear in the *Journal of the Royal Anthropological Institute* (Deeb 2009). Thanks to Esra Özyürek, Andrew Shryock, Becky Tolen, and participants at the Islamophobia/Islamophilia conference at the University of Michigan for comments.

1. For example, Ilene R. Prusher, "Through Charity, Hizbullah Charms Lebanon," *Christian Science Monitor,* April 19, 2000, p. 1. See also CNN's report from April 1, 1998, "Lebanon Rejects Israeli Pullback Plan," available at http://www.cnn.com/WORLD/9804/01/israel .lebanon.2/index.html.

2. See Andrew Shyrock's introduction to this volume for a useful overview.

3. For example, see Frances Hasso (2005) for a discussion of Israeli associations of Palestinian masculinity with violence in this vein and of its exceptions.

4. Note that I use the phrase "pious Shi'i community" or "pious Shi'i Muslims" as a gloss for those who identify with certain ideologies and practices of piety centered around Hizbullah and the prominent religious scholar Sayyid Muhammad Hussein Fadlallah. Not all pious Shi'is in Lebanon fit this description, nor is sect by any means a fixed category.

For more on the fluidity and constructed nature of notions of "sect" and sectarian identity in Lebanon, see Makdisi (2000).

5. See Deeb (2006) for a detailed elucidation of this argument.

6. For a detailed discussion of the "clash of civilizations" thesis and various critiques of it, as well as a discussion of the ways "civilization" operates as a value-laden term in relation to notions of modernity rooted in the European Enlightenment, see Jarmakani (2008).

7. When I refer to "transnational analysis," I am not referring to multi-sited research, but to the ways in which we can attend to our interlocutors' engagements with discourses that emerge in and travel through transnational contexts of power, capitalism, and militarism, today most obviously with regard to U.S. interventions in the Middle East and elsewhere. This notion of transnational feminist analysis builds on the work of Grewal and Kaplan (1994) and Moallem (2005). Such a framework is also attentive to the articulations of gender, nation, race, religion, sexuality, and class within these transnational relations of power.

8. All names are pseudonyms.

9. This is due in part to the long history of symbolic potency of the headscarf and assumptions about its relationship to limitations or facilitations of women's public participation (Abu-Lughod 2002; Ahmed 1992; El Guindi 1999; MacLeod 1991) and in part to assumptions that public participation is an accurate indicator of women's status in society. It is also related to the ways in which women's bodies are positioned in symbolic battles between colonialist and nationalist movements and to the patriarchal notion, prevalent among colonialists and nationalists alike, that women "belong to" the community or nation.

10. Practicing Shi'i Muslims choose a religious scholar who has attained a certain rank in jurisprudential learning to follow or emulate on religious matters. Scholars who are thus emulated are called *marja' al-taqlid,* literally, "source of emulation."

11. LBC, the Lebanese Broadcasting Corporation, is a Christian television station in Lebanon.

12. Note that this increased interest in Hizbullah was before September 11, 2001, and was part of a move in the U.S. media in the late 1990s to begin to understand Hizbullah as a political party and as a welfare organization. This was also a moment when Hizbullah's military activity was described as guerrilla warfare without the word "terrorism," and there were reporters from the U.S. in *al-Dahiya* interested in the non-military aspects of the party. Hizbullah itself was consciously working to capitalize on this interest and present its legitimized, post-civil-war status to the international community. While I hesitate to reify September 11 as an absolute before/after break, it was at that point that Hizbullah was returned to the "A-list of terrorism." What had been the beginnings of a move in a different direction, at least in terms of media coverage, was rapidly reversed.

13. This particular transnational parallel is a common one among women activists in the Middle East. See, for example, Strum (1992).

14. The term "Westoxication" (*gharbzadagi*) was originally coined by Iranian philosopher Ahmed Fardid, and later made popular by leftist intellectual Jalal Al-e Ahmed in his book of the same title. For discussion of "Westoxication," specifically in relation to women during the Islamic revolution in Iran, see Moallem (2005).

15. This assertion contains an echo of the statements of elite Egyptian reformers during British colonialism, like Qasim Amin (2000 [1899]), who used such arguments to argue for unveiling and for women's education—though *not* for women's participation in the political and economic realms. Similar arguments, with similar limitations, were made by Lebanese intellectuals and reformers during the nineteenth-century *Nahda*. See Traboulsi (2007: 63–67). It is also an assertion that contributes an added importance to pious Shi'i women's public participation—emphasizing that it is necessary for the development of their community and underscoring comparison with ideals that are associated with the West, especially development discourses and liberal feminist discourses.

16. See Eickelman and Anderson (1999) on the emergence of a new Muslim public sphere that has been facilitated by electronic media.

17. I use the term "neoimperialism" advisedly, taking to heart Kelly and Kaplan's cautioning that describing U.S. power as imperial or neoimperial is imprecise, and does not capture the complexities of U.S. global domination, which includes an anti-European-imperialism streak and affinities between neoliberal capitalist economies and identity-politics or rights-based movements (2001: 144–45).

18. There have been several feminist critiques of this address, most notably by Lila Abu-Lughod in her article, "Do Muslim Women Need Saving?" (2002).

19. This political and economic conflict has historical roots in the construction of Lebanon as a nation-state and the marginalization of Shi'i Muslims within that state. The contemporary manifestation of this conflict was catalyzed by the assassination of Lebanese prime minister Rafiq Hariri in 2005 and by the July 2006 war, and is also related to the polarization of Lebanon and the Middle East more generally along pro- and anti-U.S. lines.

20. Obviously, U.S. discourses are implicated in both the construction and the facilitation of this conflict. But placing Lebanon next to Iraq proves to be a puzzle. In Lebanon, Sunni Muslims are "good Muslims" and Islamophobia is meant to refer to "Shi'a" Muslims, while in Iraq, at various times, the opposite becomes the case. The Bush administration's own rhetoric shifted after 2001 to embrace notions of an internal struggle in Islam, setting the U.S. up as a space of tolerance and acceptance for those deemed moderate by its standards. Among its many problems, this strategy ignores Sunni groups affiliated with al-Qaeda that are organizing and active in Lebanon, and ignores Hizbullah's role in the political system and social fabric of the country.

21. The Christian Lebanese community seems to be divided down the middle in terms of where they are allied.

22. Hariri is a Sunni deputy from the south, sister of Rafiq Hariri, the assassinated prime minister.

Works Cited

Abu-Lughod, Lila. 1998. "Introduction: Feminist Longings and Postcolonial Conditions." In *Remaking Women: Feminism and Modernity in the Middle East,* ed. Lila Abu-Lughod, 3–31. Princeton, N.J.: Princeton University Press.

————. 2002. "Do Muslim Women Really Need Saving? Anthropological Reflections on Cultural Relativism and Its Others." *American Anthropologist* 104: 783–90.

Ahmed, Leila. 1992. *Women and Gender in Islam: Historical Roots of a Modern Debate.* New Haven, Conn.: Yale University Press.

Al-e Amad, Jalal. 1983. *Occidentosis: A Plague from the West (Gharbzadegi),* trans. R. Campbell. Berkeley, Calif.: Mizan Press.

Amin, Qasim. 2000 [1899]. *The Liberation of Women and the New Woman: Two Documents in the History of Egyptian Feminism.* Trans. Samiha Sidhom Peterson. Cairo: American University in Cairo Press.

Chatterjee, Partha. 1993. *The Nation and Its Fragments: Colonial and Postcolonial Histories.* Princeton, N.J.: Princeton University Press.

Deeb, Lara. 2006. *An Enchanted Modern: Gender and Public Piety in Shi'i Islam.* Princeton, N.J.: Princeton University Press.

————. 2009. "Piety Politics and the Role of a Transnational Feminist Analysis." *Journal of the Royal Anthropological Institute* 15 (supplement 1): S112–S126.

Eickelman, Dale F., and Jon W. Anderson, eds. 1999. *New Media in the Muslim World: The Emerging Public Sphere.* Bloomington: Indiana University Press.

Grewal, Inderpal, and Caren Kaplan, eds. 1994. *Scattered Hegemonies: Postmodernity and Transnational Feminist Practices.* Minneapolis: University of Minnesota Press.

El Guindi, Fadwa. 1999. *Veil: Modesty, Privacy and Resistance.* Oxford: Berg.

Hasso, Frances S. 2005. "Discursive and Political Deployments by/of the 2002 Palestinian Women Suicide Bombers/Martyrs." *Feminist Review* 81: 23–51.

Jarmakani, Amira. 2008. *Imagining Arab Womanhood: The Cultural Mythology of Veils, Harems, and Belly Dancers in the U.S.* New York: Palgrave.

Kelly, John D., and Martha Kaplan. 2001. *Represented Communities: Fiji and World Decolonization.* Chicago: University of Chicago Press.

MacLeod, Arlene. 1991. *Accommodating Protest: Working Women, the New Veiling, and Change in Cairo.* New York: Columbia University Press.

Makdisi, Ussama. 2000. *The Culture of Sectarianism: Community, History and Violence in Nineteenth-Century Ottoman Lebanon.* Berkeley: University of California Press.

Moallem, Minoo. 2005. *Between Warrior Brother and Veiled Sister: Islamic Fundamentalism and the Politics of Patriarchy in Iran.* Berkeley: University of California Press.

Saliba, Theresa. 2002. "Introduction." In *Gender, Politics, Islam,* ed. Theresa Saliba, Carolyn Allen, and Judith Howard. Chicago: University of Chicago Press.

Strum, Philippa. 1992. "Introduction: The Women of Palestine Will Not Be like the Women of Algeria." In *The Women Are Marching: The Second Sex and the Palestinian Revolution,* ed. Philippa Strum, 1–23. New York: Lawrence Hill Books.

Terrorism Awareness Project. 2007. "Statement Calling on Feminists to End Their Silence on the Oppression of Women in Islam." http://www.terrorismawareness.org/isla mo-fascism/69/statement-calling-on-feminists-to-end-their-silence-on-the-oppres sion-of-women-in-islam/.

Traboulsi, Fawwaz. 2007. *A History of Modern Lebanon.* London: Pluto Press.

5

Bridging Traditions: Madrasas and Their Internal Critics

Muhammad Qasim Zaman

Of the many thorny debates on issues relating to "Islam and modernity," questions of educational reform are among the most contentious. What sort of education should Muslims receive in order to meet the challenges of changing times and needs? Can "useful education"—usually understood to comprise the modern, secular, Western sciences—be combined with the traditional Islamic sciences and, if so, how and in what measure? How should Islam itself be reinterpreted in order to facilitate Muslim adaptation to modern institutions and practices? Such questions were repeatedly asked by Muslim modernists of the nineteenth and early twentieth centuries as a prelude to urging their co-religionists, as Abdullah Yusuf Ali (d. 1953)—a noted intellectual of colonial India best known for his English translation of the Quran—put it, "to make modern knowledge a living force among Muslims, as it was in their palmy days" (Ali 1941: 399). Similar concerns have continued to engage the modernizing governing elite of postcolonial Muslim societies as well. They have also figured in various ways in much Western commentary on institutions of traditional Islamic learning, often known as madrasas, which are frequently viewed as sites of illiberal indoctrination.

Prominent among those at the receiving end of such questions are the traditionally educated Muslim religious scholars, the 'ulama, as well as others of a broadly traditionalist intellectual formation. In response, many among the 'ulama have argued that the sort of virtues Muslims need to cultivate come from the Islamic religious tradition itself and not from the West; that only a return to the fundamentals of the faith would restore God's favor to them and empower them in adverse circumstances; and that efforts towards "mixing" the Islamic sciences with modern, Western forms of learning are aimed ultimately at undermining the 'ulama's ability to impart authoritative Islamic learning and thus represent a thinly disguised attack on Islam itself. Assertions of this sort are easily caricatured, lending themselves to reinforcing the deep misgivings many observers have had about what the madrasa and its stringent constructions of Islam might mean for the world around it.

Yet the 'ulama of modern times have scarcely been of one mind on whether or how to defend their institutions, or to what degree to open them up to non-traditional forms of learning. Many among them have seen efforts toward bringing the Islamic and the modern, secular sciences closer together not as undermining Islam, but rather as a necessary condition for its very survival in conditions of modernity. Against their more conservative critics, they have argued that Islam has never countenanced any sharp division between religious and secular learning, and that the two streams ought to continually replenish each other in enabling Muslims to lead lives that are as true to their faith as they are attentive to modern needs. This chapter examines the views of some of these scholars.[1] Neither "friends" of the madrasa in any obvious sense nor its "foes," these traditionally educated scholars reveal a complexity in their discourses—*even when* they are framed in blandly dichotomous terms—that is seldom recognized in public commentary on the madrasa and related in-stitutions. My purpose here is not, however, to simply document the fact that many of those who derive their authority from their traditionalist intellectual formation are among the severest critics of the sorts of institutions associated with that formation. Nor is it to try to differentiate "good" scholars, who have sought to build bridges between Islamic and modern, secular learning, from "bad" ones, that is, those railing against such efforts. It is rather to examine some of the ambiguities that inhere in the discourses even of the bridge build-ers among the traditionalist scholars. What accounts for the persistence of the discourse on bringing putatively rival traditions of learning closer together? That is, does the longevity of this discourse owe itself *exclusively* to the perceived intransigence of the conservative 'ulama? And what do this discourse and its ambiguities reveal about contested conceptions of Islam, politics, religious education, and their place in a rapidly changing world?

I

We begin with Muhammad Rashid Rida (d. 1935), a Syrian disciple of the famous Egyptian reformer Muhammad 'Abduh (d. 1905) and an influential Salafi journalist and Quran commentator. The Salafis have often critiqued the historically articulated Islamic tradition in the interest of reforming Muslim beliefs and practices by radically realigning them with the teachings of the Quran and the normative example of the Prophet Muhammad, as well as with the ways of other pious forebears (*al-salaf al-salih*). There are many orientations within the ranks of the Salafis, ranging from those committed to literalist approaches to the Islamic foundational texts and considerable hostility toward the modernization of Muslim societies, to those seeking to reinterpret Islam in view of what they see as modern challenges. The latter are best characterized as "reformist Salafis." 'Abduh and Rida are among the most important representatives of this trend, as is the Qatar-based Egyptian scholar Yusuf al-Qaradawi in the contemporary world (cf. Krämer 2006: 194–95).

Unlike 'Abduh, Rida was not educated at al-Azhar, of which, like 'Abduh, he was a lifelong critic. His intellectual formation was eclectic, yet it was sufficiently traditional to provide him with the credentials of an *'alim* (plural: 'ulama [cf. Rida 1934: 139–45]). He put these credentials to good use in issuing legal opinions (*fatwas*)—regularly published in his journal, *al-Manar*—and in his Quran commentary, the *Tafsir al-manar*. It was strategically important to flaunt his scholarly credentials in engaging with the Azhar establishment, and he did this with flair. Yet he continued to also insist on his distance from al-Azhar—his intellectual independence of the sort of tradition he took the Azhar 'ulama to represent.

Rida's view of what was wrong with his fellow 'ulama, as well as his own much-vaunted sense of intellectual independence, found frequent expression in his diatribes on *taqlid*. *Taqlid*, as Rida saw it, was not principled adherence to the methods and doctrines of earlier scholars but "blind imitation"—a way in which many modernist reformers have commonly interpreted it.[2] Indeed, it was tantamount to idolatry, for those committed to it ranked the views of the earlier masters above everything else, and even insisted on approaching the foundational texts through the hermeneutical lenses provided to them by those masters. Despite accusations to the contrary, Rida did not wish to discard the Islamic scholarly tradition any more than 'Abduh had. He did, however, challenge his contemporary 'ulama's claims as gatekeepers of this tradition. He wanted to see the scholarly tradition, and the various religious and customary practices endorsed or tolerated by the 'ulama, continually evaluated in light of the foundational texts. And he thought that *everyone* was capable of independently reflecting on the Quran, and of ordering his or her life in accordance with its prescriptions. The 'ulama had not only obstructed the free flow of God's guidance to the ordinary believers; they had also dulled people's mental faculties. Islam, Rida insisted, was an eminently "rational" religion, and it had nothing to fear from the modern sciences. The 'ulama, however, had constructed barriers to the acquisition of modern learning and to combining it with the proper study of Islam, just as they had obstructed the study of the Quran itself. In the process, they had undermined the interests of Islam. At their hands, the Muslim community had come to be divided into rival doctrinal orientations and rigid schools of law, whose adherents, under the leadership of squabbling 'ulama, typically placed their particularistic interests far above the common good of Muslims. The 'ulama, Rida thought, were a bad advertisement for Islam. Far from attracting people to it, they were helpless in preventing Muslims from turning away from Islam under the impact of Westernization and at the hands of the Christian missionaries.[3]

It was not just the 'ulama of al-Azhar that were to blame, though it was these that Rida knew best. In 1912, he had visited India and spoken at a number of educational institutions there, including the Dar al-'Ulum of Deoband, the Dar al-'Ulum of the Nadwat al-'Ulama in Lucknow, and the Muhammadan Anglo-Oriental College in Aligarh. I will say more about these institutions later in this chapter. Speaking at Aligarh, a college established by Sir Sayyid Ahmad Khan (d. 1898) in 1875 to provide English education to the Muslims of India, he blamed the 'ulama for what he saw as the sorry state of Islam in India:

> We Muslims have become an argument against our religion on account of the innovations (*bida'*) and the superstitions (*kharafat*) that have become widespread amongst us. If only we had held fast to its bond (*'urwa*) and guarded its normative example (*sunna*), it would have spread to the East and the West. The rapid spread [of Islam] in its early days was due only to the excellence of its adherents, their virtues and their actions. . . . We have reached such a low point in our decline that the heathens (*wathaniyyun*) in these lands are now more advanced than Muslims in matters of knowledge, action, and unity. . . . No Muslim nation is more in need of religion, in its political and communal life, than the Muslims of India. If they were to revive Islam amongst themselves, the heathen majority will turn into a minority and the Muslim minority will turn into a majority. . . .
> (Rida 1912c: 583; cf. Rida 1912b: 337)

But if Rida was unsparing in his critique of the 'ulama, he was no less harsh in his assessment of the westernizing Muslims (*al-mutafarnijun*). Just as the unreconstructed 'ulama blindly followed past authorities, the westernizing Muslims were equally blind in their devotion to European models. Rida considered many of them to be apostates (*malahida*), who believed that "religion in this age did not go together with politics, knowledge, and civilization" (Rida 1923: 62). Quite apart from questions of the veracity of religion, such people did not realize that religious beliefs had a crucial social role, that without it people would no longer adhere to social and moral norms (Rida 1912c: 578–80). Nor

did these imitators of "foreign traditions and innovations" (al-taqalid wa'l-bida'
al-ghariba [Rida 1912c: 585]), who had blissfully abandoned their mores, see that
Western nations had continued to remain committed to *their* norms: "In their
character and their morals," he told his audience at the westernizing Anglo-
Oriental College at Aligarh, "the English provide you a lesson unmatched by
any other; for they don't give up any of their habits and traditions, even in favor
of what is better, except under severe duress" (Rida 1912c: 586).

In the space bounded by these two extremes, Rida wanted to see the emergence of a new elite that would provide both religious and political leadership
to the community. Already in 1912, Rida had helped found an educational
institution, the Madrasat al-da'wa wa'l-irshad, in Cairo to train a corps of
religious guides actively engaged with the affairs of the community, capable
of stemming what he saw as the insidious threat of Christian missionaries in
Muslim societies, and committed to rebuilding the community's religious
foundations. As he had put it in explaining his vision for this madrasa:

> One of the things that afflict Islam [today] is the lack of a group among its ad-
> herents which is devoted to general religious guidance for the Muslims as had
> existed among our pious forebears (*salafina al-salih*) and as they exist in other
> communities, such as the Christian monks and priests. Consequently, there is
> anarchy among Muslims in matters of their religion, in their upbringing and
> their morals. . . . Some among them remain ignorant, never laying their eyes
> upon a learned guide and educator who might attend to them with instruction
> and advice; others go to Christian missionary schools or government schools
> to acquire their knowledge, manners, and morals. The Muslim community has
> seen no reform emerge from such students. Instead, it has seen numerous ills in
> the students of such schools, from their divisiveness to their bad morals to their
> calls to [particularistic] . . . ties that accord neither with their religion nor with
> their history. As for the religious schools, they, for all their small numbers, have
> turned into *worldly* schools, in which knowledge is sought only for employment
> in the judiciary, as *muftis*, or as teachers. (Rida 1912a: 924)

Though this madrasa proved short-lived (closing its doors in 1915, in the
face of opposition from many 'ulama; accusations that Rida was somehow
trying, through the preachers trained at this madrasa, to subvert the Ottoman caliphate; and a chronic lack of funds),[4] Rida would continue to devote
his considerable energy to visualizing a new religious and political elite for
Muslim societies. He offered some of his most sustained reflections on this
subject in *The Caliphate*, a treatise that he published on the eve of the demise
of the Ottoman caliphate in 1923. In the classical Sunni constitutional theory,
the election of the caliph has been entrusted to an indeterminate group of

people often referred to as the *ahl al-hall wa'l-'aqd*—"those who loosen and bind" the public affairs of Muslims. Medieval jurists differed on who made up this select group: leading religious scholars, people who wielded political and military power, or some combination of the two. To Rida,

> the *ahl al-hall wa'l-'aqd* are the elite (*sarat*) of the community, its notables and its chiefs—people whom the community trusts in matters of knowledge, action, and public interest . . . and whom it follows in whatever they decide as regards religious and worldly affairs. . . . When this segment of the community is in good order, the condition of the community at large and of its rulers is also sound. . . . Consequently, Islamic reform requires that Islam's *ahl al-hall wa'l-'aqd* be people self-sufficient in their knowledge of the *shari'a*, be knowledgeable of the community's political, social, legal, administrative, and financial interests, and that they be people of probity, of considered judgment, and of sagacity. (Rida 1923: 58)

Rida was calling here for nothing less than a new kind of public and religious intellectual, one with credible claims to religious authority yet independent of the traditional religious scholars. This vision anticipates the college- and university-educated Islamists of a later generation with the difference, however, that Rida's intellectuals would not be mere autodidacts in religious matters. Rather, the elite among them were to be educated at an educational institution specifically designed for them, acquiring there all that they needed to provide religious and political leadership to the community at large. The caliph himself would come from within the ranks of such intellectuals. Later scholars have remained uncertain about whether Rida intended his caliph to exercise any real authority or if he was meant to serve largely as a symbol of the global Muslim community. Either way, it is the new religious intellectuals who were to play the key role in reorienting Islam and Muslim societies toward a politically independent, religiously unified, and intellectually vibrant path. While the caliphate was not resuscitated, Rida's vision of a new kind of religious intellectual, one that bridged religious and worldly knowledge and combined religious authority with social and political standing, has not ceased to resonate in many circles. It has also remained elusive.

II

Among Rida's many admirers is Yusuf al-Qaradawi (b. 1926), arguably the most influential of the Sunni 'ulama in the contemporary Muslim world.[5] Like Rida, Qaradawi has long argued for a new kind of religious intellectual, one who combines Islamic and modern forms of knowledge, speaks "the language of the age" (Qaradawi 2000: 143–44, 149) and is what Qaradawi calls a "centrist," in self-conscious contrast to those given to extremes of different kinds. Qaradawi speaks with much pride of his directorship, from the school's inception in the early 1960s to the mid-1970s, of the College of Higher Religious Studies in Doha, Qatar, where he had tried to foster an educational system that "combined the old and the new." As he had put it in 1963 to Muhammad ibn Ibrahim Al al-Shaykh, the grand mufti of Saudi Arabia and the first rector of the then newly founded Islamic University of Medina, "the student should not live dissociated from his age. If he is destined to preach or to issue fatwas, he should be knowledgeable about the world of those to whom he preaches and he should be able to speak to them in their language. . . . As Ibn al-Qayyim [(d. 1350) a medieval Hanbali jurist much revered by the Salafis] has said, 'a true jurist is one who joins the "obligatory" to the "actual." . . . We cannot but live in our own age . . .'" (Qaradawi 2002–2006, 2: 441). For the next twelve years (1977–89), Qaradawi was the dean of the Shari'a Faculty of the newly founded Qatar University. The founding documents of the university had stressed its Islamic character, Qaradawi says, as well as the aspiration that "it would combine traditional authenticity and the contemporary." The Shari'a Faculty itself sought, under Qaradawi's leadership, to "produce a Muslim legal scholar who, when asked, gave fatwas on the basis of [sound] knowledge, preached with discernment, and who kept one eye on the sacred law and tradition (*al-shar' wa'l-turath*) and the other on the present age and the existing reality . . ." (Qaradawi 2002–2006, 3: 390–91).

This vision has continued to guide him. In April 2007, Qaradawi announced the establishment of the College of Islamic Studies in Qatar's Education City, which, as its name suggests, houses a number of educational institutions. The College of Islamic Studies is to offer degrees in "public policy in Islam" as well as in contemporary Islamic law (*fiqh*). The objective of the latter program, as Qaradawi has explained it, is to "prepare graduates who are intellectually, morally, and technically capable of relating our Islamic legacy with its texts, methodologies and principles to modern problems and challenges and their solutions" (*Gulf Times* 2007).

Though Qaradawi celebrates Rida for having enunciated the "golden rule" that "we should cooperate in matters on which we agree and excuse one another in things about which we disagree" (Qaradawi 1991: 100; cf. Qaradawi 2002–2006, 3: 39), Qaradawi exemplifies it much more than Rida. While Rida had spent a great deal of his energy dueling with al-Azhar and trying to sidestep or subvert that institution, Qaradawi has always insisted on the continuing relevance and authority of the 'ulama. This has had much to do, of course, with the fact that Qaradawi, unlike Rida, is himself a product of al-Azhar. And it reflects his pragmatic recognition that "the traditional religious establishment" carries much influence in many Muslim societies and that it would not serve the Islamists well to come into conflict with it (Qaradawi 1991: 184). Rida, moreover, had led an impoverished life, while Qaradawi has enjoyed the patronage of the ruling family of Qatar for many decades. Rida had once lamented that if only the rich Muslims would establish schools in which the religious and the worldly sciences were taught together, Muslims would no longer be vulnerable to Christian missionary schools and Muslim reformers would be able to promote both the religious and the political interests of Islam (Rida 1953, 10: 476). At least in this respect, Qaradawi may well be considered the sort of Muslim reformer Rida had visualized.

The most notable attempt toward the integration of various kinds of Muslim intellectuals into a shared framework is provided by the International Union for Muslim Scholars (*al-Ittihad al-'alami li-'ulama al-muslimin* [hereafter usually referred to as the 'Ulama Union]), an organization Qaradawi helped found in 2004 with its secretariat in London and, since early 2008, in Cairo. The objectives of this organization include, among other things, "[preserving] the Islamic identity of the Muslim Ummah" and "strengthening the Islamic spirit in the soul of both individuals and groups"; "stand[ing] up to internal and external destructive trends and promot[ing] Muslims' public awareness of their Ummah's role and noble goals"; and "paving the way for the application of the Islamic Shari'ah system through encouraging contemporary authentic ijtihad . . . [and by demonstrating] the validity and applicability of Islam for every time and place" (IUMS, "Constitution," articles 22–27). According to its constitution, this organization is open "to scholars who graduated from shari'ah [faculties] . . . and Islamic Studies departments at various universities around the Muslim world. It is also open to those who are highly interested in shari'ah sciences and Islamic culture and those who have [had] considerable and tangible production [in these sciences]" (IUMS, "Constitution," article 4).

What is most striking about the latter statement is, of course, the fact that it allows many more people than madrasa-trained scholars to be counted as 'ulama. The five hundred or so people listed as members on the official website of this organization do, indeed, come from many different walks of life. The list includes Muhammad Salim al-'Awwa, an Egyptian lawyer with a Ph.D. in comparative law from the University of London and currently the general secretary of the 'Ulama Union; Rashid al-Ghannushi, a leading Tunisian Islamist presently based in London; Salman al-'Awda, a prominent Saudi Salafi who came to prominence for voicing opposition to King Fahd's decision to station Western troops on Saudi soil in the wake of Saddam Hussein's invasion of Kuwait in 1990; Sayyid Salman Nadwi, the dean of the Shari'a Faculty of the Nadwat al-'Ulama in Lucknow; Zafar al-Islam Khan, editor of the *Milli Gazette*, a Muslim newspaper published from Delhi; 'Ali Muhy al-din Qarradaghi, a specialist in Islamic economics and a close associate of Qaradawi in Qatar; Fahmi Huwaydi, a prominent Islamist journalist in Egypt; Muhammad Taqi 'Uthmani, the vice president of the Dar al-'Ulum of Karachi, one of leading Deobandi madrasas of Pakistan; Muhammad Husayn Fadl Allah, the most prominent Shi'i religious authority (*marja' al-taqlid*) in contemporary Lebanon; Muhammad 'Imara, a prolific Egyptian Islamist intellectual whose many works include an edition of the collected works of Muhammad 'Abduh; Jalal al-din Haqqani, a leader of the Afghan mujahidin during and after the Afghan resistance against Soviet occupation who subsequently became part of the Taliban movement and later still emerged as a key figure in the "neo-Taliban" insurgency in the tribal areas of Pakistan's North-West Frontier Province;[6] and Muhammad 'Ali Taskhiri, an Iranian Shi'i scholar who has long been associated with efforts to bridge the differences between the Sunnis and the Shi'a.[7]

As this small sample should suggest, there are significant intellectual, political, and doctrinal differences among the people associated with the International Union for Muslim Scholars. There are journalists, lawyers, and Islamist leaders here; scholars trained in madrasas of various sorts, as well as in Western or westernized educational institutions; Shi'is and Sunnis; and even an Afghan warlord. Such differences suggest that it would not be easy to foster a consensus on substantive issues beyond vague and general pronouncements. Yet the very differences among members of the 'Ulama Union makes the rhetorically powerful point that leading scholars and activists from across the Muslim world *can* come together on a shared platform, that their intellectual and cultural differences can be bridged.

It is worth noting who is *not* listed among members of this international alliance. This can become a very long list, but suffice it to say here that the dissident Iranian intellectual 'Abdolkarim Soroush, one of the severest critics of the Iranian religious establishment and of its authoritarian claims, is not among its members. Nor is Nasr Hamid Abu Zayd, an Egyptian scholar who had to flee his native Egypt in the face of charges of apostasy for his view on how the Quran ought to be contextualized in its original historical milieu. The Syrian civil engineer Muhammad Shahrur, who has written extensively on the need to rethink Islamic juridical norms through a radical re-reading of the Quran, is also absent. So, too, is Wahid al-din Khan, a prominent Indian scholar who has been a lifelong critic of his fellow 'ulama for what he sees as their failure to adapt to the needs of changing times and for their excessively politicized interpretations of Islam. Qaradawi would probably consider such individuals as representing *incommensurable* rather than commensurable forms of disagreement—a distinction he has made elsewhere (Zaman 2004: 148). This means that while some sorts of disagreement are to be cherished, for they have enriched Islamic civilization, others contradict the very premises of a distinct Islamic identity and therefore have no recognizable place within the community.

The real divide, as Qaradawi sees it, is not between people who are products of different intellectual systems. Such divides, and the intellectual disagreements or misunderstandings arising from them, can be healed or transcended relatively easily. Indeed, as the membership roster of his 'Ulama Union makes plain, varied sorts of individuals can all be recognized as 'ulama, irrespective of their different intellectual backgrounds. The real divide is, rather, between people committed to the *totality* and non-negotiability of Islamic norms and those seen as subverting these norms—and the Islamic civilization anchored in them—from within the Muslim community and from outside. Qaradawi writes:

> Among the interpretations with which the secularists (*al-'almaniyyun*) and the modernists (*al-hadathiyyun*) calumniate [the Islamists] is the idea of "political Islam," which, without doubt, is an idea alien to our Islamic society. By [political Islam] they mean an Islam that concerns itself with the internal and external affairs of the Muslim community. [They mean by it] actions aimed at freeing the community from the foreign power that directs [Muslim] affairs, physically and morally, as it pleases. [They also mean by it] actions seeking to cleanse the community of the cultural, social, and legal sediments of Western colonialism so that the community can return once again to submission to God's law in different areas of life. They use this characterization of "political Islam" in order to alienate people from its [aforementioned] content and to frighten them away from those calling to a comprehensive conception of Islam—one that is inclusive of belief and law, worship and social interaction, proselytism and the state. (Qaradawi 2007: 93)

To look at it another way, the real divide is not between those calling for reform and those opposing it, but rather between different kinds of reform—one genuine, because it is anchored in Islam, the other insidious, for serving anti-Islamic interests. As the "Islamic Charter" (*al-mithaq al-Islami*) of the 'Ulama Union puts it, unmistakably echoing Qaradawi on this and other scores:

We believe that genuine reform (*al-islah al-haqiqi*), one that preserves the unity of the community and guides it towards excellence and progress, is internal reform (*al-islah al-dhati*), one that begins from the constants of the community and its own interests. This signifies the reform of Muslims through Islam, and not the distancing of Islam [from the lives of Muslims], its distortion, or its "development" in the name of reform. The external calls for reform really only seek to strike at the community's strengths in order to keep it weak and to maintain [foreign] control over its affairs. (IUMS, "al-Mithaq")

Precisely where the boundaries lie between those who use Islam to reform Muslim affairs and those who appeal to reform as a way of undermining Islam itself remains uncertain in the foundation documents of the 'Ulama Union as well as in Qaradawi's own writings. Qaradawi seems to be in little doubt, however, that a firm boundary does exist somewhere between the two orientations. This is a divide that his "centrism" seeks not to dilute but rather to affirm and strengthen. Qaradawi's world, as well as that of the 'Ulama Union, is one in which Islam is pitted against a Western "neoimperialism" (*isti'mar jadid*) bent upon the destruction of distinctive Islamic institutions and of Muslim identity (Qaradawi 2000: 9–86). And it is among the purposes of this organization to pool Muslim resources, to create awareness against Western onslaughts against Islam, and to think of ways of effectively combating them.

Qaradawi credits the Harvard political scientist Samuel Huntington with having reminded "defeated" people—by which he presumably means westernizing Muslims, among others—that civilizations other than the West still exist and that religion plays an important role in many of them (Qaradawi 2000: 112–14; Huntington 1996). Yet, for all of Huntington's talk of several major civilizations in the contemporary world, Qaradawi believes that it is with Islam and its challenge to the West that Huntington is really concerned (Qaradawi 2000: 115). The West, Qaradawi argues, seeks to undermine Islam and Muslim identity, and not just through political and military means. Globalization itself is a thinly veiled effort to spread Western norms throughout the rest of the world. In response to this challenge, Qaradawi seeks to refurbish not just a commitment to Islamic norms among Muslims but also, and specifically, a sense of Muslim civilizational identity. Globalization, too, can be put to use in this effort, primarily through its means of communication and its information technologies. More ambitiously, Qaradawi seems to envisage an alternate globalization, one that is not dominated by the neoimperialist West and in which Islam and Muslims can play the leadership role that properly belongs to them. Bridging religious and worldly education—or at least some of the distance between their products—is a crucial means of preparing Muslims for such roles.

III

From the Arab world, I now turn to South Asia to consider some examples of how traditionally educated scholars there have viewed the dichotomous relationship between rival intellectual traditions. Sayyid Ahmad Khan, the founder of the aforementioned Muhammadan Anglo-Oriental College (1875), which became the Aligarh Muslim University in 1920, was convinced that Muslims had no alternative but to learn English and the modern sciences, for in this way alone could they compete with the Hindus for jobs in the colonial economy. The traditional madrasas provided their graduates few avenues toward improving their economic status. What is more, the sort of Islam to which madrasas were committed had little to offer in the face of the modern challenges that confronted Muslims. Sayyid Ahmad was not only an educational entrepreneur but also a theologian, and he had initially sought to found an institution that would both equip Muslims with modern, Western forms of knowledge *and* impart a new understanding of Islam itself. The former was always a far more important goal for Aligarh than the latter, however, and the extremely low opinion the 'ulama had of Sayyid Ahmad's modernist views meant, in any case, that Aligarh's early leaders found it politic to leave aside its aspirations to becoming the beacon of a new understanding of Islam (Lelyveld 1982).[8] Henceforth, Aligarh would have to content itself with representing one side of the dichotomy of Western versus Islamic education. The other side of this dichotomy came to be typified by the Deoband madrasa, founded in 1867, in the aftermath of the formal establishment of British colonial rule in the Indian subcontinent, to provide Muslims with an education focusing on the Islamic foundational texts and Islamic law. Over the past century and a half or so, Deoband has proved to be a remarkably successful institution. Thousands of madrasas—in India, Pakistan, Bangladesh, South Africa, Britain, and elsewhere—have come to espouse its reformist orientation, producing scholars and religio-political activists who have cast a long shadow over many facets of contemporary Islam (Metcalf 1982; Zaman 2002).

As well as many staunch defenders, Deoband has produced its share of scholars who have been highly critical of the sort of learning imparted at this and related institutions. One of these critics was Manazir Ahsan Gilani (d. 1956), a prolific scholar whose writings include the official biography of one of the founders of Deoband as well as a major history of Islamic education in South Asia. Following his graduation around 1914, Gilani had briefly taught at the Deoband madrasa, though it was at the Theology Faculty of the Osmania University in

Hyderabad (founded in 1918) that he spent much of his academic career. As the ruler of the princely state of Hyderabad and patron of the university had put it in his founding decree of 1917, this institution was established in order that "the knowledge and culture of ancient and modern times may be blended so harmoniously as to remove the defect created by the present system of education . . ." (quoted in Datla 2006: 50). The medium of instruction at Osmania University, unlike Aligarh, was to be Urdu, the lingua franca of the Muslims of India.[9] And a translation bureau was set up to make Western as well as some Islamic works available to students in the Urdu language. The experience of teaching at Osmania University undoubtedly shaped Gilani's own efforts in the direction of "harmoniously blending" rival streams of learning.

Gilani's two-volume book on Islamic education, first published in 1943, sheds much light on the history of Muslim intellectual life in medieval and early modern South Asia (Gilani, *Nizam-i taʿlim*). The real purpose of this book is, however, to argue for Muslim educational reform in his contemporary India. Gilani shows that the nucleus of Muslim education in medieval and early modern India had comprised a remarkably small and stable body of religious texts.[10] He identifies these as the *Mishkat al-masabih,* a collection of the reported teachings of the Prophet Muhammad compiled by Muhammad b. ʿAbdallah al-Tabrizi (fl. 1337); a famous compendium of Hanafi law, the *Hidaya,* by al-Marghinani (d. 1196/97), together with a commentary on this work, the *Sharh al-wiqaya,* by ʿUbayd Allah b. Masʿud al-Mahbubi (d. 1346/47); and two very brief commentaries on the Quran, often treated as a single work called the "Two Jalals"—*al-Jalalayn*—because the two commentators were both named Jalal al-Din (Jalal al-Din al-Mahalli [d. 1459] and Jalal al-Din al-Suyuti [d. 1505]). Everything else, Gilani argues, was extraneous to this core curriculum, added or removed according to the exigencies of the time. Yet this small curriculum sufficed, he argues, to produce religious scholars of the highest caliber, intellectuals who were highly regarded in their own and later times not just in South Asia but also in the greater Muslim world.

The implications of this argument are obvious. Contrary to general belief both in and outside the madrasa, Gilani insisted that there was nothing sacrosanct about much of what is taught in madrasas. As long as certain key texts were retained, other texts and disciplines could be dispensed with to make room for new texts and new sciences, which is precisely what earlier generations of madrasa scholars had done all along. Particular texts were included in the curriculum of the madrasa not for their intrinsic "religious" value but rather because they had helped, in their time, to shape and hone the intellectual faculties of the students. By this criterion, there ought to be no objection to the continual revaluation and change of the madrasa curriculum in order to make room for new texts, techniques, and sciences that serve the pedagogical and intellectual concerns of the time most effectively.

But this was only half of Gilani's proposal. The other half concerned not the madrasas but the westernized institutions of learning. Just as the madrasas could easily dispense with much of their inherited textual baggage to make way for new texts and disciplines, the westernized institutions (he was clearly thinking of Aligarh here, though he did not mention it explicitly) ought to also have the same core curriculum of religious texts (cf. Gilani, *Nizam-i ta'lim*, 1: 252–57). Once these texts were in place, the rest of the westernized, secular curriculum would cease to pose any serious challenges to Muslim religious identity, and there would be no duality of intellectual traditions—no intellectual schizophrenia in Muslim societies.

This vision of Muslim educational reform expected a great deal of the 'ulama, in that they would have had to consent to the virtual demise of madrasas except as select institutions of specialized higher education.[11] But it also expected a lot from the westernized Muslim colleges and universities, which would have had to agree to a substantial curriculum in the study of Islam. They have seldom done so. In colonial India, such westernized institutions were, in any case, too few to adequately cater to the needs of all Muslims. Gilani seems eventually to have realized that his proposals would not convince many people, whereupon he came up with a considerably more modest idea. Muslims ought to enroll and study in westernized institutions of all kinds, he now suggested. Rather than spending large amounts of money on establishing new institutions of Western education specifically for Muslims—of which not only Aligarh and the Osmania University in Hyderabad, but also the Jamia Millia Islamia of Delhi were classic examples—the Muslim community ought to invest its resources in establishing boardinghouses for Muslims studying in different kinds of educational institutions. Irrespective of the nature of education they received, Muslims would be reasonably secure in their religious identity if their moral formation took place in boardinghouses that self-consciously cultivated their Islamic sensibilities. As Gilani saw it, this relatively modest proposal could enable Muslims to partake of modern educational opportunities more fully than they had done so far without constantly fearing for their faith (Nadwi 1972: 60–77).[12] The institution of the madrasa remains unmentioned in this new proposal, which suggests that Gilani saw the real threat to Muslims as coming from their exposure to Western education rather than from the intellectual schizophrenia of Muslim societies that he had lamented in his history of Muslim education.

The precise impact of Gilani's ideas remains uncertain, though some among the 'ulama have been rather more receptive to them than have Muslim modernists. In a detailed introduction to a collection of Gilani's letters, 'Abd al-Bari Nadwi (d. 1976) strongly endorsed Gilani's proposal for Muslim boardinghouses as a way of socializing the Muslim youth in Islamic norms while lamenting that neither Gilani nor anyone else had done much to put this idea into effect (Nadwi 1972: 60–77). 'Abd al-Bari was a product of the Nadwat al-'Ulama of Lucknow, which was founded in 1894; one of its goals was to reduce the distance between traditional and westernized institutions of learning.[13] Zafir al-Din Miftahi, a biographer of Gilani and the chief mufti of the Deoband madrasa, likewise applauds Gilani's proposal (Miftahi 1989: 195–96). Gilani's aforementioned ideas for a radical restructuring of the madrasa curriculum are, however, passed in silence here.

A more recent example of the continuing interest in aspects of Gilani's educational thought—in this instance, in a manner truer to the broader thrust of Gilani's ideas—is offered by a book on the curriculum of the madrasa by Sayyid Salman Nadwi (Nadwi 2004b). A product both of the Nadwat al-'Ulama and of the Imam Muhammad ibn Sa'ud Islamic University in Riyadh, Saudi Arabia, and now the dean of the Faculty of Shari'a at the Nadwat al-'Ulama, Salman Nadwi cites Gilani extensively in this work, and the book itself is guided by concerns broadly similar to Gilani's (Nadwi 2004b: 104–17). Striking a familiar note, Salman Nadwi observes that the Muslim community has suffered greatly because of its division between two very unequal groups: a small group of those representing religious life and a preponderant majority comprising those raised on an "irreligious education" (la-dini ta'lim). A consequence of this division has been an increasingly narrow concern of the religious class (tabaqa) with matters of worship, he says, with the result that the 'ulama have had little to offer by way of sound leadership in social, economic, and political matters and there is even less incentive on the part of others to heed their advice in such matters (Nadwi 2004b: 232).

While he now occupies a position of leadership at the Nadwat al-'Ulama, Salman Nadwi freely acknowledges that his institution has largely failed in its early aspiration to mitigate the divide between secular and religious learning. More remarkable than this candid admission is his observation that it is those belonging to the Tablighi Jama'at who have come to remedy the longstanding division between rival intellectual streams (Nadwi 2004b: 258–59). This is remarkable because the Tablighi Jama'at is not an educational venture in any conventional sense but rather a worldwide proselytizing movement which originated in northern India during the first half of the twentieth century with the goal of reintroducing Muslims to the fundamental norms of their faith; though focusing primarily on Muslims, it has been concerned with the preaching of Islam to non-Muslims as well (Masud 2000). The Tablighi Jama'at is largely a product of the Deobandi milieu, though unlike the madrasa-based Deobandi 'ulama, leaders of the Tablighi movement are known for their distrust of any and all scholarly pursuits. The movement largely consists of those who are not formally trained 'ulama but rather people with a modern education at various levels. As Salman Nadwi notes, the Tablighi Jama'at has influential centers at Aligarh Muslim University as well as at other institutions of modern education; and graduates of these universities have served as preachers on behalf of the Tablighi Jama'at (Nadwi 2004b: 258). Yet this movement does not have any serious ideas for solving the religious, social, economic, and political problems of the people, he says. The result is that while it has been able to reduce the "spiritual . . . gulf" (*ruhani . . . khalij*) between people of different intellectual formations, the "intellectual, civilizational, and cultural gulf" (*fikri awr tahzibi wa tamadduni khalij*) between them has remained unaffected (Nadwi 2004b: 259). This continuing distance has, for its part, enabled the college- and university-educated *Islamists* to step into this vacuum in trying to provide what Salman Nadwi sees as a less than desirable leadership to the community (Nadwi 2004b: 259).

In the aftermath of 9/11, Salman Nadwi has continued to argue for the need to bridge the divide between rival streams of education. But the defense of the madrasa itself now takes center stage. This is not surprising in view of the extensive unfavorable attention madrasas in India and elsewhere have received from the media and government circles for suspected ties to terrorism. Yet such defense has sometimes itself been articulated in strident terms. As Salman Nadwi put it in a 2007 interview, "The ulema of the madrasas, who are well-versed with the history of the Muslims and of Islam, play a crucial role in shaping the mentality of the Muslim masses and . . . [in giving] them a certain direction. America knows that this class of people can effectively mobilize opposition to its imperialistic policies and designs, and so it is seeking to undermine them. In order to legitimize its imperialist aggression against many Muslim countries, it constantly claims that the ulema are 'terrorists,' 'extremists,' 'obscurantists,' and so on" (Sikand 2007).

Such rhetoric seems to do a better job of expressing the depth of Salman Nadwi's suspicions of the outside world than it does of improving the madrasa's image in contemporary India, let alone mitigating its perceived incommensurability with rival intellectual streams. In these instances, he also sounds a good deal like Qaradawi, who, as observed earlier, anchors his efforts to transcend particular dichotomies afflicting Muslims and Islamic thought in the affirmation of a relentless cultural and political struggle between Islam and the West. Again, rather like Qaradawi, Salman Nadwi's discourses on the need to live peacefully with other communities—in his case, with the Hindu majority in India—easily shade into assertions of Islam's superiority over all others and even assertions about the need to defend Islam with the force of arms, if necessary.[14] Such echoes need not surprise us. Many Muslims, and not just among Islamists and the 'ulama, do, in fact, share a similar analysis, just as many others reject it. But echoes of Qaradawi's rhetoric surely also have to do with his own ties with the Nadwat al-'Ulama. Qaradawi is the author of a book celebrating the life and achievements of Abu'l-Hasan 'Ali Nadwi, the former rector of the Nadwa, as well as his own ties with him. Qaradawi was an honored guest at the Nadwa in Lucknow on several occasions, including the eighty-fifth anniversary of the Nadwa in 1975, and it was Salman Nadwi who translated Qaradawi's speech into Urdu on that occasion (Qaradawi 2001: 24). Like Abu'l-Hasan 'Ali Nadwi, Salman Nadwi has interacted extensively with scholars from the Arab world, and also translated many of 'Ali Nadwi's writings into Arabic. These ties, with Qaradawi and with other Arab religious intellectuals, have continued. And Salman Nadwi is not only a member of Qaradawi's 'Ulama Union, he also serves on the board of trustees of this organization (http://www.iumsonline.net/English/topic_06b.shtml).

Themes similar to those of Qaradawi and Salman Nadwi are clearly discernible in the discourses of contemporary Deobandi 'ulama of Pakistan as well. For instance, Abu 'Ammar Zahid al-Rashidi, a prominent Deobandi scholar associated with the Nusrat al-'Ulum madrasa in Gujranwala, in the Punjab, has written extensively in recent years on the need to rethink the curriculum of the madrasa and to integrate the modern sciences into it (Zahid al-Rashidi 2007). The reasoning for this is, in part, that the 'ulama have the opportunity and, indeed, the obligation to expand the sphere of their activities in society, not only because people seek their guidance but also, and in no small measure, because of the failings of state-run educational and other institutions. The 'ulama, however, cannot expand their activities in society unless they broaden their intellectual horizons (Zahid al-Rashidi 2007: 303–305). The reasoning here is also that the best of the earlier 'ulama have always striven to combat challenges to Islam by appropriating the tools of those posing the challenge in question:

When Greek philosophy had become popular in our society and had begun to affect our belief system, our leading figures like Abu'l-Hasan al-Ash'ari,

Abu Mansur al-Maturidi, Ghazali, Ibn Rushd, and Ibn Taymiyya had come to master Greek philosophy. And they had affirmed the truth and superiority of Islamic beliefs by responding to the objections and doubts created by Greek philosophy and they had done so by employing its own technical vocabulary. (Zahid al-Rashidi 2007: 306)

Like Qaradawi, Zahid al-Rashidi seems to be in little doubt that there is a civilizational conflict between Islam and the West today. Yet, he writes, "the teachers and students of madrasas . . . are unacquainted with the enemy that we are fighting—its nature, its mode of operation, its weapons, and its overall framework" (Zahid al-Rashidi 2007: 306). Islamic norms and Muslim identity are being targeted in the name of globalization and human rights, he says, sounding very much like Qaradawi.[15] And it is for the 'ulama "to expound on the intellectual, religious, and cultural aspects of this conflict, to confront this aggression with the modern weapons of philosophical and other thought, of learning and research, and to defend Muslims against this deluge by building fortifications in the form of education, proselytism, reform and intellectual awakening . . ." (Zahid al-Rashidi 2007: 298).[16]

IV

A key question presents itself in light of the foregoing discussion. How do we account for the persistence of the rhetoric about the need to bridge the duality of intellectual traditions in Muslim societies? In addressing this question, we should first note that important developments have, in fact, taken place in bringing the two streams of Islamic and modern learning closer to each other in varied contexts. In Egypt, the 1961 reforms of al-Azhar established a number of faculties for the teaching of the modern secular sciences alongside the three existing faculties devoted to Arabic and Islamic studies. Though sweeping in their effects, these reforms had built on decades of earlier initiatives in a similar direction. Madrasas in many parts of India have come to be firmly integrated into the educational "mainstream," and even those madrasas, in both India and Pakistan, that ostensibly resist governmental efforts to regulate them have often opened themselves up to the content of public schools at the elementary levels, and sometimes considerably more than that (Metcalf 2007: 96–100; Zaman 2007: 79–82). On the other end of the spectrum, public schools in many Muslim countries impart substantial Islamic education as part of their curriculum. This is the case in Egypt, for instance, as Gregory Starrett has shown (Starrett 1998), as well as in many other Muslim societies.

Further, ordinary believers have been taking their own steps toward integrating religious and secular learning. As Matthew Nelson has argued with reference to attitudes toward Islamic education in contemporary Pakistan, "the overwhelming majority do not approach their educational options (for example, religious versus non-religious education) as a zero-sum game. Instead ... most families are inclined to construct a careful balance of sorts, including both types of education at the same time" (Nelson 2009: 595). In contemporary India, Salman Nadwi's aforementioned observation about the Tablighi Jama'at serving as a bridge between religious and secular learning likewise points to informal mechanisms whereby ordinary believers have often been able to bring different streams of learning closer together.

Why, then, do discourses on the need to bridge the distance between rival streams seem to continue unabated? There are several ways of accounting for this. For one thing, for all their starkly dichotomous juxtapositions, these divides are still real: there *is* considerable contestation in segments of some Muslim societies not only on how to bring religious and secular forms of knowledge closer together but on whether to do so at all. Some of the international notoriety the Taliban gained during their short-lived rule in Afghanistan (1996–2001) came, for instance, from their shutting down of girls' schools. Though the Taliban regime collapsed not long after the terrorist attacks of September 11, 2001, groups of Taliban and those claiming affinity with them reemerged in subsequent years in both southern Afghanistan and in Pakistan's North-West Frontier Province. Foremost among the many ways in which these neo-Taliban have harassed local populations and challenged government authority is by attacking schools, especially those for girls. As one spokesman for the Pakistani Taliban was quoted as saying in July 2008, they were "not against girls' education although they opposed the system of women's education in the country" (Khan 2008a). Though it is not spelled out here, the grounds on which "the system of women's education" is opposed have to do with the Taliban's conflating non-Islamic with *anti*-Islamic, hence immoral, ways of thinking. Needless to say, such conflations don't allow much space for boys' public schools either.[17]

The Taliban and their associates represent an especially egregious instance of opposition to modern, secular learning, an extreme stance that many even among the Deobandi 'ulama—the Taliban are broadly identifiable as belonging to the Deobandi orientation—have found objectionable and embarrassing (cf. Zaman 2002: 139–40). It is surely against the not incorrect perception that at least some segments of the Muslim population—and their religio-political leaders—still oppose the integration of religious and secular learning that many 'ulama have continued to emphasize the need for such integration. Yet, even as they call for educational reform, it is not unusual for such religious scholars to go on to reserve for themselves the prerogative of determining the precise path and pace of reform. This suggests their concern to not allow the modernizing governing elite to appropriate the 'ulama's hesitant openness to reform for their own purposes; but it also reinforces the dichotomy of religious and secular learning in the very act of transcending it. Nor is thinking in terms of the religious-secular divide an innovation of the 'ulama. Many among them would assert, and not without some justice, that the terms of the debate have been imposed on them by the world they inhabit—and especially by the colonial and postcolonial modernizing elite—and that the 'ulama now seek only to mitigate its deleterious effects.

The efficacy, finally, of initiatives toward integrating the religious and the secular streams has often left many unconvinced on both sides. In a work commemorating the millennial celebrations of Egypt's al-Azhar, Qaradawi had noted, for instance, that there was little intellectual exchange between those studying in the religious and the secular faculties at al-Azhar (Qaradawi 1984: 101–102; cf. Zeghal 1999). Almost contemporaneously with Qaradawi's volume on al-Azhar, the noted Pakistani modernist Fazlur Rahman (d. 1988) lamented, with some exaggeration, that "despite a widespread and sometimes deep consciousness of the dichotomy of education, all efforts at a genuine integration have so far been largely unfruitful" (Rahman 1982: 130).

Overlapping explanations such as the foregoing are not without merit, but it is tempting to account for the sheer persistence of discourses on bridging religious and secular learning in another way too. To the extent that they have embraced the dichotomous mode of analysis underlying such discourses, could it perhaps be a means through which the 'ulama have sought to reorder some of the messiness of social, religious, and intellectual conflicts they find around themselves? This new dichotomy is not imaginary, as we have observed. Yet it also is an intellectual construct, designed to make sense of contested relations among different forms and conceptions of knowledge and among people associated with them. Contestations over particular conceptions of knowledge do not necessarily have to be analyzed, after all, in terms of this (or any other) dichotomy. The fact that they *are* so analyzed suggests that framing the issues in this way helps dislodge from center stage a number of *other* conflicts, say, between and among Muslims of different sectarian, political, and intellectual orientations, among rival schools of thought, among people of varied commitments.

Historically the Sunni tradition had learned to live with these messy, and often interminable, conflicts. As Patricia Crone has observed:

> [With the gradual emergence of Sunni Islam] mainstream Muslims came fully to accept that the umma had to consist of a wide variety of different and even antagonistic groups pursuing diverse aims and objectives under the same general Islamic umbrella. The umma ceased to be a caravan taking everyone by the same route to the same destination. Sinners and upright people, believers and sinful Muslims, adherents of one legal school and the other, people moving in quite different directions under intellectual imams of their own: all these and more came to form a single community eventually known as Sunni. (Crone 2004: 389–90)

The new conflict between religious and secular learning might be seen, then, as a way to at least rhetorically do away with some of these earlier conflicts in the interest of a simpler, more streamlined Islamic identity—one anchored in the aspiration to combine religious and worldly forms of knowledge and to unite contemporary Muslims on this aspiration. As Matthew Nelson has argued in the aforementioned study, the idea that there is a single, true, Islam, and that Muslims ought to transcend or ignore particularistic sectarian and other commitments to be united in devotion to this Islam, resonates widely among vast sectors of society in Pakistan. Much the same might be said of Muslims in many other societies. The discourse on how to bridge the gap between secular and religious learning tends to posit Islam as itself a homogeneous, shared entity (Nelson 2009), with the major remaining question being how to seamlessly combine it with modern forms of knowledge.

Yet one hardly needs to probe very deeply to see that a great deal of contestation on conceptions of politics, Islam, and the place of Muslims in the world does, in fact, lie just beneath the surface of such bland dichotomies. Even as questions of educational reform are clearly intertwined with politics, for instance, there isn't any shared, overarching conception of Muslim politics in which questions of religious education are anchored. In their different contexts, Rida and Qaradawi envisage an Islamic religio-political order, as we have observed. Bridging or collapsing the divide between the religious and the secular is, for Rida and others, a means to the emergence of a new religio-political elite. To Qaradawi, it is a necessary step toward invigorating a global Muslim consciousness—an alternate globalization—in the face of what he sees as the Western neoimperialist threat. To Zahid al-Rashidi, as to Qaradawi, it is also a crucial way of strengthening Muslim defenses in the new civilizational conflict between Islam and the West. In contemporary

India, Salman Nadwi, too, has vivid memories of Muslim political grandeur, and he, too, speaks in Manichaean terms about Islam in relation to much of the rest of the world. Even so, unlike Rida and Qaradawi, Salman Nadwi's calls for Muslim political mobilization are premised not on pan-Islam or on aspirations to establish an Islamic state, but rather on a sense of belonging to India and of claiming Muslim cultural and political rights on *that* basis (cf. Nadwi 2004a: 61–62).

In an earlier generation, Manazir Ahsan Gilani was among countless other 'ulama who decided not to emigrate from India to Pakistan at the time of the partition of the Indian subcontinent. This expressed the conviction of such 'ulama that Islam did not depend on political authority in order to thrive, a conclusion their forebears had already reached upon the establishment of British colonial rule in India. Islamic education was a crucial means of preserving Muslim identity, yet, as Gilani saw it, this education could be integrated with modern, secular disciplines—just as Muslims had done at earlier times according to the imperatives of *those* times.

There is a partial analogue to Gilani's minimalist conception of Islamic education in his view that the Quran should not be thought to contain *everything.* The implication of this point, which he credited to Anwarshah Kashmiri (d. 1933), a celebrated scholar with whom Gilani had studied at Deoband, is, of course, that efforts to find all knowledge and justifications for all human endeavors—from modern science to politics—in the Quran are misguided (Gilani, *Ihata,* 112–13, 118–29). This perspective is in marked tension with the view of many Islamists, including Sayyid Abu'l-A'la Mawdudi (d. 1979) of Pakistan, that Muslims ought to take the Quran as the starting point of all knowledge, including the natural sciences (Mawdudi 1972: 66–100, 93).[18] Gilani's view also stands in sharp contrast with Rashid Rida's conviction that the teachings of the Islamic foundational texts can be shown to be extendable, through analogical reasoning, to all facets of life. As Ahmad Dallal observes, "In an age of the ever increasing powers of the nation state, a jurisdiction that covered 'all aspects of life' [had] . . . seemed more appropriate to Rida than a legal code that did not purport to exhaust all aspects of this life" (Dallal 2000: 356–57). Like the modern nation-state, Rida also wanted the system of education to produce people with a shared culture. As he put it in a speech at Aligarh's Anglo-Oriental College in 1912, just as a building will not have a secure foundation if its stones are all of different shapes and sizes, so too will the Muslim community not succeed if its members are at odds with one another in their intellectual formation (Rida 1912c: 573). Rida seems to be officiating here at a rather peculiar marriage of the supposedly shared convictions of the pious forebears, on the one hand, and, on the other, the sort of homogeneity modern nation-states seek to foster (Gellner 1983; cf. Bowen 2007). Gilani, for his part, had a considerably less homogeneous outcome in mind when proposing his minimalist combination of modern and Islamic learning.

Among the tensions we are left with in the end is the following. On the one hand, there clearly is a broad and growing agreement within the ranks of the leading 'ulama as well as between the 'ulama and other religious intellectuals that bridging the gulf between different intellectual traditions is desirable and, indeed, a matter of great urgency. On the other hand, there is no unanimity on what precisely is the gulf that most needs to be bridged and why the effort to do so is worth making. We can see this tension in more than one way. The fact that many religious intellectuals have long continued to lament the incommensurability of intellectual traditions in their societies suggests, of course, just how intractable the problem is and how elusive the prospects for any convincing solutions to it. At issue are competing understandings of what sort of education the Muslim youth ought to acquire, how the interests of Islam are best promoted, and what vision of politics—and of the world—ought to guide educational reform. Even when the principle that secular and religious forms of knowledge ought to be brought together into a shared system of education is acknowledged, the practical application of that principle remains a matter of suspicion. And much suspicion continues to characterize the relations between those who are products of Islamic institutions of learning and those graduating from westernized colleges and universities.

A rather different way of looking at the problem is also worth considering, however. From this vantage, the perceived dichotomy between religious and secular learning, or the tension between a growing agreement to transcend this dichotomy and the lack of substantial agreement on *how* to do so, can itself be viewed as a fertile ground for new ways of thinking about Islam, education, and politics in their interrelationship. Anxieties about how to bridge rival traditions, and uncertainties about the sort of criticism—of a "neoimperialist" West, of modernists and the 'ulama, of facets of the scholarly tradition—that this effort would seem to require, are all constitutive of an evolving arena of debate and contestation which, in their scope, implications, and possibilities, extend well beyond any dichotomous constructions. In South Asia and the Middle East, not a few among the traditionally educated religious scholars continue—alongside many others—to be important contributors to the shaping of this arena.

Notes

1. Elsewhere, I have explored some of the processes through which traditionally educated Muslim scholars of colonial India came to make sharp distinctions between "religious" and "secular" learning and to conceive of their institutions of learning, the madrasas, as occupying a distinct sphere in society. See Zaman (1999) and Zaman (2002: 60–86). In the present work, I am concerned with a different problem, viz., the question of how and why the traditionally educated religious scholars have sought to *undo* or mitigate the effects of such divisions.

2. For the characterization of *taqlid* as blind imitation, see, for instance, Rida (1906: 8) (of the preface, paginated separately); ibid., 64. Rida (1906) is a work comprised of fictional dialogues between a traditionalist scholar given to "blind imitation" of his forebears and a forward-looking "reformer." The latter is clearly meant to represent Rida's own position, and I take it as such.

3. This summary of his views derives from Rida (1906) as well as his diatribes against the ʿulama throughout his Quran commentary (Rida 1953).

4. On the problems this madrasa had faced from its inception, see Rida (1912a).

5. See Qaradawi (1991: 100): "The Imam Rashid Rida was the renewer of Islam in his age. Whoever reads his [books] . . . will know that this man's thought is the lighthouse providing guidance for the journey of Islam in this contemporary age."

6. The characterization "neo-Taliban" comes from Giustozzi (2008), though he uses it primarily for the Afghan rather than the Pakistani Taliban who have been active since the fall of the Taliban regime in 2001. The boundaries between the neo-Taliban on either side of the Pakistan-Afghanistan frontier are as porous as the border itself, however.

7. For the full list, see http://iumsonline.net/articls/info/members.shtml (accessed April 16, 2008; as of September 2009 the site has been unavailable).

8. For the early history of the college, see Lelyveld (1978); on Sayyid Ahmad's theological views, see Troll (1978).

9. The language of instruction was changed from Urdu to English in 1951, not long after the merger of the princely state of Hyderabad into the postcolonial Indian union. See Datla (2006: 196).

10. Gilani (N.d. [b]) is referred to in the text as *Nizam-i taʿlim*. Gilani's attempt to bridge the distance between religious and secular learning is, paradoxically, predicated on a firm distinction between the religious and the secular, a distinction that owes much to British colonial categories of analysis. See note 1, above.

11. Gilani once complained that though he had written this book in *defense* of the ʿulama's system of education, they had generally ignored it. He had not known, he said, "that it is not just the books of their opponents that [the ʿulama] didn't read; they didn't even read the writings of those on their own side." See Rahmani (1972: 357) (letter from Gilani to Sayyid Sulayman Nadwi, dated November 10, 1944). It is hard to believe, however, that many ʿulama would have seen Gilani as being "on their own side" in this instance.

12. It is worth remarking here that Gilani's latter proposal shares an important affinity with the network of schools established in recent decades in Turkey, Central Asia, Pakistan, Europe, and elsewhere by those associated with the Turkish reformer Fethullah Gülen. These are not "Islamic schools" in any conventional sense but rather westernized educational institutions, teaching English and the modern sciences. It is in the dormitories managed by the school that an Islamic moral formation takes place, and living in such dormitories is usually mandatory for the students. See Turam (2007: 71–76, 98).

13. 'Abd al-Bari later taught at the aforementioned Osmania University as a professor of philosophy.

14. Cf. Salman Nadwi (2004a: 63): "Our religion has come [to the world] in order to remain forever; no other religion will remain forever. . . . Our sacred law (shari'at) is the last of such laws; there is no place after it for any other sacred or secular law (shari'at wa qanun). We should not despair. It is our law that will triumph. It is our religion that will triumph. God will [again] exalt the Muslim community" (from a speech delivered at a girls' madrasa in 2004). On the assertion that Islam does not limit itself to "defensive warfare," see ibid., 22–23 (from a speech at the Nadwat al-'Ulama in 1997).

15. Though he does not cite Qaradawi here, it is worth noting that Zahid al-Rashidi is a member of the International Union of Muslim Scholars founded by Qaradawi. See iumsonline.net/articls/info/members.shtml (accessed April 16, 2008; as of September 2009 the site has been unavailable). Zahid al-Rashidi's name is listed at no. 27 in the organization's list of members.

16. One instance of Zahid al-Rashidi's own efforts in this regard is his regular exposition of the United Nations Declaration of Human Rights for the benefit of his advanced madrasa students. Here he seeks to place the declaration in its intellectual and historical context and to systematically compare it with particular Islamic norms. As he sees it, "the benefit [of this exercise] is that it becomes easy for young 'ulama to understand today's global struggle between civilizations, the ongoing battle for cultural supremacy between the West and Muslims" (Zahid al-Rashidi 2007: 239).

17. In the troubled Swat region of the North West Frontier Province of Pakistan, one December 2008 estimate put the number of girls' schools destroyed by the neo-Taliban and allied groups at eighty and of boys' schools at forty-five (Khan 2008b).

18. For a discussion of this speech as well as some of Mawdudi's other ideas on education, see Ahmad (2008: 142–64). Gilani, Manazir Ahsan (N.d. [a]) is referred to in the text as *Ihata*.

Works Cited

Ahmad, Irfan. 2008. "Power, Purity and the Vanguard: Educational Ideology of the Jama'at-i Islami of India." In *Madrasas in South Asia: Teaching Terror?*, ed. Jamal Malik, 142–64. London: Routledge.

Ali, A. Yusuf. 1941. "Muslim Culture and Religious Thought." In *Modern India and the West: A Study of the Interaction of Their Civilizations*, ed. L. S. S. O'Malley, 389–414. London: Oxford University Press.

Bowen, John. 2007. *Why the French Don't Like Headscarves: Islam, the State, and Public Sphere.* Princeton, N.J.: Princeton University Press.

Crone, Patricia. 2004. *God's Rule: Government and Islam—Six Centuries of Medieval Islamic Political Thought.* New York: Columbia University Press.

Dallal, Ahmad. 2000. "Appropriating the Past: Twentieth-Century Reconstruction of Pre-Modern Islamic Thought." *Islamic Law and Society* 7: 325–58.

Datla, Kavita Saraswathi. 2006. "Making a Worldly Vernacular: Urdu, Education, and Osmania University, Hyderabad, 1883–1938." Ph.D. diss., University of California, Berkeley.

Gellner, Ernest. 1983. *Nations and Nationalism.* Oxford, U.K.: Blackwell.

Gilani, Manazir Ahsan. N.d. (a). *Ihata-yi Dar al-'Ulum Deoband men bite huwe din.* Deoband: Maktaba-yi tayyiba.

———. N.d. (b). *Pak wa Hind main musalmanon ka nizam-i ta'lim wa tarbiyyat.* Lahore: Maktaba-yi Rahmaniyya.

Giustozzi, Antonio. 2008. *Koran, Kalashnikov, and Laptop: The Neo-Taliban Insurgency in Afghanistan.* New York: Columbia University Press.

Gulf Times. 2007. "QF [Qatar Foundation] Sets Up Islamic College." April 15.

Huntington, Samuel P. 1996. *The Clash of Civilizations and the Remaking of World Order.* New York: Simon & Schuster.

International Union for Muslim Scholars (IUMS). "Constitution of the International Union for Muslim Scholars." http://www.iumsonline.net/english/topic_03.shtml.

———. "Current Board of Trustees." http://www.iumsonline.net/English/topic_06b.shtml.

———. "Al-Mithaq al-Islami li'l-ittihad al-'alami li-'ulama al-muslimin." http://www.iumsonline.net.

Khan, Hameedullah. 2008a. "Girls' School, Shops Blown Up in Swat." *Dawn,* July 26.

———. 2008b. "School Building, MNA's House Blown Up in Swat." *Dawn,* December 13.

Krämer, Gudrun. 2006. "Drawing Boundaries: Yusuf al-Qaradawi on Apostasy." In *Speaking for Islam: Religious Authorities in Muslim Societies,* ed. Gudrun Krämer and Sabine Schmidtke, 181–217. Leiden: Brill.

Lelyveld, David. 1978. *Aligarh's First Generation: Muslim Solidarity in British India.* Princeton, N.J.: Princeton University Press.

———. 1982. "Disenchantment at Aligarh: Islam and the Realm of the Secular in Late Nineteenth Century India." *Die Welt des Islams* 22: 85–102.

Manar, al-. 1898–1935. Cairo: Matba'at al-Manar.

Masud, Muhammad Khalid, ed. 2000. *Travelers in Faith: Studies of the Tablighi Jama'at as a Transnational Islamic Movement for Faith Renewal.* Leiden: Brill.

Mawdudi, Sayyid Abu'l-A'la. 1972. "Naya nizam-i ta'lim." In *Ta'limat.* Lahore: Islamic Publications.

Metcalf, Barbara D. 1982. *Islamic Revival in British India: Deoband 1860–1900.* Princeton, N.J.: Princeton University Press.

———. 2007. "Madrasas and Minorities in Secular India." In *Schooling Islam: The Culture and Politics of Modern Muslim Education,* ed. Robert W. Hefner and Muhammad Qasim Zaman, 87–106. Princeton, N.J.: Princeton University Press.

Miftahi, Zafir al-Din. 1989. *Hayat-i mawlana Gilani.* Benares: Mawlana Yusuf Academy.

Mitchell, Timothy. 1991. *Colonising Egypt*. Berkeley: University of California Press.

Nadwi, 'Abd al-Bari. 1972. "Muqaddima: Bara nadir sangam—dil wa damagh donon ka." In *Makatib-i Gilani*, ed. Minnat Allah Rahmani, 25–78. Mongir, India: Dar al-isha'at-i Rahmani.

Nadwi, Muhammad Ishaq, and Shams-i Tabriz Khan. 1983–84. *Ta'rikh-i Nadwat al-'Ulama*. 2 vols. Lucknow: Nizamat-i Nadwat al-'Ulama.

Nadwi, Sayyid Salman Husayni Nadwi. 2004a. *Azadi-yi Hind, haqiqat ya sarab* Lucknow: Jam'iyyat shabab al-Islam.

———. 2004b. *Hamara nisab-i ta'lim kiya ho?* Lucknow: Jami'a Sayyid Ahmad Shahid.

Nasr, S. V. R. 1996. *Mawdudi and the Making of Islamic Revivalism*. New York: Oxford University Press.

Nelson, Matthew J. 2009. "Dealing with Difference: Religious Education and the Challenge of Democracy in Pakistan." *Modern Asian Studies* 43: 591–618.

Qaradawi, Yusuf al-. 1984. *Risalat al-Azhar*. Cairo: Dar al-tadamun.

———. 1991. *Awlawiyyat al-haraka al-Islamiyya fi'l-marhala al-qadima*. Cairo: Maktabat al-wahba.

———. 2000. *al-Muslimun wa'l-'awlama*. Cairo: Dar al-tawzi' wa'l-nashr al-Islamiyya.

———. 2001. *al-Shaykh Abu'l-Hasan 'Ali Nadwi kama 'araftuhu*. Damascus: Dar al-qalam.

———. 2002–2006. *Ibn al-qarya wa'l-kuttab: malamih sira wa masira*. 3 vols. to date. Cairo: Dar al-shuruq.

———. 2007. *al-Din wa'l-siyasa: Ta'sil wa radd shubuhat*. Cairo: Dar al-shuruq.

Rahman, Fazlur. 1982. *Islam and Modernity: Transformation of an Intellectual Tradition*. Chicago: University of Chicago Press.

Rahmani, Minnat Allah, ed. 1972. *Makatib-i Gilani*. Mongir, India: Dar al-isha'at-i Rahmani.

Reid, Donald Malcolm. 1990. *Cairo University and the Making of Modern Egypt*. Cambridge: Cambridge University Press.

Rida, Muhammad Rashid. 1906. *Kitab muhawarat al-muslih wa'l-muqallid*. Cairo: Matba'at majallat al-Manar.

———. 1912a. "Khutbat iftitah al-ijtima' al-sanawi al-'am li-jama'at al-da'wa wa'l-irshad." *Al-Manar* 15: 921–29.

———. 1912b. "Al-Khutba al-ra'isiyya fi Nadwat al-'Ulama li-sahib al-Manar." *Al-Manar* 15: 331–41.

———. 1912c. "Al-Tarbiyya wa wajh al-haja ilayha wa taqasimuha." *Al-Manar* 15: 567–86.

———. 1923. *Al-Khilafa aw al-imama al-'uzma*. Cairo: Matba'at al-Manar.

———. 1934. *Al-Manar wa'l-Azhar*. Cairo: Matba'at al-Manar.

———. 1953. *Tafsir al-Qur'an al-hakim* (commonly known as *Tafsir al-Manar*), 4th ed. Cairo: Matba'at al-Manar.

Sikand, Yoginder. 2007. "Madrasas and Charges of 'Terrorism': Interview with Maulana Salman Nadwi," http://www.theamericanmuslim.org/tam.php/features/articles/madrasas_and_charges_of_terrorism_interview_with_maulana_salman_nadwi/ (posted October 29, 2007).

Starrett, Gregory. 1998. *Putting Islam to Work*. Berkeley: University of California Press.

Troll, Christian W. 1978. *Sayyid Ahmad Khan: A Reinterpretation of Muslim Theology.* Delhi: Vikas.

Turam, Berna. 2007. *Between Islam and the State: The Politics of Engagement.* Stanford, Calif.: Stanford University Press.

Zahid al-Rashidi, Abu 'Ammar. 2007. *Dini madaris ka nisab wa nizam.* Gujranwala: Al-Shari'a Academy.

Zaman, Muhammad Qasim. 1999. "Religious Education and the Rhetoric of Reform: The Madrasa in British India and Pakistan." *Comparative Studies in Society and History* 41: 294–323.

———. 2002. *The Ulama in Contemporary Islam: Custodians of Change.* Princeton, N.J.: Princeton University Press.

———. 2004. "The Ulama of Contemporary Islam and Their Conceptions of the Common Good." In *Public Islam and the Common Good,* ed. Armando Salvatore and Dale F. Eickelman, 129–55. Leiden: Brill.

———. 2007. "Tradition and Authority in Deobandi Madrasas of South Asia." In *Schooling Islam: The Culture and Politics of Modern Muslim Education,* ed. Robert W. Hefner and Muhammad Qasim Zaman, 61–86. Princeton, N.J.: Princeton University Press.

Zeghal, Malika. 1999. "Religion and Politics in Egypt: The Ulema of al-Azhar, Radical Islam, and the State (1952–94)." *International Journal of Middle East Studies* 31: 371–99.

Part Three Violence and Conversion
in Europe

6

The Fantasy and Violence
of Religious Imagination:
Islamophobia and Anti-Semitism
in France and North Africa

Paul A. Silverstein

In a particularly poignant moment in Matthieu Kassovitz's celebrated 1995 film, *La Haine*—a bleak, neorealist portrayal of marginalization and violence in the Parisian outer-city (*banlieue*) housing projects (*les cités*)—the white Jewish protagonist Vinz attempts to justify to his close North African Muslim buddy, Saïd, his fantasy of killing a police officer if their mutual friend Abdel, the victim of police violence, dies.

> Vinz: You want to be the next Arab (*rebeu*) killed in a police station?
> Saïd: No.
> Vinz: Well, me neither.
> Saïd: *You* neither? *You* don't want to be the next Arab killed in a police station?
> Vinz: Exactly. . . .

Ten years later, Karin Albou's *La Petite Jérusalem* explored the fractures of such cross-ethnic and cross-religious imagination. Set in another Parisian peripheral *cité*, the film relates a very different coming-of-age story—not of young men trying to survive in the shadow of police violence, but of a young Orthodox Jewish woman, Laura, trying to navigate the "religious law" of her community, her studies in Kantian philosophy, and her growing sexual desire for a Muslim man, Djamel, a refugee from Algeria's protracted civil war. If Kassovitz's film self-consciously presents a fable of class and spatial solidarity emblematized by Vinz's self-presentation as an "Arab," Albou's film—set in the midst of and portraying a series of attacks on Jewish synagogues and persons

141

that marked France during the early 2000s—presents the ultimate impossibility of such cross-ethnic and cross-religious imagination, with the failure of Laura and Djamel's relationship and the emigration of Laura's family to Israel.

What this volume terms "Islamophobia" and "Islamophilia" can perhaps best be broached by exploring how categories of ethno-religious difference are produced in and through a history of violence. Much as has occurred for African American men in the United States, in contemporary French media and political discourse, young Muslim-French men from the *cités* are demonized as culturally violent, sexist, homophobic, and anti-Semitic (Guénif-Soulaimas and Macé 2003), at the very same moment that their modes of dress, musical forms, and speech patterns are appropriated as styles of resistance by non-Muslim youth across the *banlieues* and even within bourgeois city centers. If the recently expanded rates of conversion to Islam in the *cités* and prisons of France[1] index the tentative growth of an Islamic chic, and the local characterization of Islam as a religion of social protest (Daynes 1999; Lakhdar et al. 2007)—much as Hisham Aïdi (2002, 2003) has discussed in the United States and Latin America—this putative "Islamization" of the *banlieues* has invoked alarmist concerns over the rise in Islamic fundamentalism and the increased representation of the *cités* as spaces of "jihad" (Pujadas and Salam 1995), as "lost territories of the Republic" (Brenner 2002), and as the forward outposts of an Islamic imperial "Eurabia" (Bat Ye'or 2005).

The dynamics of Islamophobia and Islamophilia in France must be understood in the context of the recent debate over the "new anti-Semitism" in France. Contrasting the reported rise of anti-Semitic attacks in France during the early 2000s to the "classical anti-Semitism" whose ties to rightist expressions of French nationalism have been carefully detailed by Zeev Sternhell (1986), many recent commentators—including Emmanuel Brenner (2002), Raphaël Draï (2001), Alain Finkielkraut (2003), Pierre-André Taguieff (2004), and Shmuel Trigano (2003)—have linked the "new anti-Semitism" to the progressive turn to Islamic identity politics by the children of North African immigrants (or Franco-Maghrebis). While careful to distinguish Islamism from Islam, these authors posit Muslim-French anti-Semitism as a continuation of an older Muslim anti-Zionism and anti-Semitism imported from North Africa by immigrants, transmitted from parent to child, and let fester by a state fearful of offending its minority populations and Arab diplomatic partners (Brenner 2002: 14; Taguieff 2004: 14–15).[2] For Trigano (2003: 91), this assessment leads to a wholesale condemnation of "Arabo-Muslim" society as in need of complete reform if it is to fit into a secular modern world (see Draï 2001: 191). These authors follow Bat Ye'or (2002, 2005) in attributing to Muslim

Europeans a political will to re-establish a transnational caliphate in which minorities like Jews would be treated as *dhimmis,* subject to the whims of the sovereign—what Trigano (2003: 106–18) calls "the Ottomanization of Europe." Indeed, they see this renewed Ottoman form of governance as already in effect in the *banlieues,* which Finkielkraut (2003: 10) has characterized as "savage lands" (*lieux féroces*), where political norms of democracy and state secularism (*laïcité*) simply do not exist.

In contrast, I conceptualize Muslims and Jews in France within the same analytic field, and approach the violence of anti-Semitism, Islamophobia, and Islamophilia together as part of a set of structural tensions within late French modernity—tensions between particularism and universalism, between individual and collective rights.[3] These tensions are embedded within French postcoloniality, within a set of unresolved and enduring struggles over French national belonging that derive from the colonization of North Africa and, more particularly, from the bitter war of decolonization that literally tore the French Republic asunder. The emigration of North African workers and their families transported memories of violence to France, and the ongoing experience of racism and marginalization of many Muslim-French citizens indicates that the Manichaean world described by Frantz Fanon (1963: 41–42) in late colonial Algeria remains a fair descriptor of the present reality. This marginalization has been exacerbated in recent years by France's "war on terror," a war that antedates September 11, with roots in the early-1990s, when fears of the Algerian civil war's spread to French soil led to the state's progressive securitization of the housing projects (or *cités*) where many of the young Franco-Maghrebis in question live, and the resulting increase in confrontations between police and *cité* youth. Moreover, this "war on terror" has largely resulted in the interpellation (in the Althusserian sense of the term) of Franco-Maghrebis as "Muslims," a hailing that has been abetted by the larger public drama around the hijab and its recent banning from public schools (see Asad 2006; Auslander 2000; Beriss 1990; Bowen 2006; Killian 2003; Moruzzi 1994; Scott 2007; Silverstein 2004a). Whereas the previous generation of Franco-Maghrebi social and political actors—that of the Beur movement of the 1980s—primarily limited their activism toward improving their daily lives as citizens of France and residents of dilapidated suburban localities, and looked to the struggles of black Americans and South Africans for their political inspiration (see Derderian 2004; Hargreaves 1995), the younger generation—acting as "Muslims" and largely disavowing the ethnonym "Beur"—rather orients their political consciousness to the occupation of Iraq or the violence in Israel/Palestine as salient analogies for their own condition in France. It is in this context that their own reaction to the French state as an ongoing colonizing force can take on the form of generalized anti-Zionism and occasional anti-Semitism, with Jews being ironically held up (via a misleading alliance with Israeli soldiers) as icons of French bourgeois success and Islamophobic practice. As Michel Wieviorka (2007: 142–43) and his colleagues have argued:

> The Jews in Israel behave towards the Palestinians as the "French" in France do towards the "North Africans." . . . In the atmosphere of racism and disaffiliation which characterises them, the "Arabs" are therefore thought to be doubly mistreated by the French Jews who repress them as Jews, reproducing the model of the Israeli Jew towards the Palestinian Arab, and as French, racist and disrespectful towards them.

The violent racialization of North African immigrants and their children as "Muslims," and the violence they confront from the French state, is sometimes responded to in violence directed back at the state and those (including Jews) who seem to represent it.[4] The January–February 2006 abduction and murder of French-Jewish cellular phone salesman Ilan Halimi provides one site to examine how this violence of identification and disidentification plays out on the ground in highly ambiguous and complex fashion. In other cases, Muslim populations in France and North Africa—particularly Berber/Amazigh activists—engage in contrasting practices of cultural imagination, identify with persecuted Jews, and adopt philo-Semitic, pro-Israel, and even Islamophobic platforms.

In reading contemporary dynamics of Islamophobia/Islamophilia and anti-Semitism/philo-Semitism as part of a larger conflict that pits young, socioeconomically marginalized, multiply surveilled, and legally suspect Muslim-French citizens against the French state, I am engaging only a particular dimension of the diverse and fragmented character of anti-Semitism and Islamophobia in France. Like Wieviorka (2007: 13), I reject any definition of these phenomena as "homogeneous or coherent." Moreover, I am explicitly sidelining a mode of explanation that treats reciprocal violence and fantasy as but a continuation of long-standing, Jewish-Muslim sectarian conflict. I am not claiming that historical relations between Jews and Muslims in North Africa are completely irrelevant; indeed, colonial governance, as I will discuss below, provided the framework through which various groups have made distinct claims to French subjecthood (Bahloul 1996; Benbassa 1999: 185–89; Hyman 1998: 193–214).

In France, while North African Jews and Muslims, particularly of the first generation, have been similarly racialized as "immigrants" (see Silverstein 2005) and found themselves inhabiting similar spaces and sharing urban services and resources (such as halal/kosher butcher shops), their differential memories of colonial and wartime Algeria guaranteed their affective distance (see Stora 1991). These relations were periodically exacerbated following the 1967 war in Israel/Palestine, particularly given the Algerian Jewish community's orientation toward Israel as a primary source of political identification (Hyman 1998: 202–205). The ongoing violence in Israel/Palestine, and the more general self-presentation (in the wake of the Algerian civil war and the French war on terror) of many North African Arabs and Berbers as first and foremost Muslims, has driven a further wedge between the populations, magnifying the vigilance of North African Jews toward anti-Semitic rhetoric and violence, and even framing their response in kind.[5]

However, this particular genealogy of modern sectarianism is far less important for younger Franco-Maghrebis, born and raised in France after the Algerian war of independence. Their historical consciousness of colonial violence in Algeria has remained for the most part limited (Stora 2006), with mobilizations since 2003 against the proposed law to require the teaching of the "positive role of colonialism," for the recognition of France's responsibility in the slave trade, and in the formation of the Indigènes de la République movement only primarily engaging an elite or educated or activist fringe of Muslim housing project youth. For this reason, it would be wrong to understand youth fantasy and violence as the mere continuation of their parents' sectarianism, or to view the nominally anti-imperial struggles of yesterday and today as in any way seamless. Nonetheless, insofar as the colonial and wartime Algerian contexts exist as key moments in the identification of North African Muslim and Jews as differential, categorical subjects, they remain an important analytical starting point.

Colonial Roots of Islamophobia

The French colonization of North Africa was understood by many of its ideologues as part of a larger duty, a "civilizing mission" as much as a military expedition (see Colonna 1975; Cooper and Stoler 1997; Guilhaume 1992; Lucas and Vatin 1975; Rosenblum 1988, but also Bullard 2000). While this contested and highly ambivalent mission was premised on a revolutionary political theory of universal citizenship, it played itself out much closer to what Jean-Loup Amselle (2003: x), referencing Michel Foucault (1997), has termed a "war between the races." In colonial North Africa, the French colonial administration formally distinguished European citizens from native subjects (termed "nationals"), legally inscribing this division in a *code de l'indigénat* that, until 1870 for Jews and 1958 for Muslims in Algeria, denied natives French citizenship and made them subject to different court systems and legal codes as standardized and officialized by the French administration. In general, access to French citizenship required the renouncing of one's religious "personal" or "local civil" status, which was understood as tantamount to apostasy and thus almost universally avoided. Yet, within this larger, racialized citizen/"national" divide, French colonial ethnologists further classified the indigenous populations according to cultural and linguistic traits, treating them as differentially assimilable into a project of civilization (Ageron 1960; Lorcin 1995; Silverstein 2004b: 35–75). In North Africa, military scholars—following the lead of earlier arguments proposed by such luminaries as Alexis de Tocqueville (1991 [1937–1847])—repeatedly reified Arab society as principally and primarily Islamic, and perceived an incompatibility of Islamic civilization with French (Christian-secular) modernity. Such a concern belied fears of Islam as a unifying political force during nineteenth-century anti-colonial revolts, a fear that was re-energized during the twentieth century by Arab nationalist movements in Tunisia and Egypt that would eventually give birth to the fight for Algerian independence.

In colonial discourse, Islam served as the prime trope for explaining two opposed characteristics of a supposed Arab personality: on the one hand, their "bellicose," "hostile" nature, attributable to their religious "fanaticism"; and, on the other hand, their "inveterate laziness," resulting from their reverent "fatalism." In the first place, French observers argued that the Arabs' "absolutism" placed them in a "permanent state of war with the infidel, a duty of eternal war which cannot be suspended" (Servier 1923: 345–46). Islam served as the main explanatory factor for the horrors of war (beheadings, tortures, mutilations) witnessed by the French expeditionary forces during their conquest of Algeria, horrors attributable to the "vindictive and cruel character" of Arabs "who know no other law than that of the strongest" (Hamelin 1833: 7). Studies conducted by military ethnographers paid particular attention to those Algerian religious organizations, like the *marabouts* and Sufi brotherhoods (*khouan*), which wielded mystical authority and were capable of organizing believers into potential violence (cf. de Neveu 1846; Rinn 1884).

In the second place, scholars focused on a contradictory aspect of Islam—"fatalism," the absolute reliance on Allah to determine one's future. They viewed it as the root cause of a long series of vices: "laziness, dissimulation, dishonesty, suspicion, unpredictability, love of voluptuousness, luxury and feasting . . ." (Van Vollenhoven 1903: 169), decrying the Muslim Arab as a professional "sun-drinker" (*buveur de soleil*) (Docteur X 1891: 55). This reverent "laziness" was understood to reciprocally weaken the Muslim's intellect, impeding all social progress toward modernity.

Moreover, French administrators perceived this essential religiosity of Arabs as an inherent stumbling block to their administrative or legal assimilation into the French nation. "In the Mahometian civilization, religion and law are too intimately confused for the juridical condition of Muslims to be identical to that of Frenchmen or Europeans" (Larcher 1903: 16). Such an assumption led to the effective suspension of *laïcité* in Algeria, in spite of the fact that the colony was officially three *départements d'outre-mer,* and hence should normally have been subject to the same legal and constitutional regime as the metropole. When in 1891 the Third Republic considered eliminating this last impediment and naturalizing all Algerians, a violent debate broke out within the Parliament. One senator, M. Sabatier, addressing the Senate on June 27, 1891, opposed the reform on the grounds that it would implicitly condone "Coranic" civil and familial practices, from "feudal" land tenure to "polygamy," which "escape French laws, not to mention French morality" (cited in Borgé and Viasnoff 1995: 18). The consideration of religion in the granting of citizenship was only eliminated after World War II, on the eve of Algerian independence.

In contrast to their categorization of Arab Muslims as "unassimilable," French colonial scholars treated certain minority populations—particularly Jews and Berbers—as more proximate to French civilization in large part because of the perceived lack of centrality of religion to these populations' cultural practices and social life. While North African Jews were originally denied French citizenship alongside Muslims, they were later enfranchised in Algeria by the 1870 Crémieux decree and were subsequently treated as distinct from the larger colonized population. In similar fashion Berbers—while not enfranchised—were repeatedly singled out for assimilation efforts (including the establishment of French public and missionary schools [Colonna 1975]), were allowed to operate according to a system of customary rather than Islamic law for civil matters, and were preferred in the recruitment for migrant labor to colonial farms, mines, and abroad to France. According to what later became known as the "Kabyle myth" (Ageron 1960), military scholars argued that Berbers, as the autochthones of North Africa, were only superficially Islamized, secular by nature, and "Puritan" in their work habits. Indeed, at various moments, the incorporation of colonial nationals into the Greater French body politic was hailed as salutary for the French nation, as alleviating a stagnant metropolitan birthrate, providing needed soldiers and factory workers during successive European conflicts, and helping to "re-barbarize" Frenchmen out of their debilitating decadence.[6] Such claims of Berber consonance with and contribution to French modernity have been reiterated in the tensions between Islamophilia and Berberophilia in the contemporary period, as today's Berber/ Amazigh activists present themselves and the Berberophone populations they speak for as the avatars of indigenous *laïcité* and the models of Islamic practice compatible with and supportive of French Republican values.

These divisions between Arabs, Berbers, and Jews played themselves out during the struggles over decolonization. As French citizens, Jews—although many were sympathetic to Algerian and Moroccan nationalists—by and large sought to maintain some form of French North Africa, and were almost universally "repatriated" (to use the French state's rhetoric) to France at the end of the 1954–62 Algerian war. While Arabs and Berbers fought together against the French, the interests of the two populations largely diverged in the course of the decolonization struggles, with Berber elites calling for a multiethnic and multiconfessional independent state, while the Arab leaders of the National Liberation Front (FLN) in Algeria and the Istiqlal Party in Morocco sought to establish Arabo-Islamic nations (Duclos 1972; Stora 1991). The Istiqlal and FLN's visions later achieved hegemony, with many Algerian Berber leaders exiled, assassinated, or marginalized for their supposed fissiparous tendencies, for being colonial "toadies" in insisting on the cultural diversity of North Africa (Lacheraf 1953; Sahli 1953; see Chaker 1990).

The wars fought in Morocco and Algeria had repercussions in France, where several hundred thousand North African men (many of whom were Berber) worked and lived, either in workers' dormitories or, as the violence in Algeria escalated, in shantytowns with their wives and children. During the war, these immigrants were subject to heavy surveillance, the criminalization of their associations and organizations, and occasional instances of police repression, such as occurred at a pro-FLN rally in Paris on October 17, 1961, when riot police opened fire on Algerian marchers; hundreds were killed and their dead bodies tossed into the Seine (Einaudi 2001; Haroun 1986). The police were under the direct control of Maurice Papon, a former high official under the Vichy regime who was later found responsible for the deportation of thousands of French Jews to concentration and death camps in Nazi Germany, and who subsequently proved his mettle by instituting a regime of state-condoned torture against members of the nascent Algerian nationalist movement when he was governor of Constantine in eastern Algeria. In this sense, state violence against Jews and Muslims is historically and intimately connected.

Postcolonial Violence

By war's end, there were over 400,000 North Africans living in France. By the early 1980s, this number had increased to approximately 1.5 million, as labor migration continued apace until 1974, and family reunification policies afterward facilitated the arrival of the wives and children of male immigrants.[7] This immigration was ambivalently portrayed by French observers in alternate terms of national contribution and violence, with tropes of "invasion" being deployed to describe the North African presence particularly during moments of economic downturn, as occurred in the 1930s, the mid-1970s, and since the mid-1990s (Wihtol de Wenden 1991). If Charles Martel, as French history textbooks proclaim, pushed back the Saracens in the battle of Poitiers in AD 732, immigration from North Africa today has been reconstrued by certain apocalyptic writers as the Saracens' revenge, whether as a "peaceful invasion" (*invasion pacifique*) or one armed with Kalashnikovs (Raspail 1973; Figueras 1983). Indeed, extreme right scholars repeatedly warn that the "Islamic subversion [may] win the new Hundred Years' War and deliver us to Islam" (Hollender 1988).

Such racist (or Islamophobic) discourse and martial representations have been formalized in actual attacks which, in particularly ritualized fashion, have sought to repel the immigrant armies. These attacks trace their genealogy to the nationalist and fascist activism of the 1920s and 1930s, particularly around Charles Maurras' Action Française movement, whose generalized anti-Semitism extended to both Jews and Muslims. During the Vichy government, Muslims, and particularly Muslim nationalists, were subjected alongside Jews to internment and deportation, both in the metropole and in the North African territories. The French-Algerian war witnessed an upsurge of popular and police violence against immigrants, principally directed at breaking down the nationalist movement, but often indiscriminately affecting North African men and women in general.[8] Emerging from this colonial history, intermittent "murderous summers" (*étés meurtriers*) claimed the lives of nearly fifty North African immigrant men and their children between 1973 and 1983 (Aïchoune 1985). In the summer of 1973 alone, fifty Algerian workers were attacked and fifteen were killed in and around Marseilles, in a style of assault known locally as a *ratonnade* ("rat hunt"). In sportlike fashion (resembling, perhaps, the aristocratic tradition of the fox hunt), a group of white *beaufs* (short for *beaux-frères*, or "brothers-in-law," the French equivalent of "good ol' boys") would set upon the "rat" (*raton*), beat him up, destroy his identity papers or pay slips (thus making his stay in France illegitimate), and leave him for dead. However, by the early 1980s, the attack ritual had transformed somewhat, with the principal prey changing from male immigrant workers to "immigrant" children (irrespective of their actual place of birth) playing in the courtyards between public housing buildings. Rather than being hunted down by packs, the children were shot at, sniper-style, by (mostly elderly, white male) neighbors from their apartment windows using .22 long rifles, primarily employed for hunting purposes (Aïchoune 1985: 141–43).

It is important to note the articulation of racism, nationalism, and sports in the attacks just described. Masculinized pleasure appears to be a central component of racist violence in France, and indeed has been central to the constitution of working-class white masculinity in certain contexts. Moreover, the attacks described above seem to constitute exclusivist enactments of the French nation (Stolcke 1995). While the intentions of individual attackers are largely inscrutable, the attacks participate in a larger symbolic history and structure. Identity papers torn up recapitulate legal expulsion; the targeting of children (and, in Germany, homes) signals acts of exclusion from the national family and from legitimate means of social reproduction. However, as Terence Turner (1995) has argued, racist attacks are as much acts of inclusion as of exclusion. Marginalized (often unemployed) "white Frenchmen" act violently as if to re-insert themselves socially as the ideological defenders of the racially circumscribed "nation" on whose behalf they appear (and sometimes claim) to act. An exclusive male citizenship is thus violently enacted through racist attacks.

This enactment of *beauf*, male nationalist agency through violence, relies on, to borrow the words of Allen Feldman (1991: 20), "novel subject positions [that] are constructed and construed by violent performances" in postcolonial France. However, it is not only the *beauf* male subject that is elaborated through violence. Indeed, Franco-Maghrebi male subjectivity is likewise engendered in the course of these same racist attacks, as mediated in the confrontation with the French state and its agents. Alongside the .22 long rifle shootings of the early 1980s developed a second attack ritual: the unnecessary use of force by police and security officers against young "immigrant" *banlieue* men. The attackers included male private guards and security forces assigned to local supermarkets and train stations, compartmentalized spaces of the French state within the housing projects. As in the case of the .22 long rifle attackers, the perpetrators often succeeded in pleading guilty to lesser sentences, if not in being acquitted altogether (Aïchoune 1985).

Largely in response to such unpenalized, "legitimate" violence, young Franco-Maghrebi men and women began in the early 1980s to mobilize collectively in opposition to the police in what subsequently became known as the "Beur movement."[9] The movement was encouraged by the newly elected socialist government of François Mitterrand, which emphasized the "right to difference" (*droit à la différence*) within French identity, legalized immigrant associations which had been banned since 1939, and provided funding for a variety of cultural and anti-racist activities. Beur activism further drew broad support from Catholic social service organizations, as well as from local Jewish groups, and thus became a space for productive interfaith dialogue. Divisions between Beurs and Jews ("*feujs*") became increasingly manifest following the Israeli invasion of Lebanon and the growing identification of several Beur actors (via their association with Trotskyist political organizations) with the Palestinian cause (see Boukhedenna 1987). The Beur movement as a larger arts and popular culture scene also spurred early fantasies of cross-racial identification via the Beur figure of the "baba cool," the long-haired urban social bandit as emblematized by the Majid character in Mehdi Charef's popular novel and film *Le Thé au harem d'Archi Ahmed* (1983).

The Beur movement likewise was the springboard for the expansion of Berberist politics in France. Kabyle academic and immigrant labor groups active in France since 1967 reconstituted themselves as cultural associations and attracted younger Beur participants with courses in Berber language (Tamazight) as well as in Berber dance, musical, and theatrical traditions. These associations laid the groundwork for contemporary Amazigh activism, which maintains the discourse of multiculturalism and secularism embedded in the Beur movement, a discourse which has earned them (and Beur activism in general) the ire of Islamist social movements which arose in the French *banlieues* during the 1990s (see Kepel 1987).

Yet, throughout, racist violence specifically targeting Franco-Maghrebis was the primary spur for Beur militancy. The first independent movement of Beurs borrowed the English name Rock Against Police (RAP) and organized free concerts to increase public awareness of the murder of three Franco-Maghrebi teenage boys by police during the preceding four months. The second concert, held on May 15, 1981, took place in the public housing complex Couzy in the Parisian suburb of Vitry, on the exact site where one of these victims, the young Kader Lareiche, had been killed by a night watchman three months earlier (Aïchoune 1985: 127–28; Jazouli 1992: 28). Likewise, the .22 long rifle assassination of a community organizer, Abdenbi Guemiah, precipitated the November 1982 foundation of the Association Gutenberg, named for the suburban Nanterre housing project in which it was founded (Boubeker and Abdallah 1993: 65).

The first French cultural association of Franco-Maghrebi women was formed in March 1981 in the Busserine outlying quarter of Marseilles under similar conditions. The association was founded by the sister of Zahir Boudjlal, who, with Lahouari Ben Mohammed, had been killed the previous month. While the association had the explicit goal of documenting racist assassinations, its first action was to organize a protest against the deportation of Djamila, a young resident of Busserine who had been arrested during the demonstration following the assassination of Lahouari. In other words, the constitution of a female Beur(ette) political subjectivity was itself historically predicated on male violence and its prevention. This movement of Beurette women to protect their "brothers" (*frères*)—literal or fictive—from the French state actually inverts standard gender relations in the *banlieues*. Drawing on their own idealization of North African domestic life and Muslim mores, Franco-Maghrebi men generally adopt the role of being the protectors of women; which is to say, they protect their own honor by regulating their sisters' (and other female kin's) sexuality. Moreover, Franco-Maghrebi women as protectors of men contrasts with a masculine Beur political subjectivity described below: the violent avenger of fallen "brothers."

Such "novel subject positions" underwrote the 1983 March for Equality and Against Racism (known colloquially as the *Marche des Beurs*), the historical touchstone and unifying event for the "Beur movement." The march, which mobilized over 100,000 demonstrators from Marseille to Paris, was to a great extent a response to the "murderous summer" of the previous months. For one participant, Ahmed Ghayet, the march formed the Beurs as a particular political and generational subjectivity: "The history of the youth, which one has baptized today as the '*banlieue* youth,' which had been baptized 'Beurs,' I would date from the 1983 March" (cited in Bouamama, Sad-Saoud, and Djerdoubi, 1994: 40). The event was organized by the Association SOS Avenir Minguettes, whose twenty-year-old president, Toumi Djaidja, had been seriously wounded several months earlier while attempting to intervene when policemen had unleashed their dogs on a group of young residents of Les Minguettes (Lyon). Male and female marchers displayed banners commemorating the young men killed during the summer and were greeted along the way with local memorials in suburban Vaulx-en-Velin (Lyon) and Nanterre (Paris) for residents killed during the previous year (Jazouli 1992: 60). In this way, the forging of the Beurs as a trans-suburban political generation corresponded to assassinations of young *banlieue* men who were seen by community organizers as "brothers" (*frères*), whether actual, as in the case of Zahir Boudjlal, or fictive kin (Bouamama et al. 1994: 50).

If many Franco-Maghrebis participated in nonviolent actions like the march, others felt such displays of passive solidarity to be ineffectual and demanded that a "blood price" (*prix de sang*) be paid (Bouamama et al. 1994: 51). However, as the actual attacker, under police custody if not a police officer himself, could not be directly punished by the victim's male kin, the community took collective action, directing their "rage" at the police force as a whole, as well as at the symbols of their economic exclusion in the *cités*. In the summer of 1981, following a police raid in the Cité de la Cayolle in Marseilles in which a number of women, children, and elderly residents were injured, young male residents fire-bombed the shopping centers and police stations throughout the area. During the same period, in Lyon, when a hunger strike protesting the expulsions of young Franco-Maghrebis failed to overturn the responsible legislation, and when shortly thereafter a young woman from neighboring Saint-Dizier was extradited to Algeria, Les Minguettes exploded in a series of violent confrontations between young men and the police. In an estimated 250 separate incidents, groups of mostly Franco-Maghrebi (but also other *banlieusards*) boys would steal a car, engage police in a chase, and then abandon and burn the vehicle.

While clearly having a pleasurable, if not sporting, quality, these "rodeos" (as they were locally called) were often (though certainly not always) understood by their participants as exercises in a particular agency delimited by the violence of the *banlieues*. According to one local resident and community activist, Djamel, "It was from the moment of police provocations that the youth began to become aggressive, because they didn't understand the police's aggressions towards them. The rodeos were to respond to everything they had undergone, they and their parents. . . . The rage they had in themselves was directed at the cars" (cited in Jazouli 1992: 21–22). Two years later, similar confrontations occurred in neighboring Venissieux (Lyon), leading to the weeklong occupation of the housing project by a regiment of four thousand police officers. During the same year, young men of the Monmousseau *cité* of Les Minguettes engaged police in a violent struggle after the latter had broken into an apartment thought to contain stolen goods. In this engagement with the police, and the French state as a whole, Beur male subjectivity became premised not only on the men's status as the objects of violence, but also on their role as the subjects of violence, as the avengers of their "brothers" and defenders of their "parents."

This form of agentive subjectivity was inherited by the younger brothers of the Beur actors, who by the 1990s found themselves further marginalized from the fruits of their parents' labors, as well as disillusioned by the failure of multicultural identity politics associated with the Beur movement. The repeated, violent confrontations between *cité* youth and the police throughout the 1990s largely involved locally delineated groups—which crossed religious, ethnic, and racial lines—responding to the killing of one of their "brothers" by representatives of the state. For instance, clashes between youth and riot police (Compagnies Républicaines de Sécurité, or CRS) occurred in November 1990 in the Mas-du-Taureau *cité* of the Lyonnais suburb of Vaulx-en-Velin after the death of twenty-one-year-old resident Thomas Claudio in a motorcycle chase with police; in March 1991 in Sartrouville (Paris) after the assassination of eighteen-year-old Djamel Chettouh by a Euromarché supermarket security guard; and in May 1991 in Val-Fourré after the death of eighteen-year-old Aïssa Ihich, who asphyxiated after being denied his asthma medicine while in police custody. As after the 1981 rodeos, the government's response to the contestation involved direct intervention into the everyday social life of the *cités* in the form of increased police presence, youth programs, and Marshall Plan–style economic measures.

Through such responses, the French state largely reinforced an image, popularized through the media and in the speeches of conservative political candidates, of a *banlieue* youth increasingly "outside the law" (*hors la loi*). Many sociologists in France, sometimes themselves former Beur activists, described the *banlieue* youth as participating in a "riot culture" (*culture de l'émeute*) characterized by a generalized historical amnesia and "hate" (*haine*) directed indiscriminately at all symbols of the French state (Aïchoune 1991: 13). If the Beurs, as hybrid political subjects, represented the utopian future of a "plural France" touted by Beur activists and socialist politicians whereby the young Franco-Maghrebi citizens served as icons of a multicultural future (Boubeker and Abdallah 1993: 43), the *banlieue* youth of the 1990s represented its dystopian obverse of dangerous social anomie. In this representation of the *cités*, multicultural, class-based community was viewed as having devolved into "ethnic and territorial gangs" involved in "endemic daily violence" that at best organized itself into a "riot" against the police (Jazouli 1992: 141–42). Increasingly, the *cités* were portrayed by the police and media as "lawless zones [*zones de non-droit*] in which the law of the Republic is totally absent" (*Le Monde*, September 7, 1995). These representations and the resulting state policies of further securitization of the *cités* continued up through and in response to the October–November 2005 wave of violence (see Silverstein and Tetreault 2006).

The point of this discussion is not to substantiate an Islamophobic portrayal of Muslim-French citizens as preternaturally or culturally violent, nor is it to claim that all violent acts are intentionally political in their enactment, but rather to argue that the subject positions of male and female housing project residents (Beurs, *beaufs,* and *banlieue* residents more broadly) are constituted themselves in no small part in and through masculinized violence, and that this violence organizes suburban spaces of marginalization. Moreover, it is to argue that this struggle is strongly local in its rubric, oriented to the specific conditions of marginalization experienced by youth at the hands of the state and its socioeconomic agents and icons; the *banlieue* youth in question were by and large *not* motivated by global ideologies of Marxism or Islamism, even if such political movements were, and continue to be, present in the housing projects in question. In this sense, it is of little wonder that the anti-police "riots" should target not only police stations, but also gymnasiums, shopping centers, schools, and other such institutions associated with state economic, political, and cultural dominance. As much as acts of destruction, these attacks entail occupation and appropriation, as local residents inscribe the sites, through graffiti and tags, as their own. Or, in the case of the growth of parallel grassroots services in the shadows of these defunct institutions, residents simply replace these sites with their own.

Wars on Terror

As Vincent Geisser (2003) has discussed in his work on *La Nouvelle Islamophobie* ("The New Islamophobia"), the ostensible social chaos of *cité* youth (dis) organization became a further source of anxiety in that it was seen to leave open a vacuum for the rise of "communitarian" organizations, particularly Islamic fundamentalist groups. Since the demise of the Beur movement and the beginning of the Algerian civil war, the monopoly maintained by the state agencies of North African countries over the organization and transmission of Islamic knowledge and worship has largely broken down. In its wake, a great diversity of Islamic associations, mosque structures, and activist organizations have prospered in France, tracing their lineage to various Sufi and Salafi movements originating from the Middle East, South Asia, and West Africa (see Bowen 2009; Cesari 1994; Kepel 1987). While religious beliefs and practices remain quite diverse, many younger Franco-Maghrebi men and women have joined evangelical Islamic groups, and have rejected the "traditionalism" of their parents for modernist, streamlined interpretations of the Quran and the science of hadith.

With the transnationalization of the violence of the Algerian civil war, general fears of a *banlieue* "generation in revolt" have been translated into particular concerns of Franco-Maghrebi *cité* youth succumbing to the "temptation of Jihad" (cf. Pujadas and Salam 1995). The life histories of two individuals in particular symbolized this fear: first, the conversion of Toumi Djaidja, organizer and icon of the 1983 *Marche des Beurs,* to a neotraditional form of Islam while serving a brief prison sentence; second, the participation of Khaled Kelkal, a Franco-Maghrebi from Mas-du-Taureau, in the 1995 attempted bombing of a rail line outside Lyon that was attributed to the Algerian Armed Islamic Group. For French government officials and media pundits, these two trajectories signified the birth of a third generation of immigrants in the 1990s, one founded in the transnational cross-linkages between youth indigenous to the French *banlieues* and those Islamist and Berberist militants who had fled the Algerian civil war to come live in France (Silverstein 2004b: 174–83).

These anxieties over suburban housing projects serving as a node in an international terrorist network that supposedly linked Algiers to Cologne to Sarajevo to Kabul to Iraq (cf. *Le Figaro,* August 16, 1995), were magnified by the post–September 11 arrest of French-Moroccan Zacarias Moussaoui as the "20th September 11th hijacker" and the discovery of several French citizens of North African parentage among Taliban forces in Afghanistan and among the "foreign fighters" in the Iraqi insurgency. In response, France's homegrown war on terror has attempted to retake control of the *cité* frontiers and reincorporate them into the state's economic and legal framework. The war has operated on two fronts that have both reinforced Franco-Maghrebi identification as particularly Muslim subjects, and have positioned this subjectivity in opposition to French social-political belonging. In the first place, the French government has increased police intervention and surveillance across the urban periphery in an explicit attempt to re-monopolize local violence. Security forces and intelligence agencies have conducted multiple sweeps (*rafles*) for suspected terrorists in the *cités,* breaking into prayer rooms and association locales. In response to the summer 1995 bombings, the French government activated the Vigipirate anti-terrorism plan to raise the level of public vigilance. Originally conceived in 1978 and first introduced during the 1991 Gulf War, the plan operates according to a logic of armed deterrence, mobilizing the military to guard schools, transportation hubs, government buildings, and centers of tourism. The plan remained in effect until the September 11 attacks, at which point it was elevated to a "reinforced" level of "high surveillance" of public institutions. Like the USA Patriot Act, the reinforced Vigipirate plan lowered the bar of probable cause and authorized extensive identity checks and property searches in public areas. North African youth have been particularly targeted by such "random searches" (*contrôles au faciès*), resulting in countless judicial detentions, arrests, and, in the case of undocumented migrants, deportations.

In such identity checks, security agents interpellate Franco-Maghrebis as potential Islamist terrorists.

These security measures have additionally focused on the *cités* as spaces of potential terror. The 1995 Vigipirate plan added 200 plainclothes inspectors to the already expanded suburban security forces to "penetrate the milieus of delinquency" (*L'Express,* November 9, 1995). In 1999, Socialist prime minister Lionel Jospin bolstered these measures, mobilizing 13,000 additional riot police and 17,000 military gendarmes to patrol these same "sensitive urban zones." Finally, in 2003, law-and-order interior minister Nicolas Sarkozy further increased the regiments of *cité* security forces and gave them new powers to search homes and vehicles, thus eliminating previous "no-go areas." In an effort to destroy clandestine mosques and Islamic associations, he likewise criminalized congregations in the entries, basements, and garages of public housing projects.

In the second place, the French war on terror has involved the official recognition *qua* containment of Islam in France. In particular, the French government has sought to determine the parameters of Islamic practice in France through the official banning of headscarves in public schools, and the creation of official French Councils of the Muslim Faith (CFCM) that would mediate between French Muslims and the state (Bowen 2006; Fernando 2005; Silverstein 2004a). These policies provide the institutions and legal norms through which the government seeks to bring Islamic practice in line with French ideologies of *laïcité*. While attempts to create such governing bodies have existed since 1989, they received a renewed push after September 11 when Sarkozy became determined to replace the *Islam des caves* ("Islam of garages and cellars") with a controllable "Islam of the mosques." However, when a substantial number of representatives from the Union of Islamic Organizations in France (UOIF) with supposed historical ties to the Egyptian Muslim Brotherhood won seats in the April 2003 elections, Sarkozy threatened to expel imams whose views did not correspond to French law and to close their mosques.

As Mayanthi Fernando (2005) has emphasized, these efforts at creating an official Islam *of* France (as opposed to Islam *in* France) blurs the distinction between a Muslim community defined by practice (particularly mosque attendance) and one defined by self-identification. By tying the CFCM to mosque structures, Islamic belief and practice that is mediated by informal organizational forms or private, domestic settings is not taken into account. Likewise, the voices of the vast majority of Franco-Maghrebis who identify culturally as Muslims but do not actively practice their religion are silenced. This tying of Franco-Islamic representation to mosques thus privileges senior men at the expense of both women and younger men engaged in *da'wa*.

Through these processes of self-identification and state interpellation, Franco-Maghrebis increasingly present themselves publicly as Muslims whose belonging to the French nation and loyalty to the French state is subsequently questioned. Whereas earlier forms of youth identification and organization during the 1980s and early 1990s had been based in shared diacritics of class and locality—being poor inhabitants of marginalized housing projects—that superseded divisions of race and religion and thus underwrote Vinz's racial cross-identification as depicted in *La Haine,* private practices and state policies have fostered a new racialization and deployment of religious categories. This is not to say that locally racialized categories of *rabeu, feuj,* or *renoi* (black) had not been part of the *banlieue* vocabulary prior to the Algerian civil war, but rather that these were relatively flexible terms of address and reference that marked personal idiosyncrasies as much as ethno-religious roots. Moreover, youth solidarity crossed these racialized boundaries, with local *bandes* (gangs) forming largely on the basis of residence. New modes of religious identification, however, outline increasingly bounded modes of sociality which, while not excluding crossings of racial or religious frontiers, mark local social struggle as expressions of a larger, transnational religious conflict which threatens to become a self-fulfilling prophecy.

In other words, when Franco-Maghrebis qua Muslims witness the events of September 11, the American occupation of Afghanistan and Iraq, or the ongoing violence in Israel/Palestine, they increasingly witness a reflection of the struggles they are undergoing in their daily lives. In spite of obvious diplomatic and policy distinctions between France and the U.S. and Israel, young French Muslims make the implicit analogy between the American army, the Israeli IDF, and the French riot police. They re-interpret, in other words, their battles with French forces of law and order as an intifada of their own, as a resistance to forces of imperialism. If their older brothers and sisters saw their struggles as intrinsically local and based in a larger fight for civic rights in France, many of today's Franco-Maghrebi youth see themselves additionally (if not primarily) as transnational Muslim subjects in solidarity with oppressed Palestinians, Afghanis, and Iraqis. As Wieviorka (2007: 112) observes in what he calls "ghetto anti-Semitism" with global reach: "The experience of Muslims [in France] becomes an illustration of what Muslims are said to experience at [an] international level and is constantly associated with images of the Israeli domination of Palestinians and the violence inflicted on the Iraqi people by the Americans." And this association of Islam with anti-imperial resistance has bolstered the Islamophilia of local youth and contributed to the increased rates of conversion to Islam in the *banlieues* as a mode of "social protest" (Daynes 1999: 316).

Moreover, this set of alliances—which racializes religion over class—implies a different orientation toward other racialized groups. If previous struggles had unified all *cité* residents in opposition to *beaufs* or bourgeois Parisians (as the latter adopted *cité* styles as a mode of their own symbolic protest), the recent generation of *cité* youth tends to approach their Jewish co-residents as representatives of international imperialism and, ironically, of an anti-Muslim French state whose own history of anti-Semitic violence is ignored. "The Jews are resented quite simply because they are said to elude injustice and, not assimilated but fully integrated, they seem to be particularly well treated by France" (Wieviorka 2007: 109). As Wieviorka (2007: 140) and his colleagues poignantly conclude: "This ghetto anti-Semitism constitutes a historical paradox: those who, in the past, lived in ghettos . . . and have endured racist hatred have today become, in an impressive turnaround, the imagined root of the evils from which they themselves have suffered."

The "New Anti-Semitism" Revisited

It is this shift in identification that helps explain the reported spike in anti-Semitic violence in the early 2000s and its attribution in part to Muslim-French *banlieue* residents. Granted, the statistical rise must be, to a certain extent, questioned given new, statewide reporting guidelines that—particularly for schools where the vast majority of reported incidents occurred—streamlined the collection of data on race-related crimes and arguably overreported minor schoolyard incidents as hate crimes. Further, the spike in reported anti-Semitic violence was accompanied by an even greater spike in racist and xenophobic violence particularly against Muslims in the wake of September 11 (Geisser 2003: 10–13), with a 150 percent increase recorded by the National Consultative Commission on Human Rights (CNCDH) during the same 2003–2004 period when anti-Semitic attacks rose 50 percent (*Le Monde*, March 21, 2005). While anti-Semitic attacks have since decreased, anti-immigrant and anti-Muslim violence has not.

In this light, the abduction and murder of the French Jewish mobile phone salesman Ilan Halimi by a multi-ethnic group of young French men and women from the *banlieues*, but spearheaded by a young Muslim from Côte d'Ivoire, can be re-examined. As Brian Klug (2003) has convincingly argued, "anti-Semitism" should be defined as the targeting of Jews qua Jews for violence, repression, or derision. In this sense, not every attack on Jews is necessarily an anti-Semitic attack, as any given attack may follow a very different economic or racial or political logic; this distinction is crucial in differentiating anti-Zionism (i.e., a political platform against a greater Israel) from anti-Semitism (i.e., a racism against a people). In the case of Halimi, the mastermind behind the abduction claimed that the kidnapping was purely motivated by financial goals—that Halimi was chosen not because he was a Jew per se, but because he was presumed to be rich. Or, as another of the abductors claimed, "Ilan was Jewish, and Jews are rich" (*Libération*, February 23, 2006). In this sense, the attack cannot be assimilated into the narrative of a "new anti-Semitism" perpetrated by Muslims and tied to events in Israel/Palestine. Rather, it seems to be connected to an older anti-Semitic stereotype of the Jew-as-financier, one which has endured in the historical rhetoric of the French far right and has been further appropriated into contemporary Islamist ideology in France and abroad, some of which has clearly been assimilated into *banlieue* common sense. Moreover, whatever the exact motivation of the attackers or their personal (old or new) anti-Semitic beliefs, the killing did raise—for both French Jews and the French state—the specter of a renewed anti-Semitism, encourage several thousand Jews to emigrate to Israel (as Laura's family did at the end of *La Petite Jérusalem*), and lead to increased social mobilization against this form of racism, all of which points to the fact that there may exist a social reality of anti-Semitism in France, regardless of the nature of any given attack.[10]

Moreover, attacks such as that on Halimi point to how some young Muslim-French citizens share ideological space with an anti-Semitic extreme right that, ironically again, has made its political bed on xenophobic and Islamophobic rhetoric. Rather than seeing acts of violence by Muslim youth on Jewish people and property as a failure of republican integration, as observers like Brenner (2002) and Trigano (2003) would have it, one could make a strong case that it is a sure sign of their very integration into a French nation premised simultaneously on a disavowal of cultural difference and on an avowal of a "True France" of the countryside (a *pays réel*) historically connected to Catholic anti-Semitism. Indeed, it is an old sociological saw (and not an inherently false one) to take an immigrant group's racism against those who arrived more recently as an index of their assimilation. In this light, it is interesting to note the timing of the clarion calls from academics like Brenner (2002), Trigano (2003), Taguieff (2004), and Finkielkraut (2003), which have appeared since 2002. Not only do these works correspond closely to the post–September 11 war on terror, to a call for greater policing of Islamism in France, but they also can be read as reactions to the incorporation of Muslim French via the state-run French

Councils of the Muslim Faith, organizations which seek explicitly, in the words of former interior minister Nicolas Sarkozy, to "bring Islam to the table of the Republic" on the same terms as the Jewish Consistories previously established by Napoléon. Indeed, Trigano (2003: 15–17) explicitly rejects comparisons of the French Muslim and Jewish "communities" as commensurable groups who can be interpreted as being in conflict. It would not be unreasonable to describe this alarmist literature as a hostile (if not Islamophobic) reaction to the incorporation of Muslims as full-fledged citizens of France.

Amazigh Imagination

Yet the mutual resentment of Muslims and Jews in France as differently positioned, differently integrated political subjects is by no means inevitable. Philia as well as phobia may characterize intercommunal relations in France. A cardinal example of the former are Berber (or Amazigh) activists in France and North Africa, whose relationship to Islam, secularism, and anti-Semitism is quite unlike that of Muslim French more commonly represented in international media.[11] As mentioned earlier, colonial ethnologists treated Berbers as exceptionally suitable for French civilization due to their supposedly minimal and superficial Islamization.[12] Many of today's Berber activists across France and North Africa—organized in cultural associations, umbrella social movements (such as the Mouvement Culturel Berbère of Algeria and the Mouvement Amazigh of Morocco), political parties (such as the Front des Forces Socialistes and Rassemblement pour la Culture et la Démocratie of Algeria), and transnational organizations (the World Amazigh Congress)—have concurred with the colonial stereotype and have embraced the heteropraxy and pre-Islamic origins of popular modes of Berber religious practice. In general, the activists have rejected Islam as their primary mode of identification, emphasizing instead the historical (if ambivalent) separation of religious and political spheres in Berber customary law and decision making. Moreover, they have rejected the generalized anti-Zionist (and occasionally anti-Semitic) politics of the Islamic world, adopting instead an avowedly philo-Semitic (if not pro-Zionist) discourse (see Silverstein 2007). In general, Jews are "good to think" for Amazigh activists, in that, like the totemic natural species Claude Lévi-Strauss (1962) analyzed, they provide the basis for the organization of social categories of Amazigh selves and others. Jews function totemically for Amazigh militants as a people similarly marginalized under the historic mantle of Arabo-Islamic hegemony in the Middle East and North Africa. More generally, activists see in the Zionist movement a model for the Amazigh struggle: the successful codification and preservation of a threatened language, and the obtaining of political and territorial autonomy with the establishment of the state of Israel. While by no means the agents of the Israeli state that Islamists occasionally accuse them of being, Amazigh militants have actively sought to reconcile Jewish and Berber populations, and have publicly advocated a normalization of relations with Israel. Beginning in the early-1990s, delegations of French-Kabyle artists and intellectuals visited Israel and published reports of their voyages in Amazigh newsletters and blogs that circulated across France and North Africa.

Perhaps the most poignant example of Amazigh philo-Semitism and ethno-religious cross-identification occurs in the southeastern Moroccan town of Goulmima, around a masquerade festival known locally as Udayen Achour (Jewish Ashura), where Berber participants literally put on Jew-face and perform a ritual of ethnic, religious, and sometimes gender inversion.[13] The festival occurs one month after Eid al-Adha and ritually closes the end of the year holiday, with the last, dried morsels of the slaughtered ram eaten in a communal couscous. After the meal, town residents gather outside the village walls, where young men, referring to themselves as *udayen* ("Jews"), sport grotesque masks and outfits designed to hide their identities, with certain performers even cross-dressing to portray female *tudayen*. They engage in hypersexualized flirting (*taqrefeyt*) with each other, as well as with the young women spectating on the periphery of the carnival. More generally they act and talk outrageously, in a manner that satirizes local religious and govern-ment authority figures, as well as more marginal characters of town life (such as beggars, prostitutes, and drug users)—behavior and speech acts that would be practically impossible under everyday social norms.

On the face of it, the masquerade replicates those inversion dramas found throughout Berber North Africa that were historically performed between the Eid and Ashura. Colonial observers, in their search for a primordial "Berber religion," typically linked these performances, in Frazerian fashion, to pagan rituals of social renewal, in which the fertility of the soil was regenerated through the symbolic death and rebirth of the agricultural god, through the expulsion of evil via scapegoats (Hammoudi 1993: 15–32; cf. Laoust 1921: 254). Personified Jews, as well as blacks (*ismakhen*, "slaves"), are generally interpreted as functioning as such scapegoats, and are uniformly portrayed by Berber Muslims in the same grotesque, sexualized fashion displayed in the Goul-mima festival. Given this imagery, Berber masquerades have, since Moroccan independence, provoked the ire of Islamic reformers who decry the events as "vestiges of paganism (*jahiliyya*)" that threaten to infect everyday social com-portment and destroy Muslim virtues (Hammoudi 1993: 89, 167).

Udayen Achour represents a pared-down version of this ritual, represented as and transformed by Amazigh activists into a celebration—rather than a mockery or symbolic expulsion—of Judeo-Berber culture. Like the colonial ethnologists and Islamic reformists, local Amazigh militants emphasize the masquerade's pre-Islamic genealogy and even attribute its origin to a *Jewish* ritual revived by activists in recent memory. Although they recognize its timing on the Islamic lunar calendar, they disassociate it from the Eid sacrifice or the larger celebrations of Ashura as the Feast of the Muslim New Year. Underlining the Jewish nature of the event, they greet each other with the supposedly Hebrew "*Tchafou*," sing songs featuring Jewish characters invoked to replenish the local river's water supply, make pilgrimages to the old Jewish quarter (*mellah*), and work Hebrew writing and six-pointed stars into their costumes. They proudly relate how in 2000 masked youth even provoked a fatwa from the local imam by carrying signs written in both Hebrew and Arabic that argued for a rapprochement with Israel.

Putting on Jew-face thus serves to strengthen Berber activists' self-presentation as modern cosmopolitans and as Europeans through their claims to solidarity, if not identification, with Jews. Such philo-Semitism (if not pro-Zionism) helps activists distinguish themselves from Arab Muslims, who have been negatively stereotyped in the West as being prone to fundamentalism, terrorism, and anti-Semitism. Through their wholehearted support for *laïcité*, Amazigh activists present themselves as the "good Muslim" immigrants, and ultimate defenders of the French Republic. In this respect, Amazigh philo-Semitism represents a racial project of national and transnational inclusion, of anti-anti-Semitism and cosmopolitan secularism, and of imagined cross-communal identification that remaps the globe in contradistinction to the "clash of civilizations" rhetoric.

Any analysis of contemporary Islamophobia and Islamophilia, as well as anti-Semitism and philo-Semitism, needs to recognize moments when categories of analysis fragment. Social positions of "Muslim" and "Jew" in the contemporary, postcolonial French Mediterranean emerge from a long history of fantasy and violence in which various actors who are today identified (and self-identify) along these taken-for-granted religious axes have been differentially placed vis-à-vis various state practices of exclusion and assimilation. The legal separation of Jews from Muslims, and later Arabs from Berbers, by the colonial administrations of North Africa—a distinction which better reflected metropolitan social castes than the state of communal interactions in pre-colonial North African societies—gained social facticity as it was reproduced in political power imbalances in newly independent Algeria and Morocco, as well as in immigrant housing and policing policies in France. Even so, the problematization and surveillance of certain Muslim subjects in relation to their potential for religious extremism only gained currency, as I discuss above, in relation to the "war on terror" waged since the mid-1990s. In France, the self-presentation and subsequent interpellation of Franco-Maghrebis as "Muslims" underwrites contemporary avowals of solidarity of *banlieusards* with occupied Iraq and Palestine, and thus the resulting anti-Zionist (and occasionally anti-Semitic) orientation of current French street politics. Yet, as I have tried to insist, even this trajectory has been contested throughout, with an outspoken Amazigh activism continuing to challenge the unquestioned pro-Palestinian orientation of Franco-Maghrebi politics, countering anti-Semitism with its own philo-Semitic and occasionally Islamophobic rhetoric.

France and its postcolonial North African periphery thus remains marked by an ambivalence of identification and disidentification, of solidarity and exclusion, as marginalized Muslim populations become at various moments embraced as fantasy objects of national regeneration or anti-imperialist protest, and at others demonized as perpetrators of violence and barbarity, and as Jews vacillate between objects of racial and religious revulsion and icons of cosmopolitan modernity. If the contemporary rhetoric of the "war on terror" has fragmented French Jews around their political support for Israel and alarmism over the rise of the "new anti-Semitism," so too has it served to divide Berbers and Arabs into "good" and "bad" Muslims—to follow Mahmood Mamdani's critique (2004)—as measured by their relative avowal of the rights of women, homosexuals, and Jews. It is the contemporary challenge of the multiply hybrid subjects around the French Mediterranean to find new spaces of solidarity and new modes of identification that avoid the extremist rhetorics of Islamophobia and Islamophilia, of anti-Semitism and philo-Semitism—that re-imagine social interaction and belonging beyond the poles of love and hate.

Notes

An earlier version of this essay appeared as the "Context of Antisemitism and Islamophobia in France" in *Patterns of Prejudice* 42(1) (2008): 1–26. The author thanks Taylor and Francis for permission to reprint. Research was funded in part by generous grants from the U.S. Institute of Peace and the Fulbright-Hays Faculty Research Abroad Program. For comments and suggestions on various drafts, the author would like to thank John Bunzl, Brian Klug, Barbara Rosenbaum, Emmanuel Saadia, Andrew Shryock, the anonymous reviewer for Indiana University Press, and the various participants in the conferences and workshops organized by the Koebner Center for German History of the Hebrew University of Jerusalem, the Austrian Institute for International Affairs, the U.K. Faculty Forum for Israel-Palestine Peace, and the Human Rights Workshop of the University of Chicago, where various earlier versions of the paper were presented.

1. French domestic intelligence reports indicate as many as 100,000 converts in France and report that Muslims constitute up to 50 percent of the prison population (Smith 2004; Whitlock 2006).

2. Note that while the category of " Muslim French" (*Français musulmans* or *Musulmans en/de France*) as deployed in France nominally includes Muslims of sub-Saharan African, Turkish, and South Asian descent, along with converts to Islam, the focus of French media and state attention has been on French North Africans considered most susceptible to Islamist preaching (*da'wa*) and most responsible for the reported rise in anti-Semitism.

3. For a parallel analysis and critique of the discourse of the "new anti-Semitism" as a form of a "new Islamophobia," see Geisser (2003: 77–93). See also Balibar et al. (2003) and Vidal (2003) for similar skepticism. Michel Wieviorka (2007) and his research team, in their comprehensive survey of anti-Semitic attitudes in France, attempt to formulate a balanced analysis that simultaneously recognizes the social challenge of increased anti-Semitism in France while warning against succumbing to the moral panic encouraged by authors like Brenner, Finkielkraut, Taguieff, and Trigano. My essay follows very much in this project. See also Peace (2009). For a discussion of the respective roles of anti-Semitism and Islamophobia in indexing positions of nationalism and pan-nationalism within the broader field of Europe, see Bunzl (2005), as well as the various commentaries which followed this article and emphasized the larger colonial/postcolonial dynamic of the various racisms. For critical discussions of the appropriateness of the terminology "(new) anti-Semitism" and "Islamophobia" for denominating current racism against Jews and Muslims in France, see Bowen (2005: 524); Peace (2009: 118–21); Wieviorka (2007: 62–68). "Anti-Semitism" technically references an older racial typology where Jews (as well as Arabs) were reviled as "Semites." "Islamophobia" registers a psychological fear of Islamic religion, rather than the structural discrimination and racialized discourse against Muslims which is at issue. Nonetheless, these are the terms in which the French debate has been addressed, and as such I continue to use them throughout this essay.

4. Note that not all contemporary public violence by children of North African immigrants necessarily follows a logic of religious interpellation and invocation, in spite of presumptions by certain Islamophobic critics (see the interview with Alain Finkielkraut in Mishani and Smotriez [2005]). In the October–November 2005 wave of urban violence in the peripheral housing projects of France, the young men on the street were primarily organized according to ties of residence and socioeconomic marginalization that transcended ethnic and religious differences. Calls for calm by local Islamic associations and even a fatwa against the violence by the supposedly fundamentalist Union of Islamic Organizations in France (UOIF) fell on deaf ears. See Silverstein and Tetreault (2006).

5. Indeed, since 2002, there has been a significant increase in anti-Arab and anti-Muslim attacks by North African Jews, whether taking place in the public spheres of pro-Israel

rallies, or "off-line" in terms of street attacks and mosque burnings (Shatz 2005). On the more general rise of anti-Muslim attacks in France since the late 1990s, see Geisser (2003: 10–13).

6. The academician Louis Bertrand (1930 [1889]: 8–13) was particularly outspoken in his fantasies of a "new Latin race" created in the fusion of French settlers and Berbers whose "barbarity" would "rejuvenate" French civilization and lead to a "national regeneration."

7. For histories and analyses of Algerian immigration to France, see Gillette and Sayad (1976); Hargreaves (1995); Liauzu (1996); MacMaster (1997); Sayad (2004); Talha (1989); and Zehraoui (1994).

8. See MacMaster (1997), Noiriel (1988), and Wihtol de Wenden (1991) for extended histories of colonial-era racism and violence against Algerians in France. For an expanded discussion of the performativity of violence in constituting categories of racial identification, see Silverstein (2008).

9. The ethnonym "Beur" was adopted in the early 1980s by young Franco-Maghrebi men and women to indicate their double separation from their parents' "Arab" culture (often characterized pejoratively) and from normative Frenchness and the expectations of cultural assimilation that attended the latter. The term is generally considered to be a double syllabic inversion of *arabe* according to the language game of *verlan,* though others have postulated that it could be an acronym for *Berbères d'Europe* (Aïchoune 1985). The term was subsequently adopted by the French media and academia, and quickly disavowed by Franco-Maghrebis, who today see the Beur movement as either a political failure or a government manipulation. The self-appellation currently in use is "rebeu" (a single *verlan* inversion of *arabe*). In this essay, I use the term "Beur" only in reference to Franco-Maghrebi activists and fellow travelers of the 1980s. Otherwise, I use the analytical appellation Franco-Maghrebi, fully in realization that such a term does not correspond to local naming practices, and that the hyphenation better indexes Anglo-American understandings of identity than French Republican expectations of the erasure of ethnic and religious diacritics from political belonging.

10. In one heavily reported and debated incident from 2004, a young woman claimed to have been attacked on a Parisian commuter train by a group of youths who drew a swastika on her chest. The event elicited cries of outrage from Jewish and anti-racist organizations, and public apologies, promises of redress, and stiffer penalties for anti-Semitic crimes from the government. When the woman later admitted that she had made up the attack, President Jacques Chirac publicly stated that what remained important was that such an attack could very well have occurred. In this sense, the attack, while purely imaginary, continued to function as a social fact with real-world effects.

11. I have discussed Amazigh *laïcité* and philo-Semitism at length in Silverstein (2007).

12. In point of fact, Amazigh activists—like Berber-speakers throughout North Africa and the diaspora—incorporate a wide variety of religious beliefs and practices into their everyday lives, with some militants engaging in regular prayer and following Islamic dietary restrictions, while others going as far as to excise all references to God from their spoken language and to harbor scarcely hidden contempt for the believers among their

ranks. However, even the most extreme atheists outwardly defend "traditional" forms of Berber Islamic practice that they claim to be flexible in application and perfectly integrated into larger cultural forms, and even the most pious Amazigh activists refuse to condone Islamist arguments for the priority of religion in political life. Such claims to Berber cultural-religious distinctiveness generally ignore movements of religious reformism and purification in which Berber groups themselves historically engaged, most particularly during the Almoravid and Almohad Berber empires of Andalusia, as well as the fact that Berber-speakers number among the ranks of contemporary Islamist militants.

13. I do not have the space here to engage in a full ethnographic description and analysis of Udayen Achour. For a brilliant ethnography of a similar masquerade in the High Atlas, see Hammoudi (1993).

Works Cited

Ageron, Charles-Robert. 1960. "La France a-t-elle un politique kabyle." *Revue historique* 223: 311–52.

Aïchoune, Farid, ed. 1985. *La Beur Génération.* Paris: Sans Frontière/Arcantère.

———. 1991. *Nés en banlieue.* Paris: Ramsay.

Aïdi, Hisham. 2002. "Jihadis in the Hood: Race, Urban Islam, and the War on Terror." *Middle East Report* 224: 36–43.

———. 2003. "Let Us Be Moors: Islam, Race, and 'Connected Histories.'" *Middle East Report* 229: 42–53.

Amselle, Jean-Loup. 2003. *Affirmative Exclusion: Cultural Pluralism and the Rule of Custom in France.* Trans. Jane Marie Todd. Ithaca, N.Y.: Cornell University Press.

Asad, Talal. 2006. "Trying to Understand French Secularism." In *Political Theologies: Public Religions in a Post-Secular World,* ed. Henk de Vries and Lawrence E. Sullivan. New York: Fordham University Press.

Auslander, Leora. 2000. "Bavarian Crucifixes and French Headscarves: Religious Signs and the Postmodern European State." *Cultural Dynamics* 12(3): 283–309.

Bahloul, Joëlle. 1996. *The Architecture of Memory.* Cambridge: Cambridge University Press.

Balibar, Etienne, et al. 2003. *Antisémitisme: L'Intolérable chantage.* Paris: La Découverte.

Bat Ye'or. 2002. *Islam and Dhimmitude: Where Civilizations Collide.* Madison, N.J.: Fairleigh Dickinson University Press.

———. 2005. *Eurabia: The Euro-Arab Axis.* Madison, N.J.: Fairleigh Dickinson University Press.

Benbassa, Esther. 1999. *The Jews of France.* Trans. M. B. DeBevoise. Princeton, N.J.: Princeton University Press.

Beriss, David. 1990. "Scarves, Schools, and Segregation: The Foulard Affair." *French Politics and Society* 8: 1–13.

Bertrand, Louis. 1930 [1889]. *Le Sang des races. Le Cycle africain.* Paris: Albin Michel.

Borgé, Jacques, and Nicolas Viasnoff. 1995. *Archives de l'Algérie.* Milan: Editions Michèle Trinckvel.

Bouamama, Saïd, Hadjila Sad-Saoud, and Mokhtar Djerdoubi. 1994. *Contribution à la mémoire des banlieues.* Paris: Editions du Volga.

Boubeker, Ahmed, and Mogniss H. Abdallah. 1993. *Douce France: La Saga du mouvement Beur.* Paris: Im'media.

Boukhedenna, Sakinna. 1987. *Journal: "Nationalité: immigré(e)."* Paris: Editions l'Harmattan.

Bowen, John. 2005. "Commentary on Bunzl." *American Ethnologist* 32(4): 524–25.

———. 2006. *Why the French Hate Headscarves.* Princeton, N.J.: Princeton University Press.

———. 2009. *Can Islam Be French? Pluralism and Pragmatism in a Secularist State.* Princeton, N.J.: Princeton University Press.

Brenner, Emmanuel, ed. 2002. *Les Territoires perdus de la République: Antisémitisme, racisme, et sexisme au milieu scolaire.* Paris: Mille et Une Nuits.

Bullard, Alice. 2000. *Exile to Paradise: Savagery and Civilization in Paris and the South Pacific, 1790–1900.* Stanford, Calif.: Stanford University Press.

Bunzl, Matti. 2005. "Between Anti-Semitism and Islamophobia: Some Thoughts on the New Europe." *American Ethnologist.* 32(4): 499–508.

Cesari, Jocelyne. 1994. *Etre musulman en France.* Paris: Karthala.

Chaker, Salem. 1990. *Imazighen ass-a (Berbères dans le Maghreb contemporain).* Algiers: Editions Bouchene.

Charef, Mehdi. 1983. *Le Thé au harem d'Archi Ahmed.* Paris: Mercure de France.

Colonna, Fanny. 1975. *Instituteurs algériens, 1883–1939.* Paris: Presses de la Fondation Nationale des Sciences Politiques.

Cooper, Frederick, and Ann Laura Stoler. 1997. *Tensions of Empire: Colonial Cultures in a Bourgeois World.* Berkeley: University of California Press.

Daynes, Sarah. 1999. "Processus de conversion et modes d'identification à l'islam: l'exemple de la France et des Etats-Unis." *Social Compass* 46(3): 313–23.

de Neveu, Edouard. 1846. *Les Khouan: Ordres religieux chez les Musulmans d'Algérie.* Paris: Guyot.

de Tocqueville, Alexis. 1991 [1837–47]. *De la Colonie en Algérie.* Ed. Tzvetan Todorov. Brussels: Complexe.

Derderian, Richard. 2004. *North Africans in Contemporary France: Becoming Visible.* New York: Palgrave Macmillan.

Docteur X. 1891. *Simples réflexions d'un colon Algérien.* Paris: Hennequin.

Draï, Raphaël. 2001. *Sous le signe de Sion: L'antisémitisme nouveau est arrivé.* Paris: Michalon.

Duclos, Louis-Jean. 1972. "Berbers and the Rise of Moroccan Nationalism." In *Arabs and Berbers: From Tribe to Nation in North Africa,* ed. Ernest Gellner and Charles Micaud. Lexington, Mass.: Lexington Books.

Einaudi, Jean-Luc. 2001. *Octobre 1961: Un massacre à Paris.* Paris: Fayard.

Fanon, Frantz. 1963. *The Wretched of the Earth.* Trans. Constance Farrington. New York: Grove Weidenfeld.

Feldman, Allen. 1991. *Formations of Violence.* Chicago: University of Chicago Press.

Fernando, Mayanthi. 2005. "The Republic's 'Second Religion': Recognizing Islam in France." *Middle East Report* 35(2): 12–17.

Figueras, André. 1983. *La France aux Français*. Paris: Publications André Figueras.

Finkielkraut, Alain. 2003. *Au Nom de l'autre: Réflexions sur l'antisémitisme qui vient*. Paris: Gallimard.

Foucault, Michel. 1997. *Il faut défendre la société*. Paris: Gallimard.

Geisser, Vincent. 2003. *La Nouvelle Islamophobie*. Paris: La Découverte.

Gillette, Alain, and Abdelmalek Sayad. 1976. *L'Immigration Algérienne en France*. Paris: Editions Entente.

Guénif-Souilamas, Nacira, and Eric Macé. 2003. *Les Féministes et le garçon Arabe*. Paris: Editions l'Aube.

Guilhaume, Jean-François. 1992. *Les Mythes fondateurs de l'Algérie française*. Paris: Harmattan.

Hamelin, M. 1833. *Notice sur Alger*. Paris: Dentu.

Hammoudi, Abdellah. 1993. *The Victim and Its Masks*. Chicago: University of Chicago Press.

Hargreaves, Alec. 1995. *Immigration, "Race" and Ethnicity in Contemporary France*. London: Routledge.

Haroun, Ali. 1986. *Le Septième wilaya*. Paris: Seuil.

Hollender, Jean-Pierre. 1988. *2004, Tous Musulmans*. Montpellier, France: Collectif Français d'Ailleurs.

Hyman, Paula E. 1998. *The Jews of Modern France*. Berkeley: University of California Press.

Jazouli, Adil. 1992. *Les Années banlieues*. Paris: Seuil.

Kepel, Gilles. 1987. *Les Banlieues de l'Islam*. Paris: Seuil.

Killian, Caitlin. 2003. "The Other Side of the Veil: North African Women in France Respond to the Headscarf Affair." *Gender and Society* 17(4): 567–90.

Klug, Brian. 2003. "The Collective Jew: Israel and the New Anti-Semitism." *Patterns of Prejudice* 37(2).

Lacheraf, Mostefa. 1953. "*La Colline oubliée* ou les consciences anachroniques." *Le Jeune Musulman*. February 13.

Lakhdar, Mounia, Geneviève Vinsonneau, Michael Apter, and Etienne Mullet. 2007. "Conversion to Islam among French Adolescents and Adults: A Systematic Inventory of Motives." *International Journal for the Psychology of Religion* 17(1): 1–15.

Laoust, Emile. 1921. "Noms et cérémonies des feux de joie chez les Berbères du Haut de l'Anti-Atlas." *Hesperis* 1(1–3): 3–66, 253–316, 387–420.

Larcher, Emile. 1903. *Traité élémentaire de législation Algérienne*. Vol. 1. Paris: Rousseau.

Lévi-Strauss, Claude. 1962. *Le Totémisme aujourd'hui*. Paris: Presses Universitaires de France.

Liauzu, Claude. 1996. *Histoire des migrations en Méditerrané occidentale*. Brussels: Complexe.

Lorcin, Patricia M. E. 1995. *Imperial Identities. Stereotyping, Prejudice and Race in Colonial Algeria*. London: I. B. Tauris.

Lucas, Philippe, and Jean-Claude Vatin. 1975. *L'Algérie des anthropologues*. Paris: François Maspero.

MacMaster, Neil. 1997. *Colonial Migrants and Racism: Algerians in France, 1900–1962*. New York: St. Martin's Press.

Mamdani, Mahmood. 2004. *Good Muslim, Bad Muslim: America, the Cold War, and the Roots of Terror*. New York: Doubleday.

Mishani, Dror, and Aurelia Smotriez. 2005. "What Sort of Frenchmen Are They? Interview with Alain Finkielkraut." *Haaretz*. November 25.

Moruzzi, Norma. 1994. "A Problem with Headscarves: Contemporary Complexities of Political and Social Identity." *Political Theory* 22(4): 653–72.

Noiriel, Gérard. 1988. *Le Creuset français: Histoire de l'immigration XIXe–XXe siècle*. Paris: Seuil.

Peace, Timothy. 2009. "*Un antisémitisme nouveau?* The Debate about a 'New Antisemitism' in France." *Patterns of Prejudice* 43(2): 103–21.

Pujadas, David, and Ahmed Salam. 1995. *La Tentation du Jihad*. Paris: J. C. Lattès.

Raspail, Jean. 1973. *Le Camp des saints*. Paris: Robert Laffont.

Rinn, Louis. 1884. *Marabouts et Khouan. Étude sur l'Islam en Algérie*. Algiers: Jourdan.

Rosenblum, Mort. 1988. *Mission to Civilize: The French Way*. New York: Doubleday.

Servier, André. 1923. *L'Islam et la psychologie du Musulman*. Paris: Challamel.

Sahli, Mohammed C. 1953. La colline du reniement. *Le Jeune Musulman*. January 2.

Sayad, Abdelmalek. 2004. *The Suffering of the Immigrant*. Cambridge, U.K.: Polity.

Scott, Joan Wallach. 2007. *The Politics of the Veil*. Princeton, N.J.: Princeton University Press.

Shatz, Adam. 2005. "The Jewish Question." *New York Review of Books* 52(14).

Silverstein, Paul A. 2004a. "Headscarves and the French Tricolor." *Middle East Report Online*. http://www.merip.org/. January 29.

———. 2004b. *Algeria in France: Transpolitics, Race, and Nation*. Bloomington: Indiana University Press.

———. 2005. "Immigrant Racialization and the New Savage Slot: Race, Migration, and Immigration in the New Europe." *Annual Review of Anthropology* 34: 363–84.

———. 2007. "Islam, *Laïcité*, and Amazigh Activism in France and North Africa." In *North African Mosaic: A Cultural Reappraisal of Ethnic and Religious Minorities*, ed. Nabil Boudraa and Joseph Krause. Newcastle, U.K.: Cambridge Scholars Publishing.

———. 2008. "Thin Lines on the Pavement: The Racialization and Spatialization of Violence in Postcolonial (Sub)Urban France." In *Gendering Urban Space in the Middle East, South Asia, and Africa*, ed. Martina Rieker and Kamran Asdar Ali, 169–206. New York: Palgrave Macmillan.

Silverstein, Paul, and Chantal Tetreault. 2006. "Postcolonial Urban Apartheid." *Items and Issues* 5(4): 8–15.

Smith, Craig S. 2004. "Europe Fears Islamic Converts May Give Cover for Extremism." *New York Times*. July 19.

Sternhell, Zeev. 1986. *Neither Right nor Left: Fascist Ideology in France*. Princeton, N.J.: Princeton University Press.

Stolcke, Verena. 1995. "Europe: New Boundaries, New Rhetorics of Exclusion." *Current Anthropology* 36(1).

Stora, Benjamin. 1991. *La Gangrène et l'oubli: La mémoire de la guerre d'Algérie*. Paris: La Découverte.

———. 2006. "The Algerian War in French Memory: Vengeful Memory's Violence." In *Memory and Violence in the Middle East and North Africa*, ed. Ussama Makdisi and Paul A. Silverstein, 151–74. Bloomington: Indiana University Press.

Talha, Larbi. 1989. *Le Salariat immigré devant la crise*. Paris: Editions du CNRS.

Taguieff, Pierre-André. 2004. *Rising from the Muck: The New Anti-Semitism in Europe*. Trans. Patrick Camiller. Chicago: Ivan R. Dee.

Trigano, Shmuel. 2003. *La Démission de la République: Juifs et Musulmans en France*. Paris: Presses Universitaires de France.

Turner, Terence. 1995. Comment on Verena Stolcke, "Europe: New Boundaries, New Rhetorics of Exclusion." *Current Anthropology* 36(1).

van Vollenhoven, Joost. 1903. *Essai sur le fellah Algérien*. Paris: Rousseau.

Vidal, Dominique. 2003. *Le Mal-Etre juif: Entre repli, assimilation et manipulations*. Marseille: Agone.

Whitlock, Craig. 2006. "Trial of French Islamic Radical Sheds Light on Converts' Role." *Washington Post*. January 1.

Wieviorka, Michel. 2007. *The Lure of Anti-Semitism: Hatred of Jews in Present-Day France*. Trans. Kristin Couper Lobel and Anna Declerck. Leiden: Brill.

Wihtol de Wenden, Catherine. 1991. "North African Immigration and the French Political Imaginary." In *Race, Discourse and Power in France*, ed. Maxim Silverman. Brookfield, Vt.: Grower Publishing Co.

Zehraoui, Ahsène. 1994. *L'Immigration: de l'homme seul à la famille*. Paris: CIEMI/Harmattan.

7

German Converts to Islam and Their Ambivalent Relations with Immigrant Muslims

Esra Özyürek

"I would never have become a Muslim if I had met Muslims before I met Islam."

I heard these words over and over again during my yearlong ethnographic research among ethnic German converts to Islam in Berlin.[1] The first time, it was uttered by a self-declared German imam who had converted to Islam while trying to convert Arabs and Turks to Christianity. The second time, the speaker was a twenty-five-year-old former East German woman who came to Islam through her Bosnian boyfriend, whose family never accepted her. The third time, the comment was made by a fifty-year-old man who converted to Islam about thirty years ago after meeting Iranians who came to Europe to collect money and organize for the Iranian revolution. After that I stopped counting. Although all of the several dozen German converts I talked to (and the dozens of converts whose narratives I read on the internet) claim that they embraced Islam in a context of significant personal relationships with Muslims,[2] a substantial portion of German Muslims are quite discontented with born Muslims, especially those of immigrant backgrounds. This paper is an attempt to comprehend the paradoxical feelings of love and hate for Islam and Muslims that many German Muslims experience. My aim in exploring this issue is to understand what it takes to be a (supposed) Islamophile in a political and social context that is highly Islamophobic.

Embracing Islam in an Islamophobic Context

Islamophobia is rapidly increasing in Europe. In the post–Berlin Wall era, the exclusion of Muslims has become an essential element of European self-definition (Asad 2003: 164), and numerous political parties, including Jörg Haider's Freedom Party in Austria (Bunzl 2005), the Flemish Interest Party in Belgium, Le Pen's National Front Party in France, and the Swiss People's Party have successfully based their election campaigns on anti-immigrant and anti-Muslim positions. Ironically, as Islamophobia becomes more prevalent, more ethnic Europeans are embracing Islam. Today there are more converts in France, Britain (Köse 1996), Italy, Sweden (Roald 2004), Denmark (Jensen 2006), the Netherlands (Van Nieuwkerk 2004), and Germany (Wohlrab-Sahr 1999) than ever before. Muslim immigrants are consistently discriminated against in Germany, as they are in most European countries, and Islam itself is not generally respected. At an institutional level, despite the fact that Islam is one of the most actively practiced religions in Germany, regional German governments have resisted granting Islam the status of a state-recognized religion, a status that would allow Muslims to teach about Islam in public schools and make use of taxes imposed on mosques by state authorities (Fetzer and Soper 2005; Jonker 2000; Özyürek 2009).

Despite these unfavorable conditions, ethnic Germans are steadily embracing Islam by reciting the Islamic creed in the presence of at least two witnesses, declaring their belief that "there is no God but God and Muhammad is the messenger of God." Because this conversion process is so simple and requires no registration, there is no reliable figure regarding the number of new German Muslims. Estimates range from 20,000 to 100,000. Regardless of their exact numbers, new German Muslims carry great symbolic weight in German society. They play a central role in Muslim organizations nationwide and have become important mediators between Muslim communities and the majority society (Özyürek 2007).[3] Furthermore, they attract negative public attention disproportional to their numbers and are often suspected of being potential threats to the nation (Özyürek 2008).

There is a budding literature on converts to Islam in the Christian-majority societies of Europe (Van Nieuwkerk 2006; Wohlrab-Sahr 1999; Roald 2004; Mansson 2002) and North America (Hermansen 1999; Jackson 2005; Rouse 2004). Although informative about the kinds of processes individuals pass through when they convert, few of these studies (Roald 2004) emphasize the fact that these converts choose to embrace a minority religion in contexts where Islam and Muslims are feared, hated, discriminated against, marginalized, and forced to assimilate. Converting to any minority religion is a difficult process. Converts coming to the minority religion from the majority religion typically face exclusion from their earlier group affiliations, suspicion from both the majority and the minority group, and new kinds of discrimination of which they were previously unaware. But when ethnic Europeans, Germans in our case, convert to Islam, the stakes are even higher, because Islam is a persistently and negatively Othered religion. The discrimination to which converts are subject often comes as a surprise to them. One German Muslim woman who converted to Islam in her early twenties and donned the Islamic headscarf described how shocking this process has been for her: "I didn't expect so many negative reactions. Before people used to call me 'sunshine' because my hair is really blond. Especially men used to always compliment me for my hair. Now when people look at me they only see an oppressed woman. Maybe someone with dark skin knows better how to deal with this feeling. But I really didn't expect things to change so fast and so dramatically."[4]

Elsewhere I have argued that German converts to Islam are under extreme pressure because they are accused of being traitors to German society and are even perceived as potential terrorists (Özyürek 2008).[5] In their personal lives, German Muslims are constantly questioned, feared, and at times subjected to acts of violence. In this essay I discuss strategies some German Muslims have developed to defend their choice in this highly Islamophobic context. Although many German Muslims identify with born Muslims and many others spend a good portion of their time fighting to improve conditions for Muslims of immigrant backgrounds in Germany, many other (and sometimes the very same) new German Muslims try to distance themselves and Islam itself from born Muslims in Germany and the Middle East. They are eager to underline the fact that Muslims and Islam are two different things. Like non-converted, non-Muslim German intellectuals, many converts believe that immigrant Muslims need to be educated, integrated, and transformed. But for them, this transformation should happen not through leaving Islamic practices behind, as atheist left-wing Germans would suggest, nor through reforming Islam, as center-right-wing Christian Democrats would support, but, on the contrary, by making immigrant Muslims leave their Middle Eastern or African cultures and traditions behind and persuading them to apply fundamental Islamic teachings in their everyday lives. In other words, the German converts argue, it is Muslims who need to change, not Islam.

Muslim Tradition and Islamic Essence

Anne Sofie Roald (2006), an ethnic Swedish convert to Islam and a professor of religious studies at the University of Lund, argues that converts go through a three-stage developmental process of love, disappointment, and maturity. In the first stage converts become fascinated with everything born Muslims do, and they believe born Muslims are expressions of perfection. In the second stage of disappointment, they become disillusioned as they realize many Muslims do not live up to normative or ideal Islamic standards. Roald claims that many new Muslims leave the religion at this stage. Gradually, converts move to the stage of maturity, where they develop a healthy distance from other Muslims and integrate Islam into their own identity. At this stage, they come to the realization that they are Scandinavian (or German, or Italian, or French) individuals who live within an Islamic frame. It is likely that any convert to a new religion or even to a new political movement goes through such developmental stages. Yet in the Northern European, and particularly the German, case, there is more reason for converts to find themselves in the second stage and to stay there for an extended period. Before their conversion to Islam, German Muslims grow up in a society where Muslim practices are seen as inferior to German practices, even if converts have never concentrated on these depictions. Muslim culture is essentialized and coded as irrational, sexist, violent, and non-democratic. After they convert, German Muslims find themselves in a position to defend anything and everything Muslims do. Moreover, converts, especially women who don the headscarf, suddenly find themselves mistaken for, or treated as, marginalized Muslim immigrants. Differentiating between "religion" and "tradition" is important for newcomers to the religion and individuals who engage in Islamic reform. However, this discourse also allows German Muslims to distance themselves from born Muslims and their stigmatized practices, all the while remaining dedicated to Islam.

Because concerns about Islam in much of contemporary Western Europe and especially in Germany are focused mainly on immigrants, debates about domestic policy relating to Muslims often center on how to regulate and control immigrant behavior in matters of gender and sexuality. Hence German Muslims often find themselves in a position to confront common public perceptions about gender relations in Islam. New German Muslims must repeatedly discuss heavily criticized practices associated with Muslims, including forced marriage, honor killing, and domestic violence. They adopt a strategy of defining these practices as immigrant cultural traditions that are not properly Islamic.[6]

Scholars of ethnic European conversion to Islam point to different reasons why converts, especially women, might be choosing Islam. Sultan (1999) in Sweden, Van Nieuwkerk (2006) in the Netherlands, and Hofmann (1997) in Germany argue that women converts find Islam's well-defined gender roles and boundaries especially attractive. Hofmann (1997) argues that strict separation of gender roles and the celebration of motherhood have been central to German culture as well, but that recent public challenges to these concepts as a result of the women's liberation movement, as well as continuing expectations that women be dedicated mothers, are troubling for many German women. According to Van Nieuwkerk (2006), the primacy given to traditional female roles and their public celebration in Islam brings a sense of balance to converts. However, sometimes converts find what fascinated them about Islamic gender roles troubling after a while, especially when they become more familiar with how these roles are practiced in Muslim communities (Badran 2006).

My friend Aarika, a German convert to Islam, is very critical of what she sees as the lower status of women in many immigrant Muslim families. She takes it upon herself to defend Islam by telling everyone that practices that lower the status of women are merely Middle Eastern and if immigrants had studied their Islam properly, they would know better; Muslim women have all the rights German women enjoy and more. When I met her, Aarika was an independent, successful, attractive woman in her forties. The fact that in her twenties she used to be a fashion model in East Berlin did not surprise me at all. Currently she is the manager of the Berlin branch of an expensive Italian fashion store. After having grown up in a typically atheist East German family, she learned about Islam a few years ago during a trip to Egypt. She also met her current husband, Hasan, on that trip; he was working as a DJ in the hotel where Aarika was staying. Even though Hasan does not practice Islam, knowing him and other people in Egypt was an opportunity for Aarika to learn about Islam. She told me that what surprised her the most about Egyptians was how giving and content they were, even though they had so little compared to her. After reading about Islam for a year or so on her own, she slowly adopted Islamic practices such as not eating pork, not drinking alcohol, fasting, and praying. Eventually she converted in a little mosque in Berlin. Her husband learned about Aarika's conversion when she wanted to have an Islamic marriage with him, and he was quite shocked. Because Aarika does not want to lose her well-paying position, she continues to live in Berlin and visits her husband four times a year in Egypt. When she does, she rents an apartment for them to stay in since her husband shares a room with several other co-workers in the hotel where he is employed. Her husband, she told me, is not interested in coming to Berlin. He asks what kind of a man he would be, unable to speak the language or find a job. Aarika defends her independent position as perfectly Islamic and the oppressed position of many Muslim women as merely a reflection of their local traditions.

One evening, when I was invited to dinner by Aarika and her mother in the house they share in Potsdam, a town just outside Berlin in the former East

Germany, I witnessed one of the frequent exchanges they have about Muslims. Aarika's mother is supportive of her new religion as long as she does not cover her hair. Like many other former East Germans, or Ossies, she cannot stand Muslim immigrants, especially Turks. When she learned that I am from Turkey, Aarika's mother started to tell me story after story about how rude Turks are. She complained that Turkish women always walk behind their husbands, never talk to Germans even when they ask for directions or the time, have too many children, and push you out of the way with their elbows in the subway or in a store. When I turned to Aarika for help in the difficult position I found myself in as a guest, I was surprised to see my friend nodding enthusiastically and not taking a step to defend the Turkish people. Then she said to me, "I always tell her that these are the traditions, and if these people were to educate themselves better as Muslims, they would know that they shouldn't behave like that. If, for example, they had read the traditions of the Prophet Muhammad, they would know that it is their duty to smile at everyone, even when they do not know the people, and that they should be nice to them." Like many other Muslim converts, or born Muslims who are part of Islamic reform movements, Aarika believes that many Muslim practices have little to do with Islam, but are products of local cultures.

Distancing from Immigrant Muslims

Almost all new German Muslims I talked to or read about had met Islam through a meaningful relationship with a born Muslim.[7] Immigrant Muslim lovers, spouses, neighbors, best friends in Germany, and romantic or friendly relationships established with born Muslims during travel to Muslim-majority holiday destinations have been crucial in transforming lives. In many cases, it is difficult to know whether these personal connections with born Muslims came out of or followed the earlier fascination of the pre-conversion German with Islam and Muslim culture. Nevertheless, most converts had significant born-Muslim individuals in their lives.

Monika Wohlrab-Sahr (1999) argues that for some German Muslims conversion becomes a means to immerse themselves in new and alien cultures. Such affiliations with Otherness might be the case for some new Muslims, especially in the earlier phases of conversion. In my experience, however, I found that many ethnic German Muslims are keen to differentiate themselves from Muslims of immigrant background and to establish their identity as German Muslims. It is likely that German Muslim identity became an option only after the ethnic German Muslim community reached a critical mass, which might not have been the case when Wohlrab-Sahr conducted her research in the early 1990s.[8]

One determining factor in a convert's decision to affiliate or disaffiliate with immigrant Muslims is location of residence. Although many German Muslims choose to live in immigrant Muslim neighborhood, especially if they are married to an immigrant Muslim, others make a clear decision to live outside these neighborhoods. Berlin houses a large number of immigrant residents, at least 200,000 of them from Muslim-majority countries, and is a very ethnically segregated city. Areas such as Neukölln, Wedding, and Kreuzberg are dominated by residents of Muslim backgrounds. Other parts of the city, especially those located on what used to be the east side of the Berlin Wall, like Pankow, did not receive "guest workers" from Turkey in the 1970s and are still occupied mainly by ethnic Germans.[9] Both for historical reasons and because many of these areas are strongholds of neo-Nazi groups, few immigrant Muslims choose to live in these neighborhoods. Because I traveled widely throughout the city, the nature of segregation did not become clear to me until I had lunch one day in the chic, newly restored Mitte, in what was formerly East Berlin. This area is now inhabited by upwardly mobile, hip, thirty-something ethnic Germans, most of whom came to the city after the fall of the Wall. As I was enjoying my lunch on a summer day on Kastanienalle, I heard some customers giggling. When I looked at what they were laughing at, I saw two young women quietly walking down the street with colorful, stylishly wrapped headscarves and long skirts. Soon most customers in the restaurant stopped their lunch to look at them. Some kept laughing and talking about them even after they had passed by. At that moment I realized that, although such women are a common sight in many neighborhoods in Berlin, they are very unlikely in the eastern neighborhoods. In fact, most Berliners do not often travel to other neighborhoods and like to do most of their shopping and dining in their own parts of the city.[10]

As a former resident of East Germany, my German Muslim friend Ada continued living in Pankow after she converted. Pankow is one of the least immigrant-friendly neighborhoods, with established "no entry" zones declared and controlled by neo-Nazis. It is not uncommon for darker-skinned people to be beaten up and harassed in these areas. Ada told me that she chose this neighborhood because it is quiet, safe, clean, and has big green parks where she can take her four-year-old son. When she moved into her current apartment building as a single mother, she was already a Muslim but was not wearing a headscarf. She found her neighbors quite nice and polite, keeping a friendly distance. After she began wearing a headscarf, which she wrapped tightly around her head, Ada's neighbors became very unfriendly to her. During a Muslim feast, she participated in a project organized by Inssan, a small Muslim organization that aims at improving dialogue between Muslims and non-Muslims. She baked cookies and attached them to each neighbor's door with a note saying, "Your Muslim neighbor greets you for the Muslim Sacrifice Feast." The idea behind the gesture was that this would be a good opportunity for Muslims to meet their non-Muslim neighbors and teach them about their practices. In her apartment building not a single neighbor said a word to Ada, although they took the sign and cookies from their door.

The worst incident that happened to Ada in her neighborhood was the morning she woke up to find that her car had been torched. The police never found the criminals. Ada herself did not conclude that this might have happened because of her lifestyle. When I asked her more questions about the incident, however, she told me that all the other cars on the street were untouched and she had never seen such a thing in her neighborhood before. When I told her what I suspected, given the high rate of neo-Nazi hate crimes in the neighborhood, she looked a little surprised but said it was possible.

After Ada complained to me so much about Pankow and her neighbors, I asked her why she does not move to another neighborhood, such as Neukölln or Kreuzberg, where it would be quite acceptable, even ordinary, to wear a headscarf. She looked at me with a flash of astonishment in her eyes, since I myself was living in the chic former East Berlin neighborhood of Mitte, and said, "Oh, I cannot live in Neukölln. That is such a dirty neighborhood! Besides, I do not want my son to grow up among immigrants."

Needless to say, Ada has very real concerns. Neukölln is an immigrant ghetto occupied mainly by Turks and Arabs. It is the poorest neighborhood in Berlin, with the lowest employment rate, highest crime, and highest school dropout rate. Even for the students who stay in school, education is so bad that the mayor of Berlin recently said, "I would never send my own children to a school in Neukölln," a statement that caused a political scandal. Some Germans, who like the lively multicultural life of such neighborhoods, and others, who cannot afford to live elsewhere, will reside in such places. But when their children reach school age they move to another neighborhood, causing the schools in these areas to be segregated. Actually, as soon as they can afford it, some immigrant families also move out of these neighborhoods in order to send their children to schools with German children, where they can have a better education and keep themselves out of trouble. For Ada, it is important not to identify and mix with immigrant Muslims, especially poor and marginalized ones. She hopes to be an educated, upwardly mobile Muslim, even though she finds it difficult to attain this status as a single mother.

Some ethnic Germans, especially those who have born-Muslim spouses, choose to live in immigrant-majority, low-income neighborhoods. Some feel at home in these neighborhoods, while others do not enjoy the experience. Miles, who converted to Shi'i Islam thirty years ago when he was nineteen, was one such example. He and his Turkish-German wife moved to Neukölln. When I met him, his wife had taken him to divorce court and was suing for custody of their only child. No doubt this turn of events contributed to his bitterness toward immigrant Muslims living in the area. He told me about his experience in the neighborhood in the following words: "At first I thought Turkish parents educate their children in Islamic way. But after living here, I wonder which trash can they come out of. They are dirty, ugly, and disgusting. I told this to my wife, but she wanted a big flat so we moved to Neukölln. I asked her, Look, who is urinating on our door? Not the German junkies but Turks. Recently a young girl was burned in a park. *Jahiliyya* [pre-Islamic ignorance] is the biggest enemy of Muslims living here. They only care about their own bellies." Like other converts, Miles saw Muslim ignorance of their own religion as the main cause of their current marginalization in society.

Sufi-oriented German Muslims spend the most time socializing with other German Muslims and keeping their distance from immigrant Muslims. One Muslim community I met during my research that made the most explicit effort to distinguish itself from immigrant Muslim communities in Berlin is the Weimar community in Potsdam. This community is a branch of the Murabitun, first established in Morocco in the late 1960s, which then spread to Christian-majority countries such as the United Kingdom, the United States, Spain, Denmark, Germany, and South Africa, as well as South America. The group lives communally and emphasizes a social welfare system, including collection and redistribution of the Islamic tax, *zakat.* By choosing to locate in Potsdam, a charming, practically immigrant-free tourist town housing Prussian palaces, the community was also deciding to isolate itself from immigrant Muslims. I participated in several of their meetings in their beautiful gathering house on Sunday mornings. These events were advertised in the German-only newspaper published by the group, *Islamische Zeitung,* inviting people to meet German Muslims. I noticed that the only foreigners were from Spain, the United Kingdom, and the United States, where there are branches of the community. Intermarriage among these branches is common. I also met one Turkish woman and one half-German, half-Egyptian woman born and raised in Germany and married to a German man. They both attended weekly meetings but were outsiders, not initiated members of the Sufi community.

The group organizes quarterly art fairs, partly as a means to proselytize. At first sight, members of the group look like hippies. The women wear long, loose, colorful skirts and colorful headscarves wrapped in a way that leaves their ears and necks exposed, quite unlike immigrant Muslim women in Germany. At the fairs, the group also has a stand decorated by batik clothes. They play Indian music. For non-Muslim Germans who carry a stereotype of how Muslims look, these Muslims probably appear more like members of an Indian-inspired religious group than like Muslims from the Middle East. Group members I talked to told me that because they are Germans, it is much easier for them to reach out to non-Muslim Germans and tell them about Islam. They also added that because there are no immigrant Muslims in Potsdam, there are no negative stereotypes about Islam either.

When I spoke to one of the leaders of the Potsdam group, it became clear to me that the group finds it quite important to differentiate itself from immigrant Muslims. While describing the effectiveness of the quarterly market they organized, a member told me how they try to teach people about true Islam at the fair. "For example," he said, "we do not charge artists for the stalls." He added, "because Prophet Muhammad said the giving hand is always stronger than the receiving hand. We should learn to practice this as Muslims." "So," he continued, "we are not like those immigrant Muslims here who constantly say, 'Give me, give me, give me,' always begging from the state without contributing anything to this society." I was astounded that an openly anti-capitalist Muslim would have such a negative view of his religious brothers. I responded by saying, "But these are the poorest and most marginalized people in society. What can they be giving?" He answered me by saying, "Well, if they do not have money, they can at least give you a smile, and they will not even do that." To my initial surprise, this Maribitun Muslim's views on immigrant Muslims were not much different from those of my friend Aarika's mother, who also lived in Potsdam. Later I would see that such negative views of immigrant Muslims are not universal but are also not uncommon among German Muslims.

Many German convert women I met were more concerned about not looking like, or being taken for, Turkish women than about living in the same neighborhood with them. Some time after converting to Islam, a great number of women develop the desire and the inner strength to wear a headscarf. I was told over and over that when they did so, they were most afraid of, and annoyed by, being mistaken for a Turkish woman. So, many came up with solutions that would prevent them from looking Turkish. One easy solution is to adopt the head-covering style of Arab women, who are much higher in the ethnic hierarchy in Berlin because of the different conditions in which Turks and Arabs came to Germany. Whereas the majority of Turkish immigrants came as untrained guest workers in the 1960s, many Arabs from more privileged backgrounds come to Germany for university education. Turkish women in Turkey and in Berlin wear their headscarves with a little plastic frame hidden in the front part of the headscarf, which holds it up almost like a baseball cap. Although this has been quite a fashion statement in Turkey in the last two decades or so, I found that this style is quite unacceptable for converts to Islam in Germany. Most new German Muslims preferred the Arab style of wearing a bonnet inside and a headscarf outside which reveals the inner bonnet. I noticed that young Turkish women who socialize in German-speaking Islamic settings also adopt this style rather than that of their mothers. Needless to say, this subtle difference was not discernible to the uneducated eyes of the non-Muslim Germans but was more of a code to be read by stylish young Muslim women.

One style of head covering that is desirable to many Germans is the African style, where the scarf is wrapped around the head leaving the neck and sometimes part of the ears exposed. The women of the Maribitun group, as I have already mentioned, cover their hair in this way. For my friend Ulrike, changing from the Arab style of head covering to the African style was what made her conversion to Islam acceptable to her parents. Ulrike converted to Islam at age seventeen after she met the Moroccan-born man who would become her husband, but it took her ten years to adopt the headscarf. She told me how she embraced the African style through conflict with her parents. "After I started wearing the hijab, I went to my parents' house. I had told this to my mother, but my father didn't know. He said, 'What is this?' in outrage. 'You look like a Turkish woman.' And I said in despair, 'No, I don't look like a Turkish woman, this is the Arabic style!' We argued for weeks. He even accused me of belonging to Al-Qaeda. A few weeks later I went to my parents' home again for my dad's birthday, with my hijab of course. He said to his friends, 'This lady sitting on the sofa is my daughter, although she doesn't look like it. She looks more like a Turk than a German.' Later my aunt walked up to me and said, 'Ulrike, did you forget to unwrap this thing from your head?' It was not a pleasant party. A few months later it was my birthday. I was crying in my room at my parents'. My mom came in and said, 'Guests are here and I do not want another argument. Do you really have to wear this thing?' At that moment I felt a little weak and I told her that I will do it like a turban and my mom said this is great! When my father saw me he had a big smile on his face and said, 'This is much better.' And I decided to do it like that from then on. So now, they have gotten used to it and it is not a problem any more." Now Ulrike wears her headscarf like an African wrap, with another scarf around her neck, since the African style does not hide her neck. She says she also feels comfortable this way; no one recognizes her as Muslim with this style. She enjoys sitting in upscale, all-German cafés, and she even goes to the lakes during summer and swims with her entire outfit on and no one mistakes her for a Turk or treats her like a traitor who converted to Islam.

It is much easier to be a male convert to Islam in Germany today—at least for now. Unless they wear the Arab-style long white dress and the prayer cap, no one can recognize male converts as Muslims. These clothes are not considered religiously necessary for new converts but more as festive mosque apparel. Nevertheless, when they out themselves as Muslims, converted men also have to defend their position as Muslims, and they also are frustrated with immigrant Muslims, who they believe give Islam a bad name.

Amir is the son of a Lebanese father and a German mother. He was raised by his Christian mother as a non-Muslim and converted to Islam several years ago. He is now married to a Polish convert to Islam. When I met them several months ago, Amir and his wife were volunteers at a mosque in Berlin run by the Turkish government, giving information about Islam to German-speaking visitors. As we sat down on the lush green carpets and started talking about the situation of Islam in Germany, the conversation came around to the issue of reform in Islam. When he heard the word "reform," Amir straightened his posture, made his voice louder, and told me firmly, "We do not need reform in Islam. What we need is a reform of Muslims. It is really shameful that these Turks have been here for more than forty years and so many of them cannot speak German. If they were good Muslims, they certainly would have read the Prophet Muhammad's traditions that say, 'If you travel in a foreign country for more than fifteen days, make sure to learn its language so you can communicate with the people there.' So if these people were better Muslims, they would have mastered German and be better integrated in society."

In the Islamophobic environment of Germany, German Muslims face the challenge of simultaneously defending Islam and differentiating themselves from immigrant Muslims, who have lower income and education levels, and are marginalized and much hated by the rest of the society. It is in this context that they sometimes feel more empowered than non-Muslim Germans to criticize immigrant Muslims for the way they practice Islam or participate in German life. Miles, who suffered from living in the low-income immigrant neighborhood, also accused immigrant Muslims of giving Islam a bad name and inhibiting Islam's spread in Germany. He told me that, before immigrant

Muslims came to Germany, Islam used to have a very good reputation. But now, he thinks, because Turks cut themselves off from society, do not practice Islam, and are simply not good citizens, people hate Islam, even though it would benefit them so much if they converted too. He said to me: "Turks do not learn German because they do not want to be part of this society. I always tell them, 'I am telling this to you as a Muslim. You should learn German.' There is a Turkish Shi'i mosque here, but everything is in Turkish. Leaders there tell me that lack of integration is their fault and they should do at least half of the sermons in German, but in the end they never do. And Islam never becomes accessible to Germans."

Relating to Muslims in Muslim-Majority Societies

Parallel to their ambivalent and sometimes surprisingly antagonistic relationship with immigrant Muslims, many converts to Islam have an undecided relationship with the indigenous Muslims living in Muslim-majority lands. Some of them idealize these populations and strongly desire to live in their countries, while others feel very content about living in Germany and believe they can experience Islam better where they are.

Regardless of whether they want to live in Germany or in the Middle East, most converts I met agree that Turks and Arabs living in Turkey and the Arab countries are much nicer—and simply better people—than the ones living in Germany. Often, I heard how especially Turks in Germany have lost their Islamic traditions and even their humanity. In after-lecture tea gatherings in the mosques, both immigrant and converted Muslims compared their impressions from visits to Muslim-majority countries, be it visits to an ancestral homeland, a spouse's homeland, to Saudi Arabia for pilgrimage, or tourist travel to North Africa or the Middle East. Even though converted German women would occasionally have complaints about local men harassing them or people not practicing Islam properly, they would often conclude that Middle Eastern and North African Muslims who have not migrated out of their homeland are better than those who have. This kind of evaluation is common among non-Muslim Germans as well, even if the criteria of evaluation are different. My being an educated, successfully employed Turk who grew up in Turkey would prompt well-traveled Germans to share their observation that, in Istanbul, Ankara, and Izmir, there are many smart, skilled, and sophisticated people, unlike the Turks in Germany. "There they are not all like the Anatolian peasants," they would say, "who came here for work." Several times I was bluntly told, "Here we got the bad Turks, not the good ones like you." Whereas non-Muslim Germans would often admire Turkish artists, intellectuals, and businessmen for their Western outlook and their social competency in Western bourgeois ways, converted Germans would admire the non-diasporic Muslims for their commitment to Islam, generosity, and hospitality.

A counter version of this idealized vision of Muslims in the Middle East exists simultaneously. Sometimes, people would go back and forth between two images. The same individuals who praised Middle Easterners would later criticize them for not practicing Islam correctly or for having been spoiled by Western influences. My friend Ada, the East German with the little boy and charred car, shared how this perspective affects the lives of converts. She said, "German sisters often want to leave Germany for their husbands' countries. I am not sure if this is such a good idea. Of course, there you can hear the call to prayer, go around in your hijab comfortably, and everything. But now Western civilization is everywhere. You can even buy alcohol in Saudi Arabia. I have a friend who recently moved to Jidda with her husband. She says Jidda is too westernized; you can even buy alcohol there. Now they will move to Mecca." Ada wanted to live in Canada or the U.S. Like many other Germans I met, converted or not, she never liked Germany or the German language. She had lived in the U.S. for one year as an exchange student and then in Canada for a year with her Bosnian boyfriend. She liked the easygoing lifestyle in both places, but she preferred Canada for its social rights. She observed that it would be very easy to live as a practicing Muslim in both countries, and she would be able to eat at Taco Bell and Cinnabon, her favorite restaurants.

Other converts had no fantasies about living in Muslim lands. Verena, who converted at seventeen after she visited a mosque during an open house with a friend, said to me, "I am proud to be a German. I love this country. I am proud that it has such a great economy and everyone wants to immigrate here. I want to live here as a Muslim." When I asked her if she ever longs to live in a Muslim-majority country, she answered with a big smile on her face: "I of course would love to live in a Muslim-majority country, but I want it to be Germany!"

Another strong tendency I observed was that of new German Muslims desiring to help and transform Muslim societies, either by alleviating their material suffering or by making them better Muslims—and sometimes both at the same time. For example, Irma, a twenty-five-year-old convert to Islam, expressed a wish to go to Africa and fight against female genital cutting among Muslims there. Irma was interested in foreign cultures and also in human suffering long before she encountered Islam through a Tunisian asylum seeker she met while she was a high school student. She decided to embrace Islam and marry her Tunisian friend, as she saw how devastating life could be when she lived in a small economically depressed Moldovan town. She told me that once she graduates from college she would like to help Muslims around the world. If she cannot go to Africa, she told me, she would like to go to Afghanistan and help women who are suffering under the Taliban and have to wear burkas. Other converted women I met also expressed a desire to help orphans in Palestine or women traders in Muslim Africa, or to work as doctors serving women in Afghanistan. They find themselves in the best position to determine what non-Islamic traditions are being used to exploit women in the name of Islam. Also, as Western women, they believe they are better equipped to eliminate practices that give Islam a bad name.

Desiring Born Muslims

Unless they are followers of a Sufi tradition, most converts to mainstream Islam want to marry born Muslims. Many, although not all, converts meet Islam in the first place through romantic relationships with a born Muslim who is either an immigrant in Europe or a local in a popular tourist destination abroad. A good number of these relationships fall apart after the German partner converts to Islam and is disappointed to find that the born-Muslim partner is not willing to reorganize his life around Islamic principles. There are also cases where born Muslims are inspired by a converted lover or partner and find Islam for themselves. These are the relationships that survive. Despite their original disappointment, survivors of the failed relationships still desire born Muslims as spouses. It is somewhat easier for converted women to find a born-Muslim husband, since there are many immigrant Muslim men without papers who urgently need to make their residence legal by marrying a German citizen. Even when they have papers, it is simply more acceptable for immigrant Muslim men to be romantically involved with German women. Converted German men, on the other hand, have an extremely difficult time finding born-Muslim wives, since most devout born-Muslim women in Germany have close ties with their families, who are less willing to accept German men, regardless of their religion.

My friend Ada blamed her boyfriend's family for the failure of their relationship. The boyfriend was the only son in the family. Because Ada was much older than he, she did not fit the ideal picture his mother had for a daughter in-law. Ada told me she did everything for the family, much more than any Bosnian bride would do. She cleaned the house, served them food, wore conservative clothes, and converted to Islam. Even after she converted, the mother of the boyfriend said, "Well, she is still German, isn't she?" Eventually, Ada realized she would not be able to persuade the boyfriend to be with her despite his mother and broke up with him. Later she married an Arab immigrant. The marriage did not last long, and it was not a good experience for Ada. When I met her, she was actively looking for a husband, but she was quite pessimistic about her prospects.

She explained to me that "all Turks and Arabs will be nice to you when they learn that you are a convert. They will say, 'mashallah, how wonderful.' But they never want you to marry their sons. They do not want you in their family." She continued, "Don't get me wrong. Of course people want to marry me. I am not ugly or stupid. But most men who propose to me need papers [to stay in Germany]. And I definitely do not want to marry someone without papers again." She realizes that such men are readily available. Because they travel to Germany alone, their families are not there to arrange their marriages. Also, they are highly motivated to marry German citizens in order to continue the new lives they establish for themselves. Ada has learned to be cautious about such people. She said, "Maybe some of them are good brothers, but I have seen the worst. Many brothers from Morocco and Tunisia marry German sisters here who know nothing about wedding contracts. Sisters do not ask for anything at the beginning. They do not even want a big wedding. And after the marriage, their husbands treat them terribly, and in the end, when they get the papers, these so-called Muslim husbands just go ahead and divorce them. I know this very well because that is what happened to me last year. Believe me, many of these marriages are terrible."

Despite her experience, Ada still wants to marry a born Muslim. When I asked her if she would consider marrying a German Muslim man, she said, "I had offers from German Muslims as well. But they were too old. I cannot marry someone without love. Besides, German men want to marry Arab or Turkish women. They think that they will know Islam better. Men think she will give them a big Muslim family. If she is Arab, she will teach him Arabic. If you marry a convert, she doesn't know Arabic herself. These German men just want to be integrated. Otherwise, it feels like you are marrying someone who lacks something." Then she challenged what she had just said, adding, "But of course those Muslims who grow up with it know much less about Islam."

One day Ada and I were sitting in a small mosque in Berlin, listening to a long and rather uninspired German-language lecture about how to prepare a dead body for burial. After a while I noticed that Ada kept glancing at the section where men sit and then lowered her eyes, blushing. When I turned to see what she was looking at, I noticed an olive-skinned, black-haired man with a white Saudi jalabiyya. He was strategically located in one of the few spots where men can see women through the screen separating the men's and women's sections of the mosque. He was staring in our direction. After the lecture, Ada asked the mosque's imam about the man. About ten minutes later, the imam appeared on the women's side with a written note from the man. After reading the note, Ada looked very disappointed. I asked her what had happened, and she told me the note was full of grammar mistakes, indicating that the man was lacking education and was probably a lower-class, recently arrived immigrant. Ada decided not to contact him. When I asked her what about him had originally captured her attention, she said, "Well, he was dressed in this fundamentally Islamic way. I was impressed by that." Then she sarcastically added, "But of course if you fear God, you shouldn't be checking out women across the room and giving them sexy looks in the first place."

Despite her search for a born-Muslim man, Ada turned this article's title, "I would never have become a Muslim if I had met Muslims before I met Islam," around and said, "I sometimes wish I knew about Islam before I knew Muslims." If this had been true, she thinks, it would be easier now for her to feel more comfortable in her faith.

In *Multiculturalism and the Jews,* Sander Gilman (2006) observes that "the line between 'anti-' and 'philo-Semitic' attitudes towards the Jews is always blurred" (2006: 226), and these sentiments are often mirror images of each other. For example, he claims, philo-Semites will compliment Jews for their intelligence, but anti-Semites will use the same stereotype to argue that Jews are cunning. Gilman argues that both positions are "just as laden with the desire to provide a form of control over the image of that construct category of the 'Jews'" (2006: 228). One can expand this discussion to the relationship between phobic and philic sentiments attributed to any feared or marginalized group and certainly to attitudes toward Muslims in Europe.

The case of German Muslims takes Gilman's discussion one step further, demonstrating that dislike and affection for a minority population can be merged in the viewpoints of a single group of people. I suggest that this complex emerges often after ethnic Germans convert to Islam only to realize that they must face unexpectedly high levels of stigma because they are associated with the country's much-hated and feared born Muslims. Scholars such as Olivier Roy (2004) and Wohlrab-Sahr (1999) argue that it is often ethnic

Europeans who already feel marginalized by society who turn to Islam as a way of rebelling against the society they live in. Roy calls these people "protest converts" (2004: 317), and Wohlrab-Sahr describes their choice as "symbolic battle." During my research, contrary to this argument, I found that a good portion of new German Muslims, although certainly not all, come from solidly middle-class families and are well educated.[11] It seems that many had little reason to protest. Moreover, most converts I met had no political aims but concentrated instead on their spiritual progress along the new path they had taken.

Hence, I would argue that only after they convert to Islam do ethnic European Muslims find themselves in a marginal position, one they never could have imagined for themselves before. Even if they could have imagined it intellectually, many found it very difficult to face in a real, day-to-day existence. As the German Muslim woman I quoted at the beginning of this piece told me, many new Muslims, especially women, felt very uncomfortable when they realized that they were being treated as stigmatized immigrants, especially once they had put on the Islamic headscarf. They pointed out to me that suddenly they were treated as individuals who do not have sufficient mental or linguistic capabilities, and who are simply oppressed women.

Being an ethnic German convert to Islam is not an easy way of being in contemporary Germany. Because of the significantly lower status of Muslim immigrants in a highly xenophobic country, and the new role attributed to Islam in the civilizational discourse of a post–Cold War, post-9/11 world, converts to Islam have an ambivalent relationship to immigrant Muslims and to "Islamic practices" as they are defined and redefined in relation to immigrants. Although Islam is almost always introduced to ethnic Germans through intimate personal connections with born Muslims and brings a greater number of born Muslims into the converts' lives, some German converts feel the need to disassociate themselves from born Muslims in the name of idealizing Islam. They assured me that Germans were more likely to listen to them and open their hearts to Islam because, unlike Turks or Arabs, they looked German and did not have an accent. Yet, in the increasingly racialized conceptualization of Islam that now prevails in contemporary Germany and in Europe generally, the space that is left for people who want to be both German and Muslim is very small. The borders they cross are less porous, and they are seen as dangerous in the new Europe. While practicing and acting on their Islamophilia, some German Muslims draw heavily on the Islamophobic discourses of German society, both to defend their difficult position and, ironically, to leave Islam untainted by a rising cultural racism.

Notes

1. Roald (2004, 264) refers to a similar statement frequently made by new Muslims in Sweden.

2. Other research with converts in Sweden (Roald 2004) and Britain (Köse 1996) has found that an overwhelming majority of Europeans convert to Islam through personal contact with born Muslims. Roald (2004) argues that because Islam is perceived so negatively in Sweden, a close Muslim contact often is necessary for Swedes to give Islam serious thought. In that sense, she argues, contact with Muslims is not the cause of conversion but a necessary first condition.

3. Roald (2004) argues that Muslim converts play an important bridge role in Scandinavian countries as well. This, however, is not the case in the United Kingdom, where immigrant Muslims are less segregated in society and are fluent in English.

4. In her book *Becoming Muslim* Anna Mansson (2002) also talks about how women converts to Islam in the United States and Sweden were shocked by, and found themselves unprepared for, the intensity of negative reactions they faced after converting to Islam.

5. Roald (2004) argues that in Sweden women converts, not men, are accused of being traitors to society. Van Nieuwkerk (2004) makes the same observation about Dutch women converts. The shift of focus from men to women in conceptualizing the Islamic threat in Europe, I believe, is a recent phenomenon.

6. How these practices came to be defined as essentially Islamic at the turn of the millennium is the topic of another paper.

7. As the German Muslim community grows, more Germans embrace Islam with German Muslims as intermediaries. Although they may exist, I never met a new Muslim who embraced Islam without any Muslim intermediaries.

8. Roald (2006) emphasizes the importance of the growth of the Swedish Muslim population in identifying Swedish converts as Swedish and Muslim.

9. After World War II, East Germany received immigrants from other socialist countries such as Vietnam and Angola. Yet they are fewer in number than Turks.

10. Jeff Jurgens (2005) notes that Berliners rarely travel outside their neighborhoods. He describes how members of the Turkish-German soccer team he was a playing with became uncomfortable when they had to travel to other parts of the city and country for tournaments.

11. Van Nieuwkerk (2004) makes the same observation for women Dutch converts to Islam.

Works Cited

Asad, Talal. 2003. *Formations of the Secular: Christianity, Islam, Modernity.* Stanford, Calif.: Stanford University Press.

Badran, Margot. 2006. "Feminism and Conversion: Comparing British, Dutch, and South African Life Stories." In *Women Embracing Islam: Gender and Conversion in the West,* ed. Karin van Nieuwkerk. Austin: University of Texas Press.

Bunzl, Matti. 2005. "Between Anti-Semitism and Islamophobia: Some Thoughts on the New Europe." *American Ethnologist* 32(4): 499–508.

Fetzer, Joel S., and J. Christoper Soper. 2005. *Muslims and the State in Britain, France, and Germany.* Cambridge: Cambridge University Press.

Gilman, Sander. 2006. *Multiculturalism and the Jews.* London: Routledge.

Hermansen, Marcia K. 1999. "Conversion Narratives of European and Euro-American Muslims." *Muslim World* 89: 56–89.

Hofmann, G. 1997. *Muslimin werden. Frauen in Deutschland konvertieren zum Islam.* Frankfurt: Universitat Frankfurt.

Jackson, Sherman A. 2005. *Islam and the Blackamerican: Looking Toward the Third Resurrection.* Oxford: Oxford University Press.

Jensen, Tina Gudrun. 2006. "Religious Authority and Autonomy Intertwined: The Case of Converts to Islam in Denmark." *Muslim World* 96: 643–60.

Jonker, Gerdien. 2000. "What Is Other about Other Religions? The Islamic Communities in Berlin between Integration and Segregation." *Cultural Dynamics* 12(3): 311–29.

Jurgens, Jeffrey. 2005. *Plotting Immigration: Diasporic Identity Formation among Immigrants from Turkey in Berlin.* Ph.D. diss., University of Michigan.

Köse, Ali. 1996. *Conversion to Islam: A Study of Native British Converts.* London: Kegan Paul International.

Lamb, Christopher, and M. Darrol Byrant, eds. 1999. *Religious Conversion: Contemporary Practices and Controversies.* London and New York: Cassell.

Mansson, Anna. 2002. *Becoming Muslim: Meanings of Conversion to Islam.* Lund, Sweden: Akademisk Avhandling.

Özyürek, Esra. 2007. "German Converts to Islam Are an Asset, not a Threat." September 13, 2007. *Spiegel Online.* http://www.spiegel.de/international/germany/0,1518,505586,00.html.

———. 2008. "German Muslims and Turkish Christians: Cultural Racism, Fears of Religious Conversion, and National Security in the New Europe." Unpublished manuscript.

———. 2009. "Beyond Integration and Recognition: Diasporic Constructions of Alevi Muslim Identity between Germany and Turkey." In *Transnational Transcendence,* ed. Thomas Csordas. Berkeley: University of California Press.

Rambo, Lewis R. 1993. *Understanding Religious Conversion.* New Haven, Conn.: Yale University Press.

Roald, Anne Sofie. 2004. *New Muslims in the European Context: The Experience of Scandinavian Converts.* Leiden: Brill.

———. 2006. "The Shaping of Scandinavian 'Islam': Converts and Gender Equal Opportunity." In *Women Embracing Islam: Gender and Conversion in the West,* ed. Karin van Nieuwkerk. Austin: University of Texas Press.

Rouse, Carolyn. 2004. *Engaged Surrender: African American Women and Islam.* Berkeley: University of California Press.

Roy, Olivier. 2004. *Globalized Islam: The Search for a New Ummah*. New York: Columbia University Press.

Sultan, Madeline. 1999. "Choosing Islam: A Study of Swedish Converts." *Social Compass* 46(3): 325–35.

Van Nieuwkerk, Karin. 2004. "Veils and Wooden Clogs Don't Go Together." *Ethnos* 69(2): 229–46.

———. 2006. *Women Embracing Islam: Gender and Conversion in the West*. Austin: University of Texas Press.

Wohlrab-Sahr, Monika. 1999. "Conversion to Islam: Between Syncretism and Symbolic Battle." *Social Compass* 46(3): 351–62.

Part Four Attraction and Repulsion in Shared Space

8

Muslim Ethnic Comedy: Inversions of Islamophobia

Mucahit Bilici

> *I see other minorities and I am jealous. They get a whole month that*
> *celebrates their heritage. Black history month, Asian awareness month,*
> *Hispanic awareness month. What do we get? We get* ORANGE ALERT!
> —Dean Obeidallah, comedian and member
> of the Axis of Evil comedy troupe

> [Little Mosque] *is appealing because it shows Muslims being normal.*
> *It humanizes Muslims. I want the broader society to look at us*
> *as normal, with the same issues and concerns as anyone else.*
> —Zarqa Nawaz, creator of the TV series
> *Little Mosque on the Prairie*

> *[By hosting Muslim comedy] we want to demystify the FBI*
> *and show people that we are human, not just cold*
> *FBI agents coming out to arrest people.*
> —Gwen Hubbard, chief recruiter for the FBI's
> National Recruiting/Testing Office

The association of Muslims with terrorism after 9/11 has prompted a search for the "comic" side of being Muslim. Do these people ever laugh? The simplistic idea that Muslims "hate us" has simultaneously produced rigid stereotypes and a countering desire to discover what those stereotypes deny: among other things, a Muslim sense of humor. Needless to say, in reasoning like this, humor usually stands for humanity. If someone has a sense of humor, then he is just like us: likable. The Danish cartoon crisis shone an uncomfortable spotlight on the Muslim relationship to humor. The degree to which the cartoons were actually funny or offensive, to whom, and for what reasons, is a complicated subject I will not explore here. Obviously, humor was not the only issue at stake. Rather predictably, however, some Western commentators saw in the Danish cartoon affair a Muslim intolerance of humor, which they equated with cultural inferiority. This kind of shortsightedness has a way of conjuring its opposite. Increasing curiosity about Muslims and their (supposed lack of) humor has created a surprising demand for Muslim ethnic comedy, especially in liberal societies where Muslims have the relative comfort to crack jokes about themselves and their non-Muslim compatriots.

Since the tragic events of 9/11, there has been an upsurge in ethnic comedy by Muslims in America. Individuals like Azhar Usman or Ahmed Ahmed and groups such as Allah Made Me Funny and Axis of Evil are appearing onstage with comic routines. They attract young Muslim audiences but also, increasingly, non-Muslim ones. Paradoxically, a tragedy that triggered widespread Islamophobia in American society seems also to have opened the field for Muslim comedy. This essay explores the intricate relationship between Islamophobia and Muslim ethnic comedy and argues that both phobic and philic sentiments arise from a loss of *common sense*. Muslim ethnic comedy in the United States thus becomes a series of inversions played out against a background of Islamophobia. A journey from fear to laughter, it aims to bridge the divide that separates Muslims from the rest of American society by reaffirming both sides' common humanity.

Muslim Comedy: "The time is right"

Muslim comedy is an emerging "market." Not only is its audience growing, but it is also a new career field for Muslim cultural entrepreneurs, mostly second-generation young people and converts. "The time is right," says Zarqa Nawaz, the Muslim producer of *Little Mosque on the Prairie,* a popular Canadian sitcom. "The marketplace has never been this curious about Muslims." These cultural entrepreneurs claim knowledge of both worlds: ethnic and mainstream. This is best illustrated in their ability to go back and forth between accented and normal speech. As arbiters of a cultural encounter and as field guides to a contact zone, these stand-up comedians are situated in a unique position. Able to "leap" from one side to the other, they practice simultaneously the two ways of seeing things. This position is often a tragic one, where a person belongs to both worlds and neither. The comic stands uneasily on the fault line, yet by standing there he becomes a sort of stitch that holds together the two sides of the cultural rift.

Muslim comedy did not begin with 9/11, but it did take on a distinctive form and quality after it. September 11 is a turning point in the history of American Muslim ethnicity as well as in the history of American Muslim comedy. Like every other ethnic group, the various Muslim communities had their internal humor, their own comedians. But they were completely obscure from the point of view of the larger society. They lacked both common language with and a reputation among mainstream audiences. The members of comedy troupes such as Allah Made Me Funny and Axis of Evil were comedians, but they were not "American Muslim comedians." They were either obscure ethnic comedians or generic mainstream ones. For example, before his Allah Made Me Funny days, Preacher Moss was producing primarily, but not exclusively, African American humor. Writing for George Lopez and Darrell Hammond, he was a mainstream comedian with an African American edge. As an individual, he was Muslim, but this was not the primary framework defining his work. Similarly, Dean Obeidallah of Axis of Evil repeatedly says that before 9/11 he was a white guy doing generic comedy. After 9/11, he says, he lost his white status and became Arab.

Islamophobia is what has made Muslim comedy a phenomenon of our times. The discrimination, prejudices, and stereotypes from which other Muslims suffer are a godsend for the Muslim comedian. Muslim comics thus represent the experience of most Muslims, but in an inverted way. They are perhaps the only beneficiaries of the *negative charisma* associated with being Muslim.

Fear and Laughter at the Airport

Let us look at the most prominent Muslim comedian in the United States: Azhar Usman. Usman, who, together with Preacher Moss, founded the troupe Allah Made Me Funny, is the very model of a post-9/11 Muslim stand-up comedian, and his jokes about the airport experience are the epitome of today's emergent Muslim comedy.

> My least favorite thing about being a comedian is all the traveling. That's right. The moment I have to walk into the airport. Heads turn simultaneously. The security . . . [As though speaking into a walkie-talkie] "We got a Mohammad at 4 o'clock." "Can I see your ID, please?" "We'll need to do an extra security check."
> Even worse is the moment I have to get onto the plane. That's right. People are shocked. They are in the middle of a conversation. "So where are you from . . . ?" And then they suddenly see me. [slightly hysterical voice] "Oh my God! I'm gonna die. [desperate whisper into cell phone] Honey, I love you. He is s-o-o hairy."

[Here Azhar takes a break from the drama and complains to his audience:]

I don't really understand why these people are so scared of me. I don't get it. Just think about it: if I were the crazy Muslim planning to hijack the plane, this is totally not the disguise I would be in [pirouetting his large, bearded self around the stage]. It doesn't exactly slip me under the radar.

[He concludes his flight story with exaggerated relief:]

Of course, once the plane safely lands, they are just looking over smiling. Ha haa ha. I am waiting for one real honest passenger to come up to me at the end of the flight . . . He says, "Excuse me sir, I thought you were gonna kill us. Ha ha. Sorry about that. Ha ha. Remember when you got up to go to bathroom? I was gonna stab you. Ha ha." That's what it feels like these days, man.

This routine provides a perfect illustration of the Muslim airport experience, where the negative charisma of being Muslim assumes full transparency. At the airport, those who have so far (in the city, at the ticket counter, and so on) been treated equally suddenly become suspect. At the internal borders of the nation, they suddenly feel their protected status begin to evaporate. Even those Muslims who do not consider themselves particularly profiled or discriminated against in everyday life suddenly begin to feel uneasy. Strip search and other security rites of passage through the border show them the hard edge of the nation. Here Muslim otherness is revealed in the most conspicuous way. Despite official efforts to present searches at the airports as random, comedians like Dean Obeidallah skeptically ask their Muslim audiences: "Are you selected for random search even when you are dropping a friend at the airport?"

The fear a Muslim inspires is associated with the unpredictability of his behavior. What if he is a terrorist? What if he hijacks the plane? What if he is only pretending to be normal? All these questions that airport authorities ask citizens to consider transform the Muslim passenger in the eyes of his fellow travelers into a source of unpredictability and danger. When a Muslim like Azhar Usman gets onto the plane, faces fall. Danger is imminent. The anxiety ends only when the plane lands. People are almost thankful to the Muslim passenger for not doing what they feared he might. Flying-while-Muslim thus becomes an extremely public event.

A crucial point here is that the airport is where Muslim experience and American mainstream experience meet. Jokes about aviation thus have a remarkable degree of transparency and universality. Muslims and non-Muslims alike can understand and laugh at airport and airplane jokes. They are at once ethnic and national, particular and universal. These jokes represent the comic surface where Muslim and American perspectives intersect most "dangerously" and with full intelligibility. Jokes about the airport experience thus constitute a significant portion of the repertoire of Muslim comedians today.

FBI's Most Wanted: Terrorist and Comedian

The Axis of Evil comedy tour started in November 2005 and gained national recognition with an appearance on *Comedy Central* on March 10, 2007. The group also put out a DVD in 2007 which features Maz Jobrani, Ahmed Ahmed, Aron Kader, and guest member Dean Obeidallah.

Ahmed Ahmed is an Egyptian American who also had an acting career in Hollywood. Dissatisfied with the parts available to Middle Eastern actors, he decided to become a stand-up comedian after 9/11. Ahmed's routine typically revolves around the absurdities of the security check at the airport. He claims that his name matches one of the FBI's most wanted terrorists. So each time he goes to the airport, he has to go through extra security checks. As he puts it:

> It is a bad time to be from the Middle East. I read a statistic on CBS.com. Right after 9/11, hate crimes against Arabs, Middle Eastern people and Muslims went up over 1,000%. Apparently that puts us in the fourth place behind blacks, gays, and Jews. You guys know this? We are still in the fourth place. So what do we have to do to be number one in something?

Ahmed Ahmed notes that often people don't believe that he is a comedian—especially when it's the airport security staff asking him what he does for a living. "They always say, 'So tell us a joke.' And I go, 'Well, I just graduated from flight school.'" Once on board, Ahmed looks around the plane. "Do you know who the air marshal is on the plane? The guy reading *People* magazine upside down while keeping an eye on me."

Otherness: Scary and Funny

The appearance and potential disappearance of ethnic comedy is linked to the location of the ethnic group in relation to the majority society. A minority group has an otherness that can seem indelible as long as the group makes some effort to maintain its distinct identity. Anxiety about identity preservation and the power differential with the majority group can combine to create a sense of "insecurity." This insecurity—a mismatch between habitus and habitat, to use Bourdieu's (1977) terms—produces cultural discord and can lead to tragic and comic outcomes. In this sense, both fear and laughter are reactions to otherness.

They represent two directions of destabilization and alienation from everyday rationality. No wonder, then, that people who experience "shocks" (from accidents to earthquakes) are prone to laughter (Brottman 2004: 76).

Discrimination or racism and ethnic comedy are two sides of the same coin. In both cases there is a breakdown—or more precisely, a deroutinization—a certain degree of alienation from common sense. Common sense here refers to a social consensus, a shared vision. The majority knows only its own view of the world, and from its vantage point the minority may look funny. But the minority has access to two visions: the majority vision, which it is obligated to cultivate in order to "fit in"; and its own, particular view. The group with the double vision, the minority, is more likely to see incongruities between the two worldviews and so finds more to laugh at. It is no wonder that many minority groups are historically famous for their humor. Behind the large body of Jewish humor lies the Jewish experience of marginality (Rappoport 2005: 66; Berger 1997: xvii). Minorities—or in our case, immigrant communities—can laugh both at the majority's taken-for-granted idiosyncrasies and at the majority's view of the minority, which they find scarily wrong or amusingly incorrect. Anthropologist Mary Douglas (1975) has rightly called humor a "play upon forms." A form that looks like unassailable truth in the majority view may turn to a tottering fiction in the eyes of the minority. The ethnic comedian basically plays on stereotypes. He critiques and destabilizes the existing "common sense" for its failure to see reality. It comes as no surprise that Aristotle declares, in his *Poetics,* that "the comic poet should assign his characters their ancestral dialect, and himself the local one" (Aristotle 1987: 45). One of Azhar Usman's airport jokes reflects the discordant vision imposed on Muslims. Dazed by the barrage of announcements warning travelers to "report suspicious individuals," he finds himself looking over at a corner of the waiting area. "I see this guy. He looks shady. I call the security guy over and he says, 'You're looking in a mirror, sir.'"

Comic vision reveals a reality different from commonsense reality. Phenomenological sociologist Alfred Schutz distinguishes between commonsense reality ("the paramount reality of the everyday life") and other realities ("finite provinces of meaning") (Schutz 1962: 207). Here, commonsense reality is objective in that it is shared by multiple social actors and is thoroughly sedimented in language and everyday symbolic structures. Other realities, however, remain subjective and partial. The comic presents an alternative reality that transcends the reality of the ordinary and helps us see things from a certain distance. What is crucial here is the relationship between *vision* and *distance.* Those who are in a position to see things differently are more likely to generate humor. Simmel's famous social type, the *stranger,* represents this ability to be both near and far and to be able to stay attached to the mainstream vision and withdraw back to the ethnic vision (Simmel 1971: 143–48).

Muslim comedians find themselves on a borderline where they can criticize both the majority and their own minority communities. "We are not a politically active community," observes Azhar Usman. "We have conference after conference about what? 'Muslim participation in the political process.' At every one a Desi uncle stands up and says: 'We need more Muslims in politics. We need Muslim politicians and journalists.' Then you ask him, 'Hey, uncle, you have three children, what do they do?' He says, 'Mashaallah, they are all doctors. I am so proud of them—even though one of them had to go to the Caribbean to get a degree.'"

"Any Syrians in the audience?" Usman often asks. "You know, I have a Syrian friend. Blond hair, blue eyes: totally blends into corporate America. Then one year he goes to the holiday party with his wife, who wears hijab. He's outed. 'Oh my God,' one of his co-workers says, 'I thought he was Jewish. I've been sending him Hanukkah cards for the past ten years.'"

As an African American Muslim, Preacher Moss is particularly well placed to comment on community divisions. "You know, I'm married to an Indian sister," he mentions in his routine, usually to applause from the audience. "All those people out there clapping," he immediately adds, "I know you're thinking: 'Thank God it's not my sister!'"

Theories of the Comic

As a uniquely human phenomenon, humor has been an object of curiosity for philosophers. Among the oldest accounts of why we laugh is the theory of superiority. According to this approach, propounded by Plato, Aristotle, and later Hobbes, we laugh at our inferiors. Laughter is seen as a means of expressing superiority over other people. Such laughter can be aggressive and is certainly self-celebratory. For our purposes here, the main insight of the superiority theory of humor is the idea of *relationality.* Superiority theory acknowledges both the power differential and the relation between two parties.

If superiority theory is a political explanation of the comic, incongruity theory provides a rather cultural one. It sees humor as an outcome of inconsistent, unexpected acts and conditions. For example, Pascal, one of the early proponents of this view, argues that "nothing produces laughter more than a surprising disproportion between that which one expects and that which one sees" (Morreal 1983: 16). Similarly, Schopenhauer describes laughter as happening in situations marked by "the sudden perception of incongruity between a concept and things themselves" (Schopenhauer 1966: 91). As Morreal puts it, summarizing Schopenhauer's perspective, "What causes laughter is a mismatch between conceptual understanding and perception" (Morreal 1983: 18). Here a concept is general and lumps together unique and particular things as if they were identical instantiations of that concept. (And isn't this the perfect definition of a stereotype?) All concepts do violence to the uniqueness of the things they claim to represent: this is a problem intrinsic to any abstraction (Nietzsche 2006: 117; Simmel 1950: 63). This violence cries out for refutation or rectification. One way to cure it is through comic treatment. Laughter, one may argue, is a product of the sudden recognition of this very gap. In this accidental encounter between reality or experience (minority vision) and the abstract metaphysics of stereotypes (majority vision), an everyday version of the destruction of metaphysics (what Derrida [1998] calls *deconstruction*) takes place. After all, what is comedy but a comic deconstruction?

Another prominent theory of humor is called the relief theory. Relief theory emphasizes the cathartic release from repression: in Aristotelian terms, a "purification" of emotions. In *Civilization and Its Discontents,* Freud explores the psychic cost of civilization for individuals. He identifies the overwhelming power and expansion of the *reality principle* over the *pleasure principle* as the main cause for the unhappiness of modern man (Freud 1961: 22). In comedy the relationship is reversed. We revert to the pleasure principle, albeit temporarily. In his discussion of jokes, Freud also links jokes to the unconscious and draws attention to the economy of psychic energy in the repression of emotions (the id) by the superego. Freud argues that the "manifest content of dreams and jokes yield pleasure through their disguised expression of unconscious wishes, resulting in partial lifting of repression and an economic expenditure of psychic energy" (quoted in Bergmann 1999: 3).

Mary Douglas (1975) and Victor Turner (1969), two prominent cultural anthropologists working within the Durkheimian tradition, rightly point to the margins and to liminality as the location of humor. Comedy is an anti-rite presented in a ritual, an anti-structure imagined as an alternative structure. Comedy, they claim, turns the world upside down by showing the audience the view from the other side. The majority's vision (structure) is temporarily and imaginarily relegated to the status of anti-structure, while the minority's vision (anti-structure) is elevated in its place. In this reversal of symbolic order, the minority is released from social classifications (e.g., stereotypes), and the majority is given the opportunity to feel like a minority (Douglas 1975: 103; Berger 1997: 72).

The idea of a reversal of symbolic order is of crucial importance for understanding the structural dimensions of ethnic comedy. Often perceived as a reversal of the relationship between the rational and the irrational, comic vision does indeed thrive on the discrepancies and interplay of two forces. For Nietzsche, these two forces were the Apollonian and Dionysian principles. The former is associated with structure, rationality, and seriousness and the latter with anti-structure, emotions, and laughter. Both comedy and tragedy originated in the cult of Dionysus, the Greek god of revelry and excess who violates all ordinary boundaries. This is why comedy is perceived as a threat to the established order—and Plato in his *Republic* famously calls for the banishment of poets (i.e., comedians and tragedians) from the ideal city.

This Dionysian element in the Greek tradition is continued by the Roman festival of Saturnalia (Nietzsche 2006: 122) and extends into the present day in the many versions of Carnival. Mikhail Bakhtin famously observed that in carnivals and other rites of passage, the ordinary world is turned upside down (Bakhtin 1968; Brottman 2004: 150; Berger 1997: 21). Laughter is therefore "one of the essential forms of truth concerning the world as a whole. . . . It is a peculiar point of view relative to the world. . . . Certain essential aspects of the world are accessible only to laughter" (Bakhtin 1968: 20).

Baber at the Bakhtinian Carnival

One episode of *Little Mosque* focuses on Baber, a protective father who is reluctant to let his daughter dress up and go trick-or-treating at Halloween. He finally decides to let her go, but only if he goes with her. So the little girl in her costume sets out with her bearded father in the religiously conservative Pakistani dress that he wears every day. But the neighborhood children greet him with shouts of "Great costume!" They think he's dressed up as Osama bin Laden. In a carnivalesque moment, the festivity that Baber had thought was foreign to his culture and potentially harmful for his children suddenly turns around and embraces him: by cultural accident, an awkward-looking immigrant guy becomes a local dressed strangely for Halloween. The carnival, according to Bakhtin, is the time and place where the world is turned upside down. Just so, it temporarily releases Baber from the tension of being his usual, strange self. For once he feels comfortable in his exotic outfit and joins his daughter in playful celebration of Halloween. Halloween becomes Halal-oween. He almost reverts to the unselfconscious pleasures of childhood, horsing around with the other kids and competing to see who can get the most candy. For a brief time the abnormal, exotic has become the normal, familiar. He feels relieved.

In this segment we see Baber oscillating between fear and laughter. The phobic and philic destinations mark the two extremes toward which he finds himself thrown. What is common to both conditions is their distance or alienation from reason/normality. It is as if he sinks below the level of commonsense rationality through fear (What is this Halloween, anyway? Can my daughter join in this pagan festival and still be a good Muslim?), and then rises above it through laughter. Once the balance is lost, it is much easier to go from fear to laughter than back to reason. There is a reason for that: while fear and reason belong to different spheres, fear and laughter (or pity, or love) share the same world of emotions. To restore reason, one emotion has to be undone by another emotion. This process of undoing the fall from reason requires catharsis (purification, purging of negative emotions). A bit of laughter can undo your fears and bring you back into the fold of rationality. This is the therapeutic function of comedy (and tragedy) that Aristotle argued for in his *Poetics*. Both tragedy and comedy, the philosopher argues, have a cathartic effect. They purify the soul and restore the balance of reason (Aristotle 1987: 45).

The FBI and Muslim Comedy

Widespread public Islamophobia and the government crackdown on Muslim institutions and individuals have deepened the alienation of Muslims from security agencies such as the FBI. In response to this problem, the FBI recently initiated an outreach program targeting Muslims. Thousands of Muslims who attended the annual convention of the Islamic Society of North America (ISNA) in south Chicago in 2007 came across an FBI booth in the bazaar section of the convention. The signs at the booth read, "Today's FBI: It's for You." Efforts to build bridges with the Muslim community in general and Arabs in particular were taken to another level when the FBI sponsored a performance by Axis of Evil at an American-Arab Anti-Discrimination Committee (ADC) convention in Washington, D.C. In an interview with Reuters explaining the rationale behind the FBI's use of ethnic comedians to reach out to suspicious Arabs and Muslims, Gwen Hubbard, the chief recruiter for the agency, said: "We want to demystify the FBI and show people that we are human, not just cold FBI agents coming out to arrest people" (www.IslamOnline.net, June 14, 2007).

The FBI's rationale for hosting Muslim comedians is strikingly similar to Muslims' own approach to comedy. When Zarqa Nawaz, the creator of the television series *Little Mosque on the Prairie,* gave a talk in Detroit, she said "[*Little Mosque*] is appealing because it shows Muslims being normal. It humanizes Muslims. I want the broader society to look at us as normal, with the same issues and concerns as anyone else."

The gulf opened between the two sides by the tragic events of 9/11 and subsequent arrests and surveillance of Muslims has disrupted the balance of rationality and citizenship. A gap has appeared between appearance and reality. From each side, one can easily become suspicious of the other. What if they are terrorists pretending to be decent citizens? What if they are after us no matter what decent citizens we are? Both sides harbor (ungrounded?) fears when it comes to the other. To pull each other out of fear back into the sphere of rationality (common sense, a sense that is common to both), they have to go through laughter. Laughter allows each to see the world through the eyes of the other. Since they no longer share a common view of the world, their redemption is possible only through putting themselves in each other's shoes. That is precisely what the Muslim comic does: he undermines the two sides' discordant visions by playing on them, making them explicit. "The comic invades and subverts the taken-for-granted structures of social life" (Berger 1997: 91).

A terrorist masquerading as a citizen versus a citizen masquerading as a terrorist. These are the FBI's bugbears and the butt of the Muslim comedian's jokes. It is as though Muslim comics engage in a game of cultural peekaboo by transmuting phobic suspicions into surprised exclamations of "Oh, he is one of us after all."

The Inverted World of Muslim Comedy

Comedy constructs a counter-world to the world of ordinary life. Because the everyday world has become extraordinary, the Muslim (an oddity in American life) becomes funny when he appears "ordinary." In other words, humor allows for a distortion of commonsense reality. Those whose reality is already distorted because of stereotypes resort to humor to rectify and reassert their own sense of what is real.

One sees a series of inversions in the practice of Muslim ethnic comedy. Let us start with some rather trivial ones. When Maz Jobrani of Axis of Evil picks up a digital video camera at the ADC convention and starts to record the FBI agents sitting around the table close to the stage, he is engaged in a symbolic reversal of the wiretapping and surveillance of Muslims by the FBI. Muslim actors like Jobrani who found no roles in Hollywood but those of terrorists switched to stand-up comedy—where they now mock the very roles they once played. Of course, this reversal of symbolic structure is not itself irreversible. Muslims tend to think that shows like *Little Mosque* are bastions of Islamophilia in a sea of hostile media, but then are surprised to discover that the actor who plays Yasir, one of the central characters, went on to play the role of a terrorist on the rather Islamophobic television series 24.

The demands of comedy may even force performers to raise their "Muslim quotient." Tissa Hami, an Iranian American comedian from Boston, who normally does not wear hijab, onstage wears an Iranian chador (a voluminous black cloak that covers her from head to toe). Sometimes she wears a slightly less full hijab—if, she jokes, she is feeling "slutty." About airport security and full body searches she notes wryly: "I was kind of hoping to save that for the honeymoon."

The discrepancy between the reality of the Muslim community and the stereotypes about it continues to be a source of concern and humor. On closer inspection one sees that the latter is an inversion of the former. An interesting outcome of the securitization of society is the ban on jokes at the airport. Making jokes in the security check area at the airport is strictly prohibited and punishable by law. According to a statement released on March 11, 2004, by the TSA (Transportation Security Agency), a woman was jailed for joking about bombs in her luggage. This particular ban makes airports a unique part of the national space. Airports are internal borders. As entry and exit points to the nation, airports provide us a unique perspective on questions of sovereignty and identity. The enforcement of no-joke zones at the airports after the tragedy of 9/11 is thus indicative of the paradoxical connection between the tragic and the comic.

An equally interesting development is the attempt on the part of Muslim ethnic comedians to turn the stage into a symbolic airport space. They do so not only by drawing much of their material from their experiences at the airport but also by literally entering the stage in a mock ritual (anti-rite) of passing through a scanner and being searched by mock TSA staff. Axis of Evil's famous performance on *Comedy Central* is the best example: they perform on a stage festooned with nuclear warning signs and each comedian is frisked by a tough-looking female security screener in full TSA regalia as he steps onto the stage. They are not the only ones to use this gimmick. In one of his performances with comedian Rabbi Bob Alper, Azhar Usman and Alper patted one another down as they took turns at the microphone. (The two comedians have toured together across the country, doing shows on college campuses and at Muslim and Jewish religious centers.)

The turning of airports into no-joke zones and the turning of the Muslim comic zone into a symbolic airport are two expressions of a single undercurrent. They are also symptomatic of the Dionysian continuum of fear and laughter, or the existential continuity between insecurity and relief. What links the no-joke zone to the comic stage is what links the tragedy of 9/11 to the emergence of Muslim comedy.

Muslim comedy is a form of code-switching in the face of situations where the language of reason is overtaken by a wrong common sense or common wrong sense. Muslim comedy reveals the space of otherness that stretches between looking scary and looking funny. By undoing otherness, Muslim ethnic comedy lifts, albeit temporarily, the restrictive limits on the self and abolishes the gulf that separates the Muslim minority from the American mainstream. It provides a relief from social classifications (a.k.a. stereotypes), which are often oppressive of the minority group. It redefines the common sense. The ability of comedy to disclose the rock bottom of our identities as "human" plays a significant role in showing the commonalities beneath the surface of "difference." That comedy reveals our humanity is well illustrated by a comment from Jewish comic Rabbi Bob Alper, who observed after a performance with Azhar Usman in Detroit on April 1, 2008, "You can't hate the person you've laughed with." Usman recalls hearing a similar sentiment from a non-Muslim audience member: "I didn't see you as a Muslim, I saw you as a human being."

Muslim ethnic comedy is part of the Americanization process: the power of comedy becomes a means of undoing otherness. The comic vision rehumanizes Muslims and allows comedians to engage in a symbolic reversal of the social order. Muslim ethnic comedy is the world of Islamophobia turned upside down.

Works Cited

Allah Made Me Funny: The Official Muslim Comedy Tour. 2005. Produced by Francisco Aguilar and Jaime Valdonado. 66 min. DVD.

Aristotle. 1987. *Poetics*. Trans. Richard Janko. Indianapolis, Ind.: Hackett.

The Axis of Evil Comedy Tour. 2007. Los Angeles: Image Entertainment. 86 min. DVD.

Bakhtin, Mikhail. 1968. *Rabelais and His World*. Cambridge, Mass.: MIT Press.

Berger, Peter. 1997. *Redeeming Laughter: The Comic Dimension of Human Experience*. Berlin: Walter de Gruyter.

Bergmann, Martin. 1999. "The Psychoanalysis of Humor and Humor in Psychoanalysis." In *Humor and Psyche: Psychoanalytic Perspectives*, ed. James W. Barron. Hillsdale, N.J.: Analytic Press.

Bourdieu, Pierre. 1977. *Outline of a Theory of Practice*. Trans. Richard Nice. Cambridge: Cambridge University Press.

Brottman, Mikita. 2004. *Funny Peculiar: Gershon Legman and the Psychopathology of Humor*. Hillsdale, N.J.: Analytic Press.

Derrida, Jacques. 1998. *Of Grammatology.* Trans. Gayatri Spivak. Baltimore, Md.: Johns Hopkins University Press.

Douglas, Mary. 1975. *Implicit Meanings: Essays in Anthropology.* London: Routledge.

Freud, Sigmund. 1961. *Civilization and Its Discontents.* Standard edition. New York: W. W. Norton & Co.

IslamOnline.net. 2007. "'Axis of Evil' Breaks FBI-Muslim Barrier," http://www.islamon line.net/servlet/Satellite?c=Article_C&pagename=Zone-English-News/NWELayout &cid=1181062753207.

Looking for Comedy in the Muslim World. 2005. Written and directed by Albert Brooks. Warner Independent Pictures. DVD.

Morreal, John. 1983. *Taking Laughter Seriously.* Albany, N.Y.: SUNY Press.

Nietzsche, Friedrich Wilhelm. 2006. *The Nietzsche Reader.* Ed. K. A. Pearson and D. Large. Malden, Mass.: Blackwell.

Rappoport, Leon. 2005. *Punchlines: The Case for Racial, Ethnic and Gender Humor.* Westport, Conn.: Praeger.

Schopenhauer, Arthur. 1966. *The World as Will and Representation.* New York: Dover Books.

Schutz, Alfred. 1962. *Collected Papers 1: The Problem of Social Reality.* The Hague: Martinus Nijhoff.

Simmel, Georg. 1950. *The Sociology of Georg Simmel.* Trans., ed., and with an introduction by Kurt H. Wolff. Glencoe, Ill.: Free Press.

———. 1971. *On Individuality and Social Forms.* Chicago: University of Chicago Press.

Turner, Victor. 1969. *The Ritual Process: Structure and Anti-Structure.* Chicago: Aldine Publishing Co.

9

Competing for Muslims: New Strategies for Urban Renewal in Detroit

Sally Howell

Masjid Muʻath bin Jabal is a Yemeni mosque located in Detroit, on the outskirts of Hamtramck, a working-class, historically Polish city that is bounded on all sides by Detroit and isolated further by a ring of industrial factories and freeways. Masjid Muʻath bin Jabal has been credited (by local Muslims and public officials alike) with having turned around one of Detroit's roughest neighborhoods at the height of the crack cocaine epidemic of the 1980s, making its streets safe, revitalizing a dormant housing market, attracting new business to the area, and laying the foundation for an ethnically mixed, highly visible Muslim population in Detroit and Hamtramck. In 1990, Muʻath bin Jabal was the only mosque in this neighborhood. Today, it is the largest of ten mosques within a three-mile radius.

In 2005, the Muslims of Hamtramck were very much in the local, national, and even international news. One of the city's newer mosques, Al-Islah Jamee Masjid, a Bengali house of worship, had requested permission from the city to broadcast its *idhan*, or call to prayer, from loudspeakers outside the mosque. This request brought to a head simmering Islamophobic sentiments in the city, attracted anti-Muslim activists from as far away as Ohio and Kentucky, and gave the rest of the United States (via an international media storm) a cathartic test of the "freedoms" we were said to be "fighting for" in Afghanistan and Iraq. Local Muslim and interfaith activists rallied around the mosque, as did city voters, support which helped pull Hamtramck's Muslims out of their immigrant parochialism and into the fray of city politics.[1] At the height of the media frenzy surrounding Hamtramck's *idhan* controversy, a story appeared in the *Detroit Free Press* (January 28, 2005) headlined "Highland Park Schools Seek More Arab, Muslim Students: Hamtramck, Detroit Intend to Keep Them." This item drew little interest outside the immediate neighborhood. It was not sensational, nor did it adhere to the "clash of civilizations" model that lurks near the surface whenever Muslims are discussed in the public sphere. The story made no mention of the "war on terror," of a community under siege, or of geopolitics. Instead it described Highland Park as a "virtually all black, overwhelmingly Christian" municipality with "one of the worst rates of crime and poverty in the state," and it posited the settlement of Muslim families in Highland Park as a corrective to the city's problems. While the *Detroit Free Press* story did not mention Masjid Mu'ath bin Jabal by name, it quoted Yahya Alkebsi, a Yemeni American consultant working for the Highland Park schools on their "Muslim package," who explained that city officials were "trying to attract families to reside in Highland Park." Alkebsi provided details on North Pointe Village, a new housing development then under way in the city. Highland Park's population shrank by 17 percent between 1990 and 2000, while Hamtramck's grew a stunning 25 percent, due overwhelmingly to immigration from Muslim-majority nations. The Masjid Mu'ath bin Jabal "miracle" was exactly what school officials wanted to reproduce in Highland Park. Public school officials in Hamtramck and Detroit were placed on high alert.

Historian Nancy Foner has cautioned that the exuberance with which immigration scholars have embraced transnational frameworks has led to an overemphasis on extraterritorial networks and transactions, while minimizing attempts to understand the complex processes by which contemporary immigrants "become American" (2001). Immigrants arriving in the U.S. today come better prepared to participate as citizens than did earlier immigrants because an increasingly globalized marketplace and mediascape have already pulled Americans and would-be Americans into common frames of reference, both encouraging migration and attuning immigrants to the expectations of contemporary American life much more than was possible in the past (Aidi 2003; Hollinger 1995; Karim 2006; Mandaville 2001). Although immigrants invest heavily in transnational circuits of communication and exchange, studying these networks to the exclusion of similar local and national circuits encourages scholars to overlook the permanency of immigrant settlement and the gradual disinvestment in transnational relations over time (Hondagneu-Sotela and Avila 1997).

Yemenis, for instance, have had a sizable presence in greater Detroit since the late 1960s, and they have participated more actively in transnational practices than have other Arab Americans (Abraham 1978; Swanson 1988; Aswad

1974), but the investment Yemenis have made in Masjid Mu'ath bin Jabal (and the American Moslem Society in Dearborn) has coincided with their shifting orientation toward a future life in America. Likewise, the local Bengali community, still relatively new to Michigan, is also intensely transnational. In recent years these populations have begun to collaborate with one another, and with other Muslims in the area, to create a new politics—a transcommunal politics—that borrows resources and ideas across lines of race, class, municipal boundaries, and ethnicity as well as across national boundaries. Peter Mandaville has defined "translocality" as a mode "which pertains not to how peoples and cultures exist *in* places, but rather how they move *through* them," disrupting "traditional constructions of political identity" and giving "rise to novel forms of political space" (2001: 50). In their work with local school boards, zoning commissions, law enforcement agencies, social workers, and one another, Muslims in Detroit (and its surrounding communities) are creating just such a new political space. Their transcommunal politics move *through* city lines and ethnic divides to create a space in which they can live comfortably *in* Detroit while simultaneously disembedding themselves from the social consequences of Detroit's particular experience of urban crisis and racialized conflict.

Both the Masjid Mu'ath bin Jabal neighborhood and the Highland Park campaign to attract Muslim students participate in this "here/not-here" struggle, with long-term consequences for the future of Islam in Michigan. They also draw from the historical legacies of Islam and the Nation of Islam in Detroit, religious traditions that have long offered themselves as different but related fixes for the city's moral, economic, and political woes, attractive especially to African Americans in times of social upheaval (Dannin 2002; Jackson 2005; Turner 1997). Islamophilia (an attraction to Islam or to Muslims) and Islamophobia (a fear or rejection of Islam or of Muslims) have long coexisted in the Detroit area in highly visible and sometimes mutually inclusive social movements.[2]

Promoting Charters and Choices

Living in a highly charged and racially demarcated cityscape, Muslims in Detroit, Hamtramck, Highland Park, and Dearborn find themselves the subjects of an intense competition by local school systems, one that is driving up the educational stakes for Muslims and non-Muslims alike. Offering packages that seem simple enough on the surface—Arabic-language instruction, halal meals, closings for Islamic holidays, and outreach liaisons to address parental concerns—these programs are designed to attract observant Muslims and make them feel at home. Yet, as this competition grows heated, more complex options are brought to the table, including "Arab" (sometimes meaning Islamic) history and culture courses, special opportunities for prayer and other religious observances at school, gender-segregated classrooms, and, increasingly, Muslim-only environments, all in ostensibly public schools.

These packages address the fears of immigrant parents by placing their children securely on the route to "delayed assimilation" (Portes and Zhou 1993). Similarly, they provide African American families the opportunity to assimilate their children into a Muslim-only educational and moral community and to opt out of (or perhaps write a new chapter in) Detroit's legacy of urban/racial crisis. The educators who develop and promote these packages are quick to point out that they replicate, in many ways, programs also available in local suburban contexts (especially Dearborn) and model themselves on Roman Catholic parochial schools, but they also worry that such packages come at a cost to the Muslim American community, potentially relegating local Muslims permanently to underclass, or minority status. Others argue that these programs offer what scholars of the left sometimes refer to as "horizontal assimilation"—a simultaneous escape from and resistance to the privileges of whiteness (Bald 2006; Jones 1963; Prashad 2001).

The competition for students between adjoining school districts was made possible in 1993 when Michigan governor John Engler signed the Charter School Act into law, and again in 1996 when he signed Schools of Choice legislation. Frustrated by decades of failure to bring about equity in public school financing and services, educational activists from a variety of political perspectives joined forces to support this legislation, which was intended to "supplement" public educational systems in Michigan; similar laws were passed across the U.S. during this period. Charter schools and schools of choice are viable because state education dollars are now distributed on a per pupil basis. The "foundational allowance" was roughly $8,400 per student in 2007–2008 (American Federation of Teachers 2007),[3] with students taking their state funding with them as they move from district to district, from building to building, and from the public system into semi-private charter entities.

Charter schools are funded by the state, yet they mirror private schools in that their spending and educational decisions are made independently of local school boards and state educational bureaucracies. As Bob Dannin (forthcoming) has pointed out in his thoughtful critique of this free-market approach to education, charter schools, voucher programs, and schools of choice have done little to improve educational outcomes, yet they have reshuffled public education dollars into the hands of private educational operators, duplicated the education bureaucracy, and internally decimated inner-city and other struggling public school systems. While these new educational offerings promise families trapped in poorly performing school districts academic rigor, a plethora of enrichment opportunities, and a retreat from entrenched and battle-weary public educators, in reality they often trap children in badly organized schools with inexperienced and unqualified instructors, little oversight, and financial resources strained by exorbitant rents and other hidden costs.

Public school systems like Detroit's now have to invest time and money advertising their free, public programs just to keep existing students. They also spend much more on remedial services now that they have to assist students who have fallen between the cracks while shifting between districts.[4] The public schools cannot turn away poorly performing students or those with disciplinary problems, whereas charter and parochial schools can and do. And, as happens wherever market forces drive choices, consumers are divided into niche markets that are easily manipulated and sometimes driven to excess. In Michigan, the charter movement, augmented by No Child Left Behind policies, has eroded the separation of church and state, most visibly within the zone where Hamtramck, Detroit, and Highland Park flow into each other, and a Muslim American market has been created. The competition for this market is intense. In this paper, I explore how the market was established, how it is viewed and manipulated from the outside, and the repercussions of this market for the transcommunal politics of Muslims in America.

The Mu'ath bin Jabal "Miracle"

In recent decades metropolitan Detroit has commonly been referred to as the most racially segregated urban area in the United States.[5] The city has lost almost a million residents since its heyday as the "arsenal of democracy" in the postwar years. Its current population is over 80 percent African American, while many suburbs, including several that share long borders with the city, like Dearborn and Warren, are over 90 percent white (and less than 3 percent black) (Southeast Michigan Council of Governments [SEMCOG] 2006). After the transformative uprisings of 1967, jobs and people left the city in record numbers, and Detroit began a downward spiral. The city's tax base, decimated by fleeing residents, forced officials to drastically reduce services like fire protection, snow removal, and community policing, which in turn encouraged more residents to leave. As rents and home values plummeted, newly arriving immigrants and poor black families were able to move into neighborhoods that were once off limits to them.

In this same period—the late 1960s—migrant workers from Yemen began to settle in Dearborn and Detroit, often near the auto manufacturing facilities where they worked. With families still in Yemen, these men were more interested in saving money to send home as remittances than in quality of life issues for themselves in Detroit. They tended to live in sparsely furnished and overcrowded rental units in neighborhoods left behind by white flight. Poletown was one such neighborhood. Still home to a working-class Polish community, it was within walking distance of the large Dodge Main factory. In 1972 Yemeni workers established the Yemen Arab Association and purchased a small club/coffeehouse on Chene Street in Poletown, which quickly became the social center of this small population. Life at the club in the early 1970s was one in which "Ramadan came and went without us noticing it," remembers Abdu Zandani, a founder of Masjid Mu'ath bin Jabal. "The *eids* came and went with no one to celebrate them, because the people weren't involved in religious gatherings. There was no place to gather" (interview with author, May 7, 2005). The only Arab Sunni mosque in Michigan at the time was the American Moslem Society in Dearborn, a mosque run by an earlier generation of Lebanese immigrants and their children. Yemeni workers worshipped there on occasion, but did not feel very welcome. This mosque, with its infamous dances and "Sunday schools," where women covered their hair only when they prayed, and where Christmas seemed almost as important as Eid al-Adha, did not strike the Yemenis as much of a mosque (Abraham 2000).[6]

In the mid-1970s, however, a visiting Jordanian pointed out to the Yemen Arab Association that they could set aside a prayer space in the corner of their club and use this space as a masjid of their own. The club's founders liked the idea and hoped it would remind their members of their religious as well as family obligations. They were also eager to strengthen their organization relative to the socialist-leaning Yemeni Benevolent Association, which had opened in Dearborn at roughly the same time. The club's members set about making a more formal prayer space in a corner of the coffee shop, holding regular prayers, celebrating Islamic holidays, and eventually raising money to purchase a small house, which they converted into a mosque of their own. Fate intervened in 1980, when Detroit and Hamtramck joined with General Motors and the Catholic Archdiocese of Detroit to tear down much of Poletown and build a new General Motors factory in its place. Jobs were on offer in an economy that had crumbled after the Arab oil embargo in the previous decade and the recent closing of Dodge Main. While local Poles resisted this campaign with vigor, the Yemenis quietly sold their mosque and club for a very competitive price and used the cash to purchase a defunct Polish funeral parlor a few blocks beyond the range of the wrecking ball and bulldozer. There they established Masjid Mu'ath bin Jabal (MMBJ) in 1980. Once it became clear that the new jobs promised by GM would not materialize, the mosque's remaining Polish neighbors moved out. Real estate prices entered freefall, and Yemeni and African American investors were able to buy houses in the area, often for as little as a few thousand dollars.[7]

The mosque, meanwhile, began to draw worshippers to the area. When shifts in the Yemeni economy made it less advantageous for men to work in the United States while supporting families in the home country, married men began to bring wives and children to Detroit. They invested in the area's decrepit housing stock, gradually turning the area around the MMBJ into a Yemeni, rather than Polish or African American, neighborhood. This transition was still new and fragile in 1985, when the crack cocaine epidemic hit Detroit. The neighborhood's numerous abandoned homes made it a center of drug-related crime. As men came and went from the mosque in the evening, they were frequently mugged, carjacked, or propositioned by women looking for their next fix. One morning the dead body of a naked woman was found hanging from a tree. For a Muslim community in the midst of a religious revival, the turmoil on display outside the mosque greatly reinforced its commitment to the moral economy that Islam represented within.

Through disciplined effort, the mosque's members began to assert control over area streets. They petitioned local police and the Wayne County Sheriff's Department for more protection. They joined with other neighborhood residents to report on local crack houses and follow up with law enforcement until the houses were cleaned out. They patrolled their own streets at night and around prayer times, to make sure worshippers could come and go on foot to the mosque. They purchased security systems for their vehicles. People from the surrounding neighborhoods began to take notice of the mosque, not simply as a gathering of foreigners to be victimized, but as a viable alternative to drugs and crime. Families from a mix of backgrounds began renting in the neighborhood again. The streets came back to life. When the Catholic church across the street from MMBJ went up for sale in 1987, its priest was eager to hand the facility over to the mosque. MMBJ's leaders decided it was time to move again.

This new facility has served the community well. It has undergone tremendous renovation and expansion, most recently in 2005, when work was completed on the now doubled prayer space. The mosque can (and on most Fridays does) accommodate 1,800 male worshippers and up to 500 women in a spacious balcony. In 1991 the former parochial school next to the mosque was renovated by the newly reorganized Al-Ikhlas Training Academy, formerly the Sister Clara Mohammed School, a Muslim parochial school that had previously served a majority African American population but now draws Yemeni and Bangladeshi students as well.[8] By this time, the crack epidemic had cooled in Detroit, and the neighborhood around the masjid had begun to turn around. As Yemeni immigration picked up in the 1990s, the neighborhood drew new Arab immigrants who could not yet afford Dearborn housing prices. It also drew African American Muslims and Bengali immigrants who appreciated the safety of the neighborhood, the rising property values, the "Islamic culture" on display in the streets, and proximity to the mosque and school. The neighborhood drew non-Muslim Detroiters as well.

As population grew, Yemeni travel agencies began opening in the neighborhood, followed by barber shops, groceries, social service agencies, cell phone centers, and medical clinics. Today, the neighborhood is home to auto workers and store owners, to the unemployed and seasonally employed, to doctors, lawyers, and schoolteachers. On block after block of crowded row houses, satellite dishes, all pointing in the same direction, vie for space on rooftops and facades. The MMBJ parking lot is filled on summer evenings with dozens of ice cream trucks owned by Yemeni drivers who gather at the mosque after finishing their routes. When the call to prayer is broadcast, the neighborhood responds. Men and boys, walking arm in arm, assemble to worship and hear the day's news. After a lull in foot traffic, women and girls take to the streets, visiting back and forth among houses.

Eventually, other mosques began to spring up in the vicinity of MMBJ, mostly small establishments organized by Tijanis (a Sufi order) or Tablighis (a reformist missionary movement), by African American women, or by rival Yemeni factions. Many of these smaller mosques did not survive. Little is left of them except faded signs and handmade shoe racks weathering on unkempt lawns. The Bengali community's first mosque, Baitul-Islam Jamee Masjid, opened a few blocks away from MMBJ in 1995. Today, there are four Bengali mosques in and around Hamtramck, all of which can trace their origins to MMBJ and Baitul-Islam. Two Bosnian mosques and an Indian mosque have also opened nearby, as well as two Yemeni mosques. Some observers might conclude (as do many area residents) that this community of roughly 12,000–16,000 Muslims is highly contentious, and that one mosque should suffice for all, especially the capacious MMBJ. The mosque's leaders, for their part, are sanguine about the diversity of religious institutions they have inspired in the area. They understand that each ethnic community prefers to have services in its own language, and to worship and celebrate Islamic holidays according to its own customs. They also encourage the development of "satellite mosques," places where Muslims who reside outside the immediate neighborhood can easily walk to daily prayers, but still join the larger congregation for Friday prayers and holidays.

On any given evening, MMBJ itself attracts over a hundred worshippers. The mosque serves as a community center as well. Boys play soccer in the parking lot; adult men meet there to socialize, politicians to canvas voters, and missionaries to galvanize the young. Increasingly, officials from local charter schools come by to discuss their offerings with parents and listen to concerns about the future of the mosque's children. Because MMBJ serves a congregation that is primarily Yemeni and new to the U.S., it has attracted the unwelcome attention and presumed surveillance of the FBI. The mosque's leaders do not downplay the injustice of this attention, but they also believe it has strengthened their commitment to represent Islam accurately and well, to serve as mediators between the neighborhood and the larger society, and to engage actively in the education, both religious and otherwise, of the next generation.

Highland Park and Hamtramck: A Study in Contrasts

Highland Park, Michigan, was home to the first mosque built in America, the Moslem Mosque, which opened its doors in 1921, when Henry Ford's assembly line was revolutionizing automobile production and the city itself was a symbol of American industrial might, modernity, and efficiency. Ironically, Ford had already begun to transfer his capital investments several years earlier from Highland Park to Dearborn, where he was building the River Rouge complex, a much larger, vertically integrated complex of factories. By 1921, many of the Syrian workers for whom the mosque was built had moved several miles away to be closer to this new source of employment. The mosque failed, in part because of this population shift, and was sold in 1927,[9] the same year Ford's Highland Park assembly plant closed its doors to automobile production. While the city held on to its middle-class status for decades, it suffered the same plight Detroit suffered after the 1967 riots, with middle-class families fleeing to the suburbs, taking jobs and tax dollars with them.

Today the city's housing stock is crumbling. Its McGregor Public Library, a beautiful Carnegie building, is boarded up with its books and records still inside, covered in dust, mold, and rodent droppings. Faced with bankruptcy, the city's administration and school district were taken over by the State of Michigan in 2001. The city lost 20 percent of its population between 1990 and 2005, dropping to just 16,000 residents, less than a third of whom own their own homes. Many in the renting population are transient, so school adminis-trators cannot place children effectively in classrooms until after the first week of school each year, according to Belvin Liles, the director of the Highland Park Career Academy. Forty percent of residents live below the poverty line, and the city today is 98 percent African American (SEMCOG 2006). Having transitioned from model city to postmodern dystopia, Highland Park now has one of the worst per capita crime rates in the country. Detroiters, whose city is often described in similar language, joke about skirting Highland Park for safety reasons when they cross town. Currently, the city is home to one small Tablighi mosque, Masjid al-Nur, whose congregation, unlike that of MMBJ, avoids politics, the public schools, and most interaction with outsiders. The remnants of several mosques can be found around the corner from Masjid al-Nur, on Hamilton Avenue, one of the city's main thoroughfares. These ruins, like those of a former Nation of Islam temple, are gradually being reclaimed by nature.

Highland Park and Hamtramck are a study in contrasts. They were created under remarkably similar circumstances; both are small islands embedded within Detroit (Highland Park comprises 2.9 square miles, Hamtramck 2.2), but Hamtramck was associated directly with the Dodge Main factory, which remained in production until 1979, and with one ethnic group rather than many. The city's Polish American community, which was large and politically influential, especially in local labor politics, did not abandon the city as rapidly as other groups, enabling Hamtramck and Poletown to postpone the white flight that sealed Highland Park's fate in the 1970s. But as Poletown's families were forced to relocate in the 1980s, they drew Hamtramck's residents into the northern suburbs along with them. Hamtramck began its own rapid decline (Kowalski 2002, Radzilowski 2006), a trend that enabled immigrants from Ye-men, Bangladesh, Africa, Bosnia, and India to afford housing in Hamtramck. While Highland Park and Hamtramck share a common border, Hamtramck has benefited most from the arrival of newcomers from the Muslim world. The city's population has increased by 25 percent since 1990, and its housing stock has risen correspondingly in value. In 2000, Hamtramck residents were 60 percent white (including Arabs), 14 percent black, and 12 percent Asian, with only 23 percent living below the poverty line. The percentage of households in the higher income brackets tripled between 1990 and 2000 (SEMCOG 2006).

Unlike Highland Park, whose school population is over 98 percent African American, the Hamtramck Public Schools are filled with immigrants from Muslim-majority nations. In 2006–2007, their classrooms boasted students from twenty-four countries of origin. Several first languages, including Bengali

(25%), Arabic (20%), Bosnian (10%), Polish (4%), and Albanian (2%), were spoken in the hallways alongside English (Hamtramck Public Schools 2008). It is difficult to find educators in Hamtramck who speak positively about the challenges this diversity creates. Yet the public schools, overtaxed by non-English-language communities and riddled with ethnic tension among teens, are nonetheless eager to prevent the loss of their Muslim students to charter schools, or to Highland Park.[10] It is at this intersection between Detroit, Hamtramck, and Highland Park that the competition for Muslims is being waged.

Free-Market School Reform, Muslim American Style

The Highland Park Schools (HPS) did their homework before launching a pilot program designed to attract Muslim students to their district. They had begun accepting Detroit and Hamtramck students through the Schools of Choice program almost as soon as it was passed into law and had been very successful at drawing large numbers of non-resident students into their district, largely through a simple but well-timed advertising campaign. In 2003 alone, 45 percent of their student population was non-resident, adding over $2 million to their budget, staving off significant school closings, and keeping the HPS administration out of the hands of state authorities. Many of the non-resident students who matriculated in Highland Park had serious disciplinary, academic, or personal problems. The HPS developed a flexible program to help underachieving students graduate or complete GED certification. Known as the Career Academy, it was led by Belvin Liles. In 2003 HPS brought in a new superintendent, Dr. Theresa Saunders, who was eager to expand the district's policy of attracting students from Detroit and Hamtramck, but she was also under tremendous pressure to raise standardized test scores in the city. The school board sought to bring in a new population of non-resident students, one that would reflect the increasing diversity found in adjoining communities and might also improve discipline and standardized test scores in Highland Park.

With these goals in mind, Dr. Saunders was steered toward the Masjid Muʿath bin Jabal model by members of the Highland Park City Council and the Highland Park Development Authority (HPDA), who also had their eye on the immigrant enclaves thriving across their borders in Hamtramck and Detroit. The HPDA was planning a large single-family housing development in the city, North Pointe Village, but was concerned about attracting new residents, given the municipality's crime rate, low percentage of owner-occupied homes, and abysmal test scores in the public schools. To find buyers for these new homes, which would be priced at two and three times the average value of existing houses in the city, they pinned their hopes on the Muslim immigrants who were buying up properties in Hamtramck and Detroit. According to one observer, the project was driven by an "if we build it, they will come" mindset: "If we bring the students, the students will bring their families. They will buy houses, one after the other." Saunders hired Yahya Alkebsi, a Yemeni American educator, to research the types of programs Muslims in neighboring communities would like to see and then to design a curriculum and other programs to tempt them across city lines.

In most of this work, the Highland Park Schools replicated the techniques local charter schools use to attract Muslim students. They begin by offering Arabic-language instruction, which means Arabic-speaking teachers as well. As the competition for Muslim students has heated up over the years, these simple offerings are augmented by an expanding array of options and accommodations, a process that contrasts sharply with that followed by districts like Dearborn and Detroit. Over a period of thirty years, the Dearborn and Detroit districts developed Arabic-language programs, policies regarding prayer in the schools and the observation of Muslim holidays, and rules regarding female modesty in sports or physical education, among many other issues, all in close collaboration with students, parents, teachers, and administrators. Change has sometimes been painful, but the growing presence of Arab and Muslim teachers and administrators within these districts has eased the process of accommodation. HPS, like a dozen or more local charter schools, sought to outmaneuver more experienced districts by hiring an Arab Muslim consultant, treating Muslims families more directly like consumers, and agreeing to segregate Muslim students from mainstream classrooms, a policy that is routinely denied in Highland Park, but is also very much on display in local charter schools.[11]

When Alkebsi began his market research on the needs and desires of local families, he began in Hamtramck, and the list of services he created reads like a direct critique of the Hamtramck Public Schools. Here I explore the educational options Highland Park developed, providing background into how such programs evolved in other area districts and their current availability. In greater Detroit, Muslim enclaves are acutely aware of the rights and privileges Muslims residing in other communities have achieved, just as non-Muslims are aware of accommodations being made in their municipalities. This knowledge informs the political issues around which Muslims and their adversaries organize, and "special accommodations" in area schools are commonly posed as evidence of changing levels of Islamophobia and Islamophilia in greater Detroit.

1. Arabic-language instruction. The Dearborn Public Schools, with a student body that is currently over 75 percent Arab American/Muslim, pioneered Arabic-language instruction at the elementary and high school levels in the early 1980s. While it has been taught in at least one of its high schools ever since, at the elementary and middle school levels Arabic is provided in only a few schools as part of a highly praised dual-language program. Much of the campaign to provide Arabic to younger students came from education specialists who had long tried to improve performance for English as a Second Language (ESL) students. The program was highly controversial throughout the 1990s, but was eventually embraced by administrators under pressure to stave off competition from charter and parochial schools.

In Detroit, where Arabic speakers are a small minority of students, Arabic-language instruction was not available until mandated by parent activism and competition created by charter schools in the mid-1990s. Arabic and Bangla are now offered as second languages of instruction in neighborhood schools with a sizable Yemeni, Iraqi, or Bengali population. Only one elementary school, in an Iraqi area of town, offers these programs during the regular school week. The others make Arabic available more sporadically, after school and on weekends, through grants provided by the No Child Left Behind Act that President George W. Bush signed in 2002. These services are usually contracted out to the Arab Community Center for Economic and Social Services (ACCESS), which is based in Dearborn.

Hamtramck Public Schools have not yet offered Arabic or Bangla instruction, despite having lost over four hundred Arab and Bengali students to charter schools in the 2003–2004 year alone. Parent requests and lobbying by area mosques and other institutions have not been successful on this front. The district's guidance counselor, Virindar Chaudery, worked up a lengthy position paper on the subject in 2004–2005, advocating for including both languages in the high school curriculum, but his effort was widely resisted in the schools. Hamtramck's new superintendent of schools, Dr. Felix Chow, was also approached about providing Arabic-language courses in the high schools. He responded to a committee of concerned Muslim leaders by saying that he did not want to bring "religion" into the schools, a comment that greatly offended those on hand.[12]

It was in this heated environment that Yahya Alkebsi first began his research for HPS. He originally set out to create a foreign-language magnet school, School A, which would offer a diverse array of second-language options. As Alkebsi interviewed Muslim families, however, he found that even families from non-Arab regions of Africa, Asia, and Europe tended to rank Arabic second on their list of choices, while Arabs and African Americans ranked it first. When he was unable to identify a qualified teacher of Bengali, he established Arabic as the school's second-language priority, but promised to add additional languages once the program was off the ground and more teachers could be hired.

2. *Islamic holidays.* The campaign to have the Dearborn Public Schools close for the two principal Islamic holidays, Eid al-Adha and Eid al-Fitr, began in the early 1980s with parents "kicking and screaming," according to Wageh Saad, director of student services, to have their holidays accommodated in the same way Easter and Christmas were. This move met a great deal of resistance among teachers, the school board, and administrators, but by 1985, as the Arab populations continued to increase and Muslim students began staying home regardless, Dearborn began allowing Muslims to be absent on these holidays without penalty. (Several school buildings had been 95 percent empty on Muslim holidays prior to 1985.) In 1994, when school finance reform was passed in Michigan, the state began mandating a minimum number of school days with an attendance rate set at 80 percent or higher. Given that more than half the student population was already taking off for Islamic holidays, Dearborn adopted a districtwide policy of closing for Islamic holidays rather than forgoing state revenue for these days.

Detroit established a policy of absence without penalty for Islamic holidays (two days each) around 1990. The Hamtramck Public Schools had a difficult time making this concession, even though it is now mandated by law through No Child Left Behind legislation. In 2004, they officially changed their policy to allow Muslim students one day's absence without penalty for each eid, but roughly 40 percent of their student body observed a two-day holiday, so they changed their policies again in 2006 to accommodate two-day holiday observances. The Highland Park magnet package mirrored Dearborn's policy. The school would close two days for each holiday.

3. *Arabic culture classes.* Parents also requested that an Islamic history and culture course be offered as an elective in the HPS magnet. These courses are regularly offered at private Islamic schools, and many immigrant parents are familiar with such offerings from their own educational experiences overseas. African American parents also expressed interest in such an offering, to counter the Eurocentrism and negative bias about Africa and Islam that lingers in textbooks used in public school curricula. Alkebsi wanted to offer such a class as an elective in the high school and to incorporate it into the social studies curriculum at lower grades. Administrators in HPS balked at this suggestion, expressing concern that it veered into the teaching of religion. As a compromise, they accepted a course on "Arabic history and culture." (Each

of my informants, regardless of perspective, regarded this course as a Trojan horse for bringing religious instruction into the classroom.)

4. *Halal meals.* Despite the abundance of halal butchers and groceries in the Detroit area today, it has been very difficult for public schools to offer halal meals to Muslim students. In Dearborn, vegetarian alternatives to non-halal meals have been provided districtwide since the early 1980s, but only a few schools offer strictly halal products. The city has tried to negotiate contracts with several distributors, but cannot get the prices down to an affordable level. A few schools in Dearborn have managed to locate discretionary funds to defray some of these additional costs, but for the most part, even in Dearborn, halal meals are not an option. Alkebsi promised families he would provide halal meals in Highland Park, but he was not able to deliver on this promise. Vegetarian meals were offered instead.

5. *Community liaisons.* Public school systems in districts undergoing tremendous population shifts are often troubled by conflict, and their administrators, knowingly or not, are prone to identify with the status quo. Dearborn and Detroit first hired second-generation Arab American teachers in the 1950s and 1960s, when their ethnicity was not especially relevant to their jobs. But by the late 1970s and early 1980s, when immigration to Michigan from the Middle East brought thousands of new students to both districts, they began hiring Arabic speakers, first in their bilingual programs, and then gradually in mainstream classrooms throughout their districts. In the 1970s and 1980s these teachers acted as go-betweens for Arab families and the schools. Today this work is handled not only by classroom teachers, but by administrators at all levels of the system and by professional liaisons as well.[13]

Hamtramck, however, which has seemed to lack flexibility, has refused to hire a liaison for either the Arab or Bengali populations, arguing that "we have students from 32 different cultural areas in our schools. We cannot afford to hire 32 different community liaisons." In fact, the district's guidance counselor, Dr. Chaudery, has played this advocacy role with sensitivity and acuity, but even he suggests it is time for someone else to take on this responsibility (interview with author, 2006). This is one of the district's most egregious offenses from the perspective of Muslim immigrant families, who point out the Polish and other surnames of the district's staff. As one teacher told me, "In Hamtramck Bengali and Arab students make up half of the student body, but they are not respected by the board, or by the superintendent. I don't mean that if you are Polish you should study Polish, or French, French, but the community should be approached and be a partner in making policy and getting them involved in the schools. And the administration, they don't have a clue at all."

Parents, teachers, and administrators all seemed to agree that the number one advantage of Highland Park's plan was its hardworking and dynamic consultant/liaison.

6. *School prayer.* Prayer in the public schools has long been a hotly contested legal issue. The No Child Left Behind Act made it much easier for Americans to practice their religion within the confines of public schools, as long as the schools themselves do not endorse or require such participation. Michigan law allows for students to spend up to two hours a week in religious instruction off site, provided it does not detract from the amount of time they spend in class.

Dearborn began allowing high school students to attend Friday prayers during Ramadan in the early 1990s. After a period of trial and error, the schools adopted a policy requiring students to return from the mosque with a note from the imam vouching for their attendance.[14] Most other districts now accommodate similar absences, although given the irregularity of prayer times throughout the year, and given the amount of travel time required between school and mosque, only a handful of students in any area high school take advantage of this allowance. Students are allowed to pray individually or to organize group prayers on site as long as teachers do not encourage or lead the process, and most local districts interpret state and federal statutes as requiring them to offer space to students for prayer. High schools in Dearborn and Detroit often have spaces set aside for prayer during the school day.[15] In Hamtramck, Dr. Chaudery's office is used for students who wish to pray during the school day, but Asian students are often hesitant to pray there, perhaps because Chaudery is Hindu.

The Highland Park offer accommodated prayer on and off site.[16] School staff would not lead the prayer, but it would be accommodated on site. Several of the newer charter schools close early on Fridays or are closed entirely on Fridays so students can attend congregational prayers with their families.[17]

7. *Gender segregation.* As long as both sexes are provided equal instruction within the same school, gender segregation is possible in Michigan. In Highland Park, Henry Ford Academy already segregates its classes by sex. In low-income districts, sex segregation is thought to increase student performance and is often considered an attractive alternative to mainstream classrooms. The practice is not followed in Dearborn, in the majority of Detroit schools, or in Hamtramck, although in certain cases in both Dearborn and Detroit students voluntarily sit on separate sides of the classroom, segregating themselves by gender (Sarroub 2005). Islamic parochial schools in the area do not segregate their classrooms by gender either. This offering was not one the HPS volunteered to Muslim

families. The idea was proposed to Alkebsi during the research phase of his program's development. Once he saw that for many families this matter was a large selling point, he began promising it to others. The idea took on a life of its own for the Muslim magnet and became a key marketing point and locus of controversy concerning the school. Several charter high schools in the area are now also offering gender-segregated classrooms, most notably Riverside Academy–West, which is housed in a former Muslim parochial school adjoining the Islamic Institute of Knowledge, a well-established, conservative Dearborn mosque.

Pitch, Success, and Backfire

In promoting School A's bundle of services, Superintendent Saunders had to move carefully. She did not want to give the appearance that she preferred immigrant students over African American students, or Muslim students over Christian or non-religious ones. Once her staff decided that the Arabic-language package might work for the city, they commissioned a public opinion survey of residents to find out if the program would raise objections among voters. It did not. Yahya Alkebsi was then hired to market School A to Muslim families in the area. He went door-to-door in immigrant neighborhoods, revisiting families he had spoken to during his market survey, reassuring them that their voices had been heard. Much of his time was spent addressing people's fears about the safety of Highland Park and the quality of the HPS. "We are not satisfied with the schools here in Hamtramck or Detroit, and you are talking about Highland Park? Are you crazy? You need to have your head examined," were refrains Alkebsi heard over and again. He also presented the Highland Park package in local media and received generous coverage in English, Arabic, and Bengali.

It is worth noting that Alkebsi's Arabic-language stories emphasized Islamic observances and gender segregation at the academy, while English-language stories made no mention of these, and highlighted instead the foreign-language emphasis of the program and Highland Park's desire to attract Muslim residents.[18] He also promoted the plan actively in local mosques, an activity he found personally troubling. Gaining the support of mosque leadership, especially the imam, "puts you in an enviable position [relative to the competition], because he [the imam] will really help, but some people understand that if you are going into the mosque, then you are trying to bring religion into the schools" (interview with author, February 22, 2006).

Administrators in Hamtramck and Detroit were fully aware of the HPS campaign and, again, drew parallels between the Highland Park model and the campaigns undertaken by area charter schools. Amal David, a bilingual coordinator with the Detroit Public Schools (DPS), had the following to say about HPS's publicity campaign, as well as that of local charters: "Highland Park was superaggressive in their campaign. They said 'yes' to halal foods, 'yes' to prayer in school, 'yes' to Arabic instruction. . . . Like the charters, they can afford to hire people whose job it is just to promote their programs to students. They visit mosques, speak from the pulpit, distribute multilingual flyers, even offer cash incentives to families" (interview with author, April 14, 2006). Al-Ikhlas Training Academy also lost several families to the Highland Park campaign, and the school's director, Nadir Ahmad, was more direct in stating his reservation about what the Highland Park campaign offered Muslim families. He told me that many of the more conservative Yemeni families, in particular, who had begun sending their children to Al-Ikhlas Academy when it moved into the Mua'th bin Jabal facility, took their daughters out of school when they reached high school because they did not like a co-ed environment, even in a Muslim parochial school. It was these families who, in the end, were willing to send their children to Highland Park, not for the Arabic classes or the halal meals, but because HPS had gone further than any local charters or Islamic schools by offering gender segregation. This factor, Ahmad suggested, put School A at the apex of the Muslim niche market in Detroit (interview with author, April 17, 2006).

Amal David agreed, adding that most of the Bengali and Yemeni families who leave the DPS are doing so not just because of language or food issues, but because "they want the whole environment to be Muslim or of their ethnicity. They are worried about the moral contamination they see on display in the DPS and are afraid for their children's future." "The ban on premarital sex," David continued, "is very strong among Yemenis, in particular, who prefer sex-segregated classrooms. Many of them still take their daughters out of school at middle school age and send them back to Yemen. The girls in this community still marry very young, for the most part, and sex for them would spoil their character as a whole, their future, so it is too important a matter to leave to chance. Most of those who opt for charters do so because they feel lost in this new culture. Others feel the DPS are not safe because they have heard of a violent fight at school, or because of ethnic tensions or discrimination, but for most families it is a question of being in an environment where the teachers and the students understand about this moral contamination and will not let it happen."

Alkebsi agreed that this conservative tendency, a fear of the larger society and its potential to contaminate the vulnerable and the young (especially females), was indeed at the core of what attracted many parents to the HPS campaign. He also admits that the competition to attract Muslim families to Highland Park produced outcomes he found personally disturbing. While his education and temperament encouraged him to appreciate the advantages of America's multicultural society, he found himself catering to isolationist trends in his own ethnic (Yemeni) community. Similarly, while the Highland Park Schools had sought to create a "universal academy" that would bring ethnic, and perhaps class, diversity to their town, they instead found themselves managing a school program that raised new barriers between Muslim non-resident and non-Muslim resident populations.

The city's initial attraction to the qualities on display in the Masjid Muʻath bin Jabal neighborhood—two-parent households, reduced drug-related crime, and entrepreneurialism—qualities they viewed in economic terms and sought to attract to Highland Park, were connected to the same qualities Detroit's Muslim families viewed in moral terms and about which they felt intensely protective; namely, the sexual inaccessibility of their population's unmarried females. HPS wanted intact families to contribute to upward mobility, owner-occupied houses, strong ethnic co-residence, and the development of an immigrant enclave in Highland Park. Muslim families sought to extend the gender-segregated spaces they had established around the mosque into the public schools. They saw their neighborhood's conservative gender norms as an invaluable defense against the qualities of American life most threatening to them: crime, violence, teen sex, drug use, contempt for parents. While School A offered Arabic classes and other tools students could use to understand, practice, and interpret Islam for themselves, it was the school's offer to isolate Muslim students from the mainstream population that ultimately accounted for its success. It was this same isolation that also brought about the school's rapid demise.

As advertised, School A opened in the fall of 2005 with over three hundred students. Their Arabic instruction was more thorough than that of local charters, their rules more open to the everyday practice of Islam, their faculty made up of certified teachers from diverse cultural backgrounds, their classrooms segregated by gender. While HPS had marketed the school to non-Muslims in the area as well as Muslims, and to their own residents, only Muslims from surrounding communities applied. "I am proud to say that I brought to Highland Park diversity," asserts Alkebsi. "If you saw the students that we had (and if things had been allowed to continue they would have grown)—white

American Muslims, black American Muslims, Africans, Senegalese, Somalis, Bengalis, Pakistanis, Indians, Hispanics. When you visited the school you saw all this diversity inside."

Yet as HPS officials looked on, they saw something else. They saw a rejection of Highland Park rather than an integration of it. "It looked and acted and felt like a charter school," said Belvin Liles, "not a public school, a charter school, or even a parochial school." In this respect it made teachers and administrators outside the school intensely uncomfortable. Alkebsi found himself listening to hostile statements about Islam. One school board member asked the superintendent if the Department of Homeland Security had approved their plans for the school. Non-Muslim teachers, meanwhile, were given a crash course on Islamic practices like *wuduu* (ritual bathing of the extremities in preparation for prayer), which left bathroom floors wet and dangerous. Tensions mounted.

The HPS system had expected one hundred students to enroll in School A during its first year, then for the program to expand incrementally over several years. When over three hundred students showed up on opening day, the district had to scramble to make both classrooms and teachers available. The district was overwhelmed and also stunned by what Alkebsi's campaign had wrought. In the words of Belvin Liles, "The African American community said, 'Look, if you want to do this, fine. We want our kids to be a part of it. We don't want a segregated group. We want real diversity. We want to make—we need to make—small class sizes, religious freedom, religious inclusion and all that stuff for everybody. If you want to start it in this school, fine. But we want everybody to be able to be included in this school.' And the Muslim population said, 'That is not what we were promised.'" At this point the superintendent, citing budget shortfalls and the lack of enrolled Highland Park residents, pulled the plug on School A. The experiment had succeeded and failed. HPS had won the competition to attract Muslim students, but lost the war.

"If they had given us a chance for the program to go on, I think it would have been good for them," Alkebsi argued. "There were a lot of challenges from both sides . . . but from the school side, they weren't ready for this. They need money and stable leadership." The Muslim students who had put their faith in the HPS campaign wound up returning to the public schools in Hamtramck and Detroit for the remainder of the year. In 2006–2007 many tried their luck in one of several new charter schools that opened in and around Hamtramck, also offering Arabic instruction, accommodating prayer, closing for Islamic holidays, and prominently displaying Muslim leadership and staff. These schools continue to compete with one another, with Al-Ikhlas Academy, and with the public schools for Muslim students.

Meanwhile, North Pointe Village, the housing development Highland Park officials had initially hoped to fill with Muslim families, is also a failed endeavor. It is unclear if a single Muslim family bought into the development, but by June 2008, a scant three years after construction began on the first house, most of the finished units stand boarded up, empty, and foreclosed. Constructed by a fly-by-night contractor, the houses never lived up to expectations. They suffered from plumbing and wiring problems, shoddy workmanship and shoddy materials. While initially placed on the market for as much as $155,000, today they can be bought for as little as $5,000. Perhaps the majority of them have been condemned (*Detroit Free Press,* June 19, 2008, p. 1B).

School A failed, but the demise of Highland Park's campaign to attract immigrants to their city took place in a larger context, in which Muslim inclusion and incorporation proceed at a rapid pace. Throughout the Detroit area, Muslims are acutely aware of the rights and privileges they have achieved, just as non-Muslims are aware of the religious accommodations being made where they live or work. This knowledge shapes the political issues around which Muslims and their adversaries organize, and special accommodations in area schools are commonly posed as evidence of changes in the social position of Muslims—their acceptability—in each local municipality. These educational projects are an important stage on which Muslim identities are performed, evaluated, and reconfigured. They are also important stages on which Muslims perform their American identities, assert their rights, and manage the phobic and philic tendencies that shape the way non-Muslims view them and, to a growing extent, the way American Muslims view each other.

In Detroit, these identity projects require Muslims to collaborate across racial and ethnic lines, across classes, across urban and suburban boundaries, across sectarian divides, and across the gaps that separate immigrants and their children from those with deeper American roots. Al-Ikhlas Academy, with its African American history and its multicultural present, is supported as much by the donations of wealthy suburbanites as it is by tuition from inner-city families. CAIR-Michigan has an articulate, energetic director, Dawud Walid, who seems to be in all places at once, speaking about Sunni-Shi'a unity, urban-suburban unity, immigrant and American born unity; and championing the civil rights of Muslims when these are threatened or denied. Mosque bulletin boards and websites are crowded with notices of fund-raising campaigns for new mosque construction, comedy tours, youth programs, or appeals to support poor and war-torn communities around the globe. Detroit's Muslim population is active, often progressive, and incorporated into local political and economic structures in ways that have provided genuine protection from hate crimes and discrimination in the period following the 9/11 attacks, even as the Justice Department has tried to remake Detroit as the centerpiece of its domestic "war on terror."

Yet the extent of Muslim incorporation in Detroit cannot fully protect this local population from a national climate in which Islam is routinely represented as dangerous and Muslims as a security threat. Detroit's Muslims contend with local bigotry and ignorance, often manifest in the self appointed "anti-Islamist" activists who hound community leaders in the blogosphere, stirring up suspicion when Muslims open a mosque in a new municipality, run for political office, or achieve new forms of public accommodation for their faith. Curiously, Highland Park's School A project was not caught up in this web of sensationalism. Perhaps this was due to Highland Park's relative invisibility. Perhaps it was due to the way the story was initially framed—not as a tale of Muslims demanding rights from beleaguered school officials, but instead as one of beleaguered school officials fighting hard to attract Muslim students. Perhaps the story did not seem controversial enough. Public schools throughout Detroit are filled with Muslim students, many are managed by Muslim teachers and administrators, and many accommodate Muslims with minimal conflict. These schools are indistinguishable from those with few or no Muslim students.

In New York City, where an equally large, diverse, and historically significant Muslim population resides, educators who sought to create an Arabic-language magnet school recently fared very differently. Debbie Almontaser, an award-winning educator and interfaith activist, was appointed to establish the Khalil Gibran International Academy in New York in 2007. The Gibran Academy was modeled on the city's other foreign-language magnet schools, none of which had been controversial, and most of which were prompted by a loss of students to newly opening charter schools. Almontaser was slandered as a "radical," a "jihadist," and a "9/11 denier" in a vicious media campaign that greeted the public announcement of the school's opening. The Gibran Academy's most adamant critic, Daniel Pipes, justified his attack in the *New York Times,* arguing that it "is hard to see how violence, how terrorism will lead to the implementation of sharia. It is much easier to see how, working through the system, the school system, the media, the religious organizations, the government, businesses and the like you can promote radical Islam" (April 28, 2008). The crisis surrounding the school was so intense that Mayor Bloomberg's office eventually stepped in and forced Almontaser to resign (see chapter 2).

The Khalil Gibran Academy, unlike Highland Park's School A, benefited from excellent planning, modest objectives, and a solid funding stream. Yet strong opposition to the school emerged that was totally unlike the negative reaction that doomed School A. Critics of the Gibran Academy wanted to disempower and silence Muslims, to challenge their fitness for citizenship, and to banish them from the public stage on which legitimate American identities are constructed. In Highland Park, by contrast, School A failed because it was seen as a valuable resource rather than a threat, as a site of opportunity and social mobility that was not as accessible to the larger public as school officials had intended it to be. The city planners of Highland Park actually admired the communities Muslims have created for themselves in Hamtramck and Detroit; they were not threatened by Muslims, or by the community-building potential of immigrant enclaves. In the end, however, they realized that tapping into this potential might empower Muslims without producing any tangible gains (at least in the short run) for Highland Park's non-Muslim, native-born, African American majority. This important contrast should attune us to the uneven incorporation of Muslims as citizens of the United States, and encourage us as scholars to look beyond the crisis writ large to explore how things work at the local level—the level at which ethnographers and social historians have always done their best, most distinctive work.

Miranda Joseph has cautioned those who participate in the work of community to think about how "community," as an idea, is used to supplement the marketplace rather than correct its deficiencies. In my experience, many community activists describe their projects in precisely the supplementary terms Joseph decries. In Michigan, public schools compete with one another for students, the communities they represent, and for capital from the state. The Highland Park Schools had little more to offer in this competition than their willingness to compete. What they wanted from this exchange was a resource Muslim immigrant communities in the area seem to embody, a cultural capital both precious and fragile. Manifest in their conservative social values, religious orthodoxy, ethnic solidarities, and willingness to work so hard and sacrifice so much to be in Detroit, this cultural capital is all most working-class immigrant Muslims have. African Americans in Highland Park suspected that the students and teachers at School A were not willing to share this cultural resource with non-Muslims. In short, they opposed the school because the moral advantages it represented, and the economic and political renewal it promised for Highland Park, did not seem genuinely public. Ironically, this conclusion is drawn by many educators who are now deeply skeptical of charter schools, whose benefits (such as they are) tend to come at the expense of mainstream public schools.

It is still not clear who the winners in the current educational competition for local Muslims will be. Highland Park's North Pointe housing development has failed. Hamtramck continues to struggle with its transformation into a twenty-first-century, new-immigrant, and working-class enclave. The public schools there have begun to target advertising campaigns toward Detroit's students in an effort to replace the large number of Hamtramck residents who now study in area charter schools. Together, these Detroiters continue to search for a way beyond the urban crisis that engulfs them. Suburban communities, including those with affluent, well-established Muslim residents, look on and draw lessons from Hamtramck and Detroit about who Muslims in America are and what kind of neighbors they are likely to make.

And the White House looks on as well. In 2006 President Bush announced a new initiative, the Less Commonly Taught Languages Program, that provides financial support for Arabic second-language instruction in target districts throughout the country. Why? Because U.S. foreign policy has generated a need for more Arabic-speakers who can translate the volumes of intelligence information captured daily in Arabic. If you doubt that the federal government is also competing for local Muslims, come to the Dearborn International Arab Festival in June, or open any of the Arabic-language or Arab American newspapers published in Detroit. There you will find the prominent sponsorship of the U.S. Armed Forces, the FBI, and the CIA. Transnational, translocal, transcommunal—the competition for Muslims is on. And the stakes are as high as, or higher than, the urban renewal of Detroit.

Notes

1. Today Muslims (African American, Bengali, and Yemeni) hold half of the city council seats in Hamtramck.

2. Such as the Nation of Islam itself, which appropriated much of Islamic doctrine and practice while rejecting even more, thereby preventing the participation of more orthodox Muslims within the movement.

3. The exact amount differs from one district to the next based on a complicated formula intended to redress imbalances between wealthy and poor districts. Additional funds are provided to support districts with declining enrollments, those with large bilingual education programs and those with other special needs; see http://aftmichigan.org/takeaction/capitol/capitolNO07.html.

4. Author interviews with Amal David (March 6, 2006) and Belvin Liles (May 17, 2006).

5. It is beyond the scope of this paper to trace the origins of Detroit's segregated land-scape. For recent work on this subject see especially Sugrue (1996), Farley, Danziger, and Holzer (2000), and Hartigan (1999).

6. The Albanian Islamic Center, the Islamic Center of America, and Masjid al-Mumineen were also functioning in the Detroit area in the early 1970s, but they were not attractive to the Yemenis for linguistic, ethnic, and sectarian reasons.

7. This narrative of Masjid Mu'ath bin Jabal's history and that of its neighborhood is drawn from author interviews with Salah al-Ghanaim and Abdu Zandani, leaders, founders, and spokesmen for the mosque (December 2005). I also interviewed Imam Mohammed Musa, who led the American Moslem Society in Dearborn from 1981 to 2001 and owns a rental property near MMBJ (October 2005).

8. In many ways this is the first "Islamic" school in the country. It descends directly from the University of Islam established by Fard Mohammed in 1933, developed and man-aged over the years by Mohammed's Temple #1 (now Masjid Wali Mohammed), and spun off as an independent school in 1991.

9. A history of the Highland Park mosque is available in my dissertation (Howell 2009).

10. At the outset of the 2007–2008 school year, Bridge Academy and Frontier Academy, two Arabic-focused charter schools operating in Hamtramck, had a combined enroll-ment of 879. Both schools are managed by Global Educational Excellence and chartered by Central Michigan University, despite being headquartered in Ann Arbor, Michigan. Established by Mohammed Issa, the group currently operates six schools (of which two are in Hamtramck, two in Dearborn, and two in Washtenaw County) that concentrate on Arabic-language instruction and a "character building" curriculum that focuses on "respect, cooperation, honesty and integrity, safety, perseverance, responsibility, conservation, and consideration." Their high school in Dearborn offers gender-segregated classrooms. The group has recently opened a school that emphasizes Spanish rather than Arabic as a second language. Hamtramck Academy, chartered by Bay Mills College, has an enrollment of 428 and also emphasizes a values curriculum. They do not offer Arabic as a second language. See http://hamtramck.heritageacademies.com/.

11. HPS administrators do not deny that the magnet school they established to attract Muslim families segregated Muslims from others in their district; instead, they deny that this was ever their intention. They contend that Alkebsi's marketing strategy offered more than the HPS was comfortable with, and might have reached beyond what is allowable by law.

12. This statement was controversial because it acknowledged (rightly) the Arabic lan-guage's pivotal role in prayer and other Muslim devotional practices. It is the language in which the Quran was revealed and in which most Islamic jurisprudence has been written. Dr. Chow overlooked the fact that Arabic is also the first language of twenty-five countries and is spoken by over 300 million people worldwide. The multiethnic coalition that has petitioned repeatedly for Arabic instruction in Hamtramck, however, is uniformly Muslim. Hamtramck and Detroit Public Schools administrators have also noted the lack of qualified

Arabic instructors available in the area and have mentioned this as one reason they have been slow to offer second-language instruction in their districts.

13. Most suburban districts also have liaisons for the Arab and Chaldean populations and for other immigrant populations as determined by demographic need. The Dearborn Public Schools in the 2007–2008 school year had Arab American principals in ten of their twenty-nine schools.

14. Prior to this policy it was found that the majority of the students who left school to attend prayers were actually truant from both school and mosque. Very few students take advantage of this program, and many have argued that it is more appropriate for students to make up their prayers after school hours. See Sarroub (2005) for a different take on Dearborn's experience of this policy and many of the others described above.

15. One Dearborn high school, Fordson, has two prayer spaces, one used by Shi'a and one by Sunni students.

16. The latter concession was won after Alkebsi shared a hadith with school officials suggesting that if you were within a certain distance of a mosque on Friday, you were obligated to attend the mosque for prayer.

17. This latter concession is not popular with parents of young children, who are forced to provide additional child care on Fridays due to their work schedules or other obligations.

18. Coverage of Alkebsi's efforts appeared in the *Detroit Free Press, Community Forum and Link, Arab American News,* and *Hamtramck Chronicle,* among other media outlets.

Works Cited

Abraham, Nabeel. 1978. *National and Local Politics: A Study of Political Conflicts in the Yemeni Immigrant Community of Detroit, Michigan.* Ph.D. diss., University of Michigan.

———. 2000. "Arab Detroit's 'American' Mosque." In *Arab Detroit: From Margin to Mainstream,* ed. Nabeel Abraham and Andrew Shryock, 279–309. Detroit: Wayne State University Press.

Aidi, Hisham. 2003. "Let Us Be Moors: Islam, Race and 'Connected Histories.'" *Middle East Report* 229: 42–53.

American Federation of Teachers. 2007. "School Aid Report 2007–2008." AFT Capital Report, November 2007. AFT Michigan: Lansing. http://aftmichigan.org/takeaction/capitol/capitolNO07.html.

Aswad, Barbara. 1974. "The Southeast Dearborn Arab Community Struggles for Survival against Urban 'Renewal.'" In *Arabic Speaking Communities in American Cities,* ed. Barbara C. Aswad, 53–84. New York: Center for Migration Studies.

Bald, Vivek. 2006. "Overlapping Diasporas, Multiracial Lives: South Asian Muslims in U.S. Communities of Color, 1880–1950." *Souls* 8(4): 3–18.

Dannin, Robert. Forthcoming. *Charting a New Path: Islam and Educational Reform in the United States.* New York: Oxford University Press.

———. 2002. *Black Pilgrimage to Islam*. New York: Oxford University Press.

Farley, Reynolds, Sheldon Danziger, and Harry Holzer. 2000. *Detroit Divided*. New York: Russell Sage Foundation.

Foner, Nancy. 2001. "Immigrant Commitments to America, Then and Now: Myths and Realities." *Citizenship Studies* 5(1): 1–15.

Hamtramck Public Schools. 2008. "2006–2007 District Report Card." *Hamtramck Horizon*. Available at http://www.hamtramck.k12.mi.us/drc0607.pdf.

Hartigan, John. 1999. *Racial Situations: Class Predicaments of Whiteness in Detroit*. Princeton, N.J.: Princeton University Press.

Hollinger, David. 1995. *Postethnic America: Beyond Multiculturalism*. New York: Basic Books.

Hondagneu-Sotelo, Pierrette, and Ernestine Avila. 1997. "'I'm here, but I'm there': The Meanings of Latina Transnational Motherhood." *Gender and Society* 11(5): 548–71.

Howell, Sally. 2009. "Inventing the American Mosque: Early Muslims and Their Institutions in Detroit, 1910–1980." Ph.D. diss., University of Michigan.

Howell, Sally, and Amaney Jamal. 2008. "Detroit Exceptionalism and the Limits of Political Incorporation." In *Being and Belonging: Muslims in the United States since 9/11*, ed. Katherine Ewing, 47–79. New York: Russell Sage Foundation.

Jackson, Sherman. 2005. *Islam and the Blackamerican: Looking toward the Third Resurrection*. New York: Oxford University Press.

Jones, Leroi (Amiri Baraka). 1963. *Blues People*. New York: Morrow Quill.

Joseph, Miranda. 2002. *Against the Romance of Community*. Minneapolis: University of Minnesota Press.

Karim, Karim H. 2006. "American Media's Coverage of Muslims: The Historical Roots of Contemporary Portrayals." In *Muslims in the News Media*, ed. Elizabeth Poole and John Richardson, 116–27. New York: I. B. Tauris.

Kowalski, Greg. 2002. *Hamtramck: The Driven City*. Chicago: Arcadia.

Ladner, Michael. 2000. "Public Schools Learn Their Lessons about Competition." In *Michigan Privatization Report*. Mackinac, Mich.: Mackinac Center for Public Policy.

Mandaville, Peter. 2001. *Transnational Muslim Politics: Reimagining the Umma*. New York: Routledge.

Portes, Alejandro, and Min Zhou. 1993. "The New Second Generation: Segmented Assimilation and Its Variants." *Annals of the American Academy of Political and Social Science* 530(1): 74–96.

Prashad, Vijay. 2001. *Everybody Was Kung Fu Fighting*. Boston: Beacon Press.

Radzilowski, Thaddeus. 2006. *Hamtramck: A Community Profile*. Hamtramck, Mich.: Piast Institute.

Sarroub, Loukia. 2005. *All American Yemeni Girls: Being Muslim in a Public School*. Philadelphia: University of Pennsylvania Press.

Southeast Michigan Council of Governments (SEMCOG). 2006. *Community Profiles: Southeast Michigan 2005*. Detroit: SEMCOG.

Sugrue, Tom. 1996. *The Origins of the Urban Crisis: Race and Inequality in Postwar Detroit*. Princeton, N.J.: Princeton University Press.

Swanson, Jon. 1988. "Sojourners and Settlers in Yemen and America." In *Sojourners and Settlers: The Yemeni Immigrant Experience,* ed. Jonathan Friedlander, 49–68. Berkeley: University of California Press.

Turner, Richard Brent. 1997. *Islam in the African American Experience.* Bloomington: Indiana University Press.

Contributors

Moustafa Bayoumi is Associate Professor of English at Brooklyn College, City University of New York. His published work includes *The Edward Said Reader;* essays in *The Nation,* the *London Review of Books, Interventions,* and *Middle East Report;* and *How Does It Feel to Be a Problem? Being Young and Arab in America.*

Mucahit Bilici is Assistant Professor of Sociology at John Jay College, City University of New York. His essays have appeared in the *Muslim World, Islam and Christian-Muslim Relations, The Blackwell Companion to Contemporary Muslim Thought, Islam at the Crossroads,* and *New Public Faces of Islam.*

Lara Deeb is Associate Professor of Anthropology at Scripps College. She is author of *An Enchanted Modern: Gender and Public Piety in Shi'i Lebanon* and numerous articles on the transformation of Shi'ism in Lebanon. Deeb is a member of the editorial committee for *Middle East Report.*

Sally Howell is Assistant Professor of History and Arab American Studies at the University of Michigan (Dearborn). Her published work includes *Citizenship and Crisis: Arab Detroit after 9/11* and essays in *Visual Anthropology, Diaspora, Anthropological Quarterly,* and the *International Journal of Middle East Studies.*

Tomaž Mastnak is Director of Research at the Institute of Philosophy in the Scientific Research Centre of the Slovenian Academy of Sciences and Arts. Currently he is Visiting Researcher in the Department of Anthropology, University of California at Irvine. His publications include *Crusading Peace: Christendom, the Muslim World, and Western Political Order; Europe: A History of the Political Concept* (in Serbian); and *Hobbes's Behemoth: Religion and Democracy.*

Esra Özyürek is Associate Professor of Anthropology at the University of California at San Diego. Her books include *Nostalgia for the Modern: State Secularism and Everyday Politics in Turkey* and *The Politics of Public Memory in Turkey*.

Naamah Paley is Dorot Foundation Fellow in Israel, where she is currently doing research on Arab education policy in the Wadi Ara region and in Haifa.

Andrew Shryock is Arthur F. Thurnau Professor of Anthropology at the University of Michigan. His books include *Nationalism and the Genealogical Imagination: Oral History and Textual Authority in Tribal Jordan; Off Stage/ On Display: Intimacy and Ethnography in the Age of Public Culture;* and *Citizenship and Crisis: Arab Detroit after 9/11.*

Paul A. Silverstein is Associate Professor of Anthropology at Reed College. His published works include *Algeria in France: Transpolitics, Race, and Nation* (Indiana University Press, 2004) and *Memory and Violence in the Middle East and North Africa* (Indiana University Press, 2006).

Muhammad Qasim Zaman is Niehaus Professor of Near Eastern Studies and Religion at Princeton University. His books include *Ashraf 'Ali Thanawi: Islam in Modern South Asia* and *The Ulama in Contemporary Islam.*

Index